Conflicts in Interpretation

Advances in Optimality Theory

Editors: Ellen Woolford, University of Massachusetts, Amherst, and Armin Mester, University of California, Santa Cruz

Optimality Theory is an exciting new approach to linguistic analysis that originated in phonology but was soon taken up in syntax, morphology, and other fields of linguistics. Optimality Theory presents a clear vision of the universal properties underlying the vast surface typological variety in the world's languages. Cross-linguistic differences once relegated to idiosyncratic language-specific rules can now be understood as the result of different priority rankings among universal, but violable constraints on grammar.

Advances in Optimality Theory is designed to stimulate and promote research in this provocative new framework. It provides a central outlet for the best new work by both established and younger scholars in this rapidly moving field. The series includes studies with a broad typological focus, studies dedicated to the detailed analysis of individual languages, and studies on the nature of Optimality Theory itself. The series publishes theoretical work in the form of monographs and coherent edited collections as well as pedagogical texts and reference texts that promote the dissemination of Optimality Theory.

Published:
Hidden Generalizations: Phonological Opacity in Optimality Theory
John J. McCarthy

Optimality Theory, Phonological Acquisition and Disorders
Edited by Daniel A. Dinsen and Judith A. Gierut

Modeling Ungrammaticality in Optimality Theory
Edited by Curt Rice

Phonological Argumentation: Essays in Evidence and Motivation
Edited by Steve Parker

Forthcoming:
Understanding Allomorphy: Perspectives from Optimality Theory
Edited by Bernard Tranel

Conflicts in Interpretation

Petra Hendriks, Helen de Hoop, Irene Krämer,
Henriëtte de Swart and Joost Zwarts

LONDON   OAKVILLE

Published by
UK: Equinox Publishing Ltd., 1 Chelsea Manor Studios,
Flood Street, London SW3 5SR
USA: DBBC, 28 Main Street, Oakville, CT 06779
www.equinoxpub.com

First published 2010

British Library Cataloguing-in-Publication Data
A catalogue record for this book is available from the British Library.

ISBN   978-1-84553-437-0 (hardback)
ISBN   978-1-84553-438-7 (paperback)

Library of Congress Cataloging-in-Publication Data
Conflicts in interpretation / Petra Hendriks ... [et al.].
     p. cm. -- (Advances in optimality theory)
  Includes bibliographical references and index.
   ISBN 978-1-84553-437-0 -- ISBN 978-1-84553-438-7 (pbk.) 1.
Semantics. 2. Pragmatics. 3. Constraints (Linguistics) 4. Optimality
theory (Linguistics) I. Hendriks, Petra, 1964-
   P325.C564 2009
   401'.43--dc22
                                        2008052638

Typeset by Catchline, Milton Keynes (www.catchline.com)
Printed and bound in Great Britain and the USA

Contents

Acknowledgements

This book presents the results of the NWO Cognition project 'Conflicts in Interpretation', in which the authors collaborated between 2002 and 2006. The authors acknowledge the Netherlands Organisation for Scientific Research (NWO) for financial support (grant 051-02-070). Henriëtte would like to thank NIAS for their great hospitality during her sabbatical year (2005-2006). NWO grant 365-70-015 provided financial support for her sabbatical, which is hereby gratefully acknowledged. Furthermore, the authors thank the following people for inspiring discussions on issues addressed in this book: Geertje van Bergen, Reinhard Blutner, Gerlof Bouma, Ad Foolen, Wilhelm Geuder, Lotte Hogeweg, Angeliek van Hout, Monique Lamers, Sander Lestrade, Torgrim Solstad, Jennifer Spenader, Peter Svenonius, Peter de Swart, Matthias Weisgerber, Yoad Winter, and Henk Zeevat. Special thanks go to Richard van Gerrevink for his editorial assistance. Parts of this book were used as course material for the ESSLLI course 'Bidirectional OT in natural language' in Hamburg, Germany, in 2008. The participants of this course are thanked for their insightful questions and useful comments. The authors also thank the audiences at various workshops and conferences where material from this book was presented for useful questions and discussion. Finally, the book greatly benefited from the comments provided by two anonymous reviewers.

1 Optimization of interpretation

1.1 Optimization

Many things we do in daily life involve processes of optimization. Usually we want to do things in the best possible way, given certain limitations. For example, if you are in a pizza restaurant, you will presumably want to order the pizza you like best. Of course, your choice will be limited by the selection of pizzas on the menu, or the list of possible toppings. Nevertheless, there will still be many options left to you. To determine your final choice, you will have to reject most of the available options on the basis of certain heuristics or constraints. For example, if you are a vegetarian, a pizza with bacon, pepperoni, chicken or shrimp will be out of the question. If you are allergic to fish, you won't choose a pizza with anchovies or tuna. Perhaps you prefer mushrooms to green pepper or onion. And if you've already had artichoke yesterday, you may not want to have artichoke on your pizza today. Even though you may not have time to consider all options, or your constraints may leave you with several good options, you will try to make the best selection possible under the circumstances. Most of the times when you go to a pizza restaurant, you end up with one particular pizza that you think was the best choice.

Speaking and understanding seem to be subject to the same principles of optimization as many other things we do. When we speak, there are in principle infinitely many ways in which we can package our message. Nevertheless, we end up selecting one particular form that expresses the message that we wish to convey best. We must decide whether or not to use an article (did John go to jail or did he go to the jail?), where to put the direct object in the sentence, and which word to emphasize by sentence stress. All these decisions are made unconsciously and at once, apparently without even thinking about the different options. Similarly, when we hear an utterance, there are in principle infinitely many meanings that this utterance may have. Does the pronoun *him* refer to the subject of the sentence or to someone else? Does the speaker talk about a particular individual or about just any individual? Does the speaker wish to express a causal relationship between two events or merely indicate their temporal order? Again, we usually end up choosing one particular meaning that we think fits best with the form that we just heard and the context in which this form was uttered. Often we don't even realize that other interpretations were possible.

This chapter provides an introduction to optimization approaches to language. Under an optimization approach, speakers select the optimal form for expressing a given meaning, and hearers select the optimal interpretation for a given form. The optimal form and optimal meaning are determined through the application of constraints of various sorts, which typically conflict. The optimal form or meaning is the form or meaning that satisfies the total set of constraints best. In addition to balancing between the demands of conflicting constraints, we argue that hearers also have to balance between their own demands and the demands of the speaker, and vice versa. This bidirectional perspective restricts the possible forms and meanings of a language even more, and will have substantial implications for the acquisition of a first language as well as for the possible variation among languages, as is shown in later chapters. Not only does the optimization approach introduced in this chapter provide a new way to tackle old problems in the areas of compositional semantics, lexical semantics, language acquisition and language typology, but such an approach may also allow for the integration of linguistic results with results from the wider field of cognitive science.

The view of speaking and understanding as processes of optimization is a core property of the linguistic framework of Optimality Theory. In the next section, we will introduce this linguistic framework and discuss its most prominent characteristics. As we will show in Section 1.3, the linguistic processes of speaking and understanding sometimes are dependent on each other. This observation has given rise to various models of bidirectional optimization, which are discussed here. Section 1.4 relates Optimality Theory to the larger field of cognitive science. Section 1.5, finally, presents an overview of the remainder of the book.

1.2   Optimization in Optimality Theory

One of the central aims of artificial intelligence is to develop an artificial system that can perform intelligent tasks similar to those performed by the human brain. Because it was contended that symbolic rules do not reflect the processes actually used by humans, in the 1980s the field of connectionism, or neural network modelling, arose. Within this field, artificial neural networks were developed which model the human brain. It was shown that these neural networks could learn to perform cognitive tasks as diverse as recognizing faces, performing a medical diagnosis, driving a car, playing a game, financial forecasting and portfolio management, and recognizing handwritten characters (Murray, 1995; Widrow, Rumelhart and Lehr, 1994).

Artificial neural networks consist of a large number of nodes and connections between these nodes, and establish a relation between an input pattern and an output pattern. The connections between nodes have weights and can be seen as implicitly representing constraints of varying strengths. Connections between input nodes and output nodes with positive weights resemble constraints promoting a particular input-output relation, whereas connections with negative weights resemble constraints prohibiting a particular input-output relation. When an input pattern is presented to the network, the pattern of activation of the network strives to maximize harmony. The harmony of a pattern of activation is a measure of its degree of conformity to the constraints implicit in the network (Smolensky, 1986). The pattern with the maximal harmony is the pattern that optimally balances between the conflicting constraints.

An important step in linguistics was the realization in the early 1990s that the concept of grammaticality in linguistics could be equated to optimization in neural network modelling (cf. Legendre, Miyata and Smolensky, 1990a,b; Prince and Smolensky, 1993, 1997; Smolensky and Legendre, 2006). A grammatical structure is then one that best satisfies the total set of constraints defining the grammar. This grammatical structure is the optimal structure. All other structures are suboptimal and hence unrealized.

1.2.1 Violable constraints

The optimization view on grammar started off in the domain of phonology (Prince and Smolensky, 1993; McCarthy and Prince, 1993a,b), but gradually spread to other linguistic domains such as syntax (e.g., Barbosa, Fox, Hagstrom, McGinnis and Pesetsky, 1998; Bresnan, 2000; Grimshaw, 1997; Legendre, Grimshaw and Vikner, 2001; Sells, 2001), semantics and pragmatics (e.g., Beaver, 2004; Blutner, de Hoop and Hendriks, 2006; Blutner and Zeevat, 2004a; de Hoop and de Swart, 2000; Hendriks and de Hoop, 1997, 2001). One of the main characteristics of an optimization approach to grammar is the assumption that linguistic rules are not hard and inviolable, but rather soft and violable.

In certain languages, the subject of the sentence may be omitted. The presence or absence of a subject can be explained through the interaction of the following two violable constraints (cf. Grimshaw and Samek-Lodovici, 1998):

(1)　SUBJECT: All clauses must have a subject.

(2)　FULL-INTERPRETATION: All constituents in the sentence must be interpreted.

The first constraint, Subject, tells us that every clause must have a subject. The second constraint, Full-Interpretation, requires each word in the sentence to be meaningful. A conflict between these two constraints arises if there is no semantic need for a subject. This happens with verbs such as *to rain*. The event of raining does not require an individual which performs or undergoes some action. So semantically, the verb *to rain* does not require a subject. However, the constraint Subject expresses the requirement that sentences must have a subject. So what do we do in this case? Do we leave out the subject, or do we insert a meaningless word to fill the subject position?

In Optimality Theory (henceforth OT), it is hypothesized that languages share the same set of constraints but differ in the ranking of these constraints. In languages such as English, the constraint Subject ranks above the constraint Full-Interpretation. As a result, Full-Interpretation may be violated in order to satisfy Subject. Because it is more important in English to have a subject in the sentence than to have only meaningful words in the sentence, the English solution to the conflict among the two constraints is to allow for a meaningless element to fill the subject position. This element is the expletive *it*, which does not have any meaning. The interaction between the constraints Subject and Full-Interpretation can be depicted in the following tableau:

Tableau 1.1: Subjects in English

Input: "It is raining"	Subject	Full-Interpretation
☞ It is raining.		*
Is raining.	*!	

The top left-hand cell in this tableau presents the input representation for which we want to find the best output. In this case, the speaker wants to express the meaning that it is raining. Two relevant candidate forms are given in the leftmost column. The speaker could say *it is raining*, or alternatively could choose to utter the sentence *is raining*. These two candidate forms are in competition with each other. Only the optimal candidate is a grammatical form. The constraints are ranked across the top, going from the highest ranked constraint (in this case Subject) on the left to the lowest ranked constraint (Full-Interpretation) on the right. An asterisk (*) in a cell indicates a violation of a constraint. In this example, the sentence *it is raining* violates the constraint Full-Interpretation because it contains a meaningless word, *it*. Furthermore, the sentence *is raining* violates the constraint Subject because this sentence does not have a subject. Because Subject is stronger than Full-Interpretation in English, the latter constraint violation is fatal. This is indicated by the exclamation mark (!). As a result of this constraint violation, the candidate form *it is raining* is the optimal candidate, which is indicated by the pointing hand (☞).

Whereas in English it is more important to have a subject than to avoid meaningless words, in languages such as Italian, on the other hand, it is more important to have only meaningful words in the sentence than to have a subject. The Italian solution to the conflict between the constraints SUBJECT and FULL-INTERPRETATION therefore is to leave out the subject.

Tableau 1.2: Subjects in Italian

Input: "It is raining"	FULL-INTERPRETATION	SUBJECT
EXPL piove.	*!	
☞ Piove.		*

EXPL stands for 'expletive'. Since Italian does not have expletives, there is no lexical item we can put here. However, if in Italian the form EXPL *piove* were the optimal form, surely some existing word would have been drafted to serve as an expletive (Grimshaw and Samek-Lodovici, 1998). As can be seen from the tableau, each candidate form violates a constraint. The form EXPL *piove* violates FULL-INTERPRETATION, whereas the form *piove* violates SUBJECT. Because in Italian the constraint FULL-INTERPRETATION is strongest, the optimal form in Italian is a sentence without a subject.

This example shows that differences between languages can be explained through a different ranking of the same set of constraints. This is called typology by re-ranking. Because English and Italian differ in their constraint ranking, these languages have different optimal solutions to the conflict posed by the same input. In both languages, optimal candidates may violate one or more constraints. Nevertheless, such violations are allowed because there is no better way to satisfy the constraints.

In OT, candidates that compete for expression are generated by the mechanism of GEN, which stands for 'Generator'. GEN creates possible output candidates from a given input. These candidates are then evaluated on the basis of the set of ranked constraints, called EVAL (for 'Evaluator'). It is assumed that the candidate set created by GEN must be infinite because GEN may be unfaithful to the input, for example by adding, deleting or rearranging segments. This property of the infinity of the candidate set poses serious problems for computational models of OT. In addition, it is of course psychologically highly implausible. However, efforts have been made to circumvent this problem. For example, smart computational strategies might eliminate suboptimal candidates as a group rather than on a one-by-one basis. As soon as a candidate has been excluded due to its violation of some constraint, all other candidates that violate this constraint even more severely can also be excluded. Alternatively, the candidate set may be infinite in principle but finite in practice, bounded by cognitive principles. Also, one may view the infinite candidate set as only being virtually infinite. At the level of neural processing underlying OT models, these candidates are not actually physically represented, but can be said to be possible outcomes on the basis of the possible strengths of the neural connections (cf. Smolensky and Legendre, 2006). Under this latter view, it may be better to talk about an output space rather than a candidate set.

In this subsection, we looked at sentence production, or OT syntax. The input is a particular meaning, from which GEN generates a candidate set consisting of possible forms expressing this meaning. The optimal form becomes the output. In the next subsection we consider sentence comprehension, or OT semantics. Here, the input is a given form, from which GEN (also called INT for 'Interpreter') generates a candidate set of possible meanings for this form. The optimal interpretation for the given form becomes the output.

1.2.2 Constraints on interpretation

In Italian, not only subjects of weather verbs such as *to rain* are omitted, but also pronominal subjects if they refer to the topic of the discourse, that is, the entity the discourse is about. So if two people are talking about John and what he might be doing right now, one of them may say:

(3) Telefona.
     telephones
     'He/she telephones.'

In the first line, the Italian sentence is given. The second line presents its gloss (i.e., its word by word translation). The third line presents its translation into English. The event described by the verb *telefona* does require a semantic subject, in contrast to the weather verbs discussed in the previous section. If we talk about the event of telephoning, there must be some individual who performs this action. In Italian, however, this subject can be omitted from the sentence, violating SUBJECT, but only in order to satisfy a stronger constraint (cf. Grimshaw and Samek-Lodovici, 1998). Such a stronger constraint might be:

(4) DROP-TOPIC: All subjects or objects that are co-referential with the topic must be omitted.

The constraint DROP-TOPIC promotes the omission of subjects and objects that refer to the topic of the discourse. This constraint is in conflict with the constraint SUBJECT when the subject is co-referential with the topic (i.e., refers to the same individual as the discourse topic). In this situation, the speaker can decide to pronounce the subject (in violation of DROP-TOPIC) or to omit the subject (in violation of SUBJECT). In case of such a conflict, the stronger constraint wins. So in Italian, the best form for the input meaning 'John, whom we are talking about, telephones' is the form *telefona*, which satisfies the stronger constraint DROP-TOPIC.

Now what about the hearer? How does the hearer understand that *telefona* means 'John, whom we are talking about, telephones', and not 'someone telephones'? The hearer will notice that this clause does not have a subject, in violation of the constraint SUBJECT. If the hearer knows the meaning of the verb, he will also know that there must be someone who telephones. But obviously this is not enough to warrant the conclusion that this someone is John. The constraints we formulated to account for possible sentences in English and Italian are not sufficient to explain the interpretation of these same sentences. These constraints refer to aspects of form, such as the presence or absence of a subject, an object or an expletive. They distinguish between candidate forms, and punish certain forms in favor of other forms. However, other constraints are necessary to distinguish between candidate meanings for a given form. That is, constraints on speaking (production constraints) are partly different from constraints on understanding (comprehension constraints), although there may be constraints that play a part both in speaking and in understanding.

What do these comprehension constraints look like? If a noun phrase were present in subject position, obviously this noun phrase must be interpreted as the individual performing the action of telephoning. The following constraint, which has been shown to account for certain interpretational preferences in the online (i.e., word-by-word, from left to right) comprehension of sentences as well (cf. de Hoop and Lamers, 2006; Lamers and de Hoop, 2005), has this effect:

(5) SUBJECT-FIRST: The first noun phrase in the sentence must be interpreted as the subject.

Obviously, this must be a violable constraint because not all first noun phrases are subjects, especially not in languages such as Dutch and German that allow objects to be fronted under certain conditions. Under these conditions, the constraint SUBJECT-FIRST is violated in order to satisfy stronger constraints (see de Hoop and Lamers, 2006; Lamers and de Hoop, 2005, for examples and a discussion of these stronger constraints). But what happens if no noun phrase is present in the sentence, such as in (3)? In this situation, the topic of the discourse fulfils the role of the semantic subject of the verb.

(6) SUBJECT=TOPIC: The subject must be interpreted as the discourse topic.

The interaction between these two constraints can again be depicted in an OT tableau:

Tableau 1.3: Subjectless sentences in Italian

Input: Telefona. Topic = John	SUBJECT-FIRST	SUBJECT=TOPIC
"someone telephones"		*!
☞ "John telephones"		

In this tableau, the input is a certain form for which we want to find the best interpretation. The candidates are possible interpretations for this input form. Because there is no noun phrase in the sentence, the constraint SUBJECT-FIRST is satisfied vacuously. As a result, the weaker constraint SUBJECT=TOPIC decides between the candidate interpretations. This accounts for the observation that *telefona* is interpreted as meaning that the person on the telephone is the one whom we are talking about, and not just any person. If a noun phrase were present in the sentence, the constraint SUBJECT-FIRST would pick out this noun phrase as the subject. So depending on which constraint is strongest, a subject can or cannot be omitted from the sentence. Furthermore, the semantic subject of a verb is interpreted from the discourse, unless an overt subject is present in the sentence. This latter pattern results from the interaction of constraints that differ in strength too.

Usually, only the effects of the stronger constraints are visible within a language. However, sometimes a lower ranked constraint becomes crucial. This happens, for example, when all relevant candidates equally violate or satisfy higher ranked constraints. In OT, this phenomenon is called 'emergence of the unmarked'. This happens in Tableau 1.3 with the lower ranked constraint SUBJECT=TOPIC, whose effects become visible only when the sentence does not contain a noun phrase. In this situation, the constraint SUBJECT-FIRST is satisfied vacuously by both candidates in the tableau. If, on the other hand, the sentence does contain a noun phrase in subject position, the stronger constraint SUBJECT-FIRST tells the hearer to interpret this noun phrase as the subject. Because a violation of SUBJECT-FIRST is more serious than a violation of the weaker constraint SUBJECT=TOPIC, the overt noun phrase is taken to be the subject, even though it may not be the discourse topic. So if the sentence contains a noun phrase in subject position, we see no effects anymore of the weaker constraint SUBJECT=TOPIC.

Now that we have seen how OT constraints interact, let us take a closer look at the constraints themselves and their properties.

1.2.3 Markedness constraints versus faithfulness constraints

An important concept in OT is the concept of markedness. Certain forms are preferred to other forms because they are unmarked, for example because they are shorter, less complex, ordinary, the default choice in a particular situation, or because they occur in many languages. Similarly, certain meanings are preferred to other meanings because they are unmarked, for example because they require less effort by the hearer, or are less complex or more stereotypical. Although it is difficult to exactly define the notion of markedness (see later chapters for a more detailed discussion), markedness is encoded in the constraints. Markedness constraints have the effect that the relation between input and output is not as straightforward as it could be. As a result, certain forms are preferred to other forms, irrespective of their meaning, and certain meanings are preferred to other meanings, irrespective of their form. Markedness constraints refer to the output only and are blind to the nature of the input. An example of a markedness constraint is the constraint SUBJECT, which is a constraint on forms penalizing subjectless sentences. Irrespective of whether the input meaning involves an event such as raining or an event such as telephoning, output sentences without an overt subject violate this constraint. Thus subjectless sentences are the marked forms. This corresponds to the observation that, cross-linguistically, sentences with a subject are the default forms, whereas subjectless sentences only occur under special licensing conditions (Samek-Lodovici, 1996).

The constraint SUBJECT clearly illustrates that markedness is a concept which may be not be easy to define. Although sentences with a subject seem to be more frequent than subjectless sentences, subjectless sentences are shorter than sentences with a subject. Furthermore, for speakers the production of sentences with a subject requires more effort than the production of subjectless sentences. So if shortness of expression or speaker effort were the determining factor here, subjectless sentences should have been the unmarked forms.

In addition to markedness constraints, OT also has faithfulness constraints. Faithfulness constraints require the relation between input and output to be as straightforward as possible. In OT phonology, where the input is an underlying form stored in the mental lexicon and the output is a surface form as it gets pronounced in a particular utterance, faithfulness amounts to identity of form. In OT syntax, where the input is a meaning and the output is a form, faithfulness cannot simply be identity between input and output, because forms and meanings are different entities. The same holds for OT semantics, where the input is a form and the output is a meaning. Rather than a relation of identity, faithfulness in OT syntax and semantics can be viewed as a relation of association. Although the input and the output in OT syntax and semantics are different entities, the relation between input and output can be said to be as straightforward as possible if there is a one-to-one mapping between forms and meanings. Such a one-to-one mapping between forms and meanings is promoted by constraints that associate a particular form with a particular meaning. These constraints thus have a similar effect as faithfulness constraints in OT phonology. Blutner and Zeevat (to appear) refer to constraints that associate a particular form with a particular meaning as 'linking constraints'. Mattausch (2004), in the context of language change, terms constraints that refer to specific pairs of form and meaning 'bias constraints'. These bias constraints will be discussed in more detail in Chapter 6. In the present chapter, however, we will continue to use the term 'faithfulness constraints' for all constraints associating a particular input with a particular output, to emphasize the similarities with OT phonology.

So faithfulness constraints in OT syntax and OT semantics associate a particular form with a particular meaning. Whereas markedness constraints only take into account the output (which can be either a form or a meaning, depending on the direction of optimization), faithfulness constraints take into account both the input and the output. The constraint FULL-INTERPRETATION can be viewed as an example of such a faithfulness constraint. This constraint requires that each word in the output sentence has a counterpart in the input meaning. The behavior of a form with respect to this constraint cannot be established without taking into account its meaning.

1.3 Bidirectional optimization

In the previous section, we looked at optimization in sentence production (OT syntax) and in sentence comprehension (OT semantics). In our brief discussion, we treated them as two separate processes of optimization. However, a very general phenomenon in natural language which seems to require the intricate interaction between production and comprehension, is the phenomenon of blocking. In this section we will show how OT is able to account for blocking phenomena by combining OT syntax and OT semantics. The resulting system of bidirectional optimization formalizes the intuition that hearers not only proceed from their own hearer's perspective but also take into account the speaker's perspective (Blutner, 2000; Blutner, de Hoop and Hendriks, 2006). Conversely, speakers not only proceed from their own speaker's perspective but also take into account the hearer's perspective. When a hearer hears a certain form, he will of course first have to determine the optimal meaning corresponding to this form. But in addition he will also have to check whether this optimal meaning indeed produces the heard form in production. In other words, the hearer will have to check whether, if he were a speaker, he would indeed select the heard form to produce this meaning. If not, this meaning could not have been intended by the speaker and hence another meaning should be selected by the hearer. Similarly, when a speaker produces a certain form on the basis of an intended meaning, she will have to check whether this form, when interpreted, will yield the intended meaning. If not, the form is not recoverable for the hearer and hence should not be used by the speaker.

1.3.1 Strong bidirectional optimization and total blocking

If a meaning can be expressed by two different forms, but one of these forms is less marked, often the other form is blocked for this meaning. For example, two possible ways to realize the comparative form of *good* is as the regular form *gooder* or as the irregular form *better*. Because the irregular form *better* is somehow preferred, the regular form *gooder* is blocked as the comparative form of *good*. This type of total blocking can be accounted for under the following definition of optimization:

(7)　Strong bidirectional optimization (adapted from Blutner, 2000):
　　　A form-meaning pair <f, m> is bidirectionally optimal iff:
　　　(a)　there is no other pair <f', m> such that <f', m> is more harmonic than <f,m>.
　　　(b)　there is no other pair <f, m'> such that <f, m'> is more harmonic than <f,m>.

The term *harmonic* in this definition refers to the notion of harmony, which is a measure of the degree of conformity of a pattern of activation in a neural network to the constraints implicit in the network. Here, the term indicates how well an output candidate satisfies the constraints of the grammar. Under the definition in (7), we do not consider forms or meanings separately. Instead, we consider pairs consisting of forms and their corresponding meanings. A form-meaning pair is an optimal pair if there is no pair with a better form or better meaning. Only optimal pairs are realized in language. Such optimal pairs block all other pairs in the same competition.

This blocking effect can be illustrated on the basis of the non-linguistic example of a dance. Imagine a situation in which women are supposed to dance with men, better female dancers are preferred to less good female dancers, and better male dancers are preferred to less good male dancers. Obviously, the best pair is the pair consisting of the best female dancer and the best male dancer. For the best female dancer, the best male dancer would be the best choice, and for the best male dancer, the best female dancer would be the best choice. All other imaginable pairs of female and male dancers are less good, because they consist of a less good female dancer, a less good male dancer or both. Because the pair consisting of the best female dancer and the best male dancer is better in comparison to all other pairs, all other pairs are blocked.

Returning to the *gooder – better* example, because *better* (form f) is preferred to *gooder* (form f') for the comparative meaning of *good* (meaning m), the form *gooder* (form f') is blocked. In other words, the pair <*better*, comparative meaning of *good*> is more harmonic than the pair <*gooder*, comparative meaning of *good*>. Because there is no pair which is more harmonic than this pair, the pair <*better*, comparative meaning of *good*> is the bidirectionally optimal pair.

1.3.2 Weak bidirectional optimization and partial blocking

Under strong bidirectional optimization, there will only be one dancing pair: The best pair, which is the pair consisting of the best female dancer and the best male dancer. However, it is not hard to imagine a situation in which other dancers are allowed to dance as well. For the next-to-best female dancer, as for all female dancers, the best dance partner would be the best male dancer. But if the best male dancer already forms a pair with the best female dancer, he cannot at the same time dance with someone else. So all imaginable pairs in which the best male dancer dances with someone else than the best female dancer will be blocked. Similarly, all imaginable pairs in which the best female dancer dances with someone else than the best male dancer will be blocked. As a result, the next-to-best female dancer will end up with the next-to-best male dancer. Crucially, pairs which do not consist of either the best female dancer or the best male dancer will not be blocked. And if even more dancing pairs are allowed to be formed, the two-but-best female dancer ends up with the two-but-best male dancer, and so on. This situation arises from the following, recursive, definition of bidirectional optimality, which is called super-optimality:

(8) Weak bidirectional optimization (adapted from Blutner, 2000):
A form-meaning pair <f, m> is super-optimal iff:
(a) there is no super-optimal pair <f', m> such that <f', m> is more harmonic than <f, m>.
(b) there is no super-optimal pair <f, m'> such that <f, m'> is more harmonic than <f, m>.

This situation has been argued to exist in natural language as well, and to give rise to what is called Horn's division of pragmatic labor (Horn, 1984): Unmarked forms are used for unmarked meanings, and marked forms are used for marked meanings. As an example of partial blocking in the lexical domain, consider the derivational process by which nouns are derived from verbs by means of an affix (Kiparsky, 1983; see Blutner, 2000, for an OT perspective). This process is responsible for words like *informant – informer, refrigerant – refrigerator, contestant – contester, commandant – commander, stimulant – stimulator.* The second noun of each pair is derived on the basis of the highly productive affix *-er/or*, the first noun of each pair on the basis of the much less productive affix *-ant*. The meaning of the first noun of each pair partially blocks the meaning of the second noun. For example, because *refrigerant* refers to the substance, the meaning of the word *refrigerator* is confined to what is not covered by the word *refrigerant*. In general, the special (less productive) affix occurs in some restricted meaning and the general (more productive) affix picks up the remaining meaning. As a result, blocking is not total but partial.

A way to represent the competing forces of production and comprehension is by means of an arrow diagram. Suppose that, as a result of certain markedness constraints, f_1 is a better form than f_2, and m_1 is a better meaning than m_2. The following ordering relations between form-meaning pairs can be derived, represented in an arrow diagram, where the arrows point to the preferred pairs:

Diagram 1.1: An arrow diagram of bidirectional optimization

$$\begin{array}{ccc}
\langle f_1, m_1 \rangle & \leftarrow & \langle f_2, m_1 \rangle \\
\uparrow & & \uparrow \\
\langle f_1, m_2 \rangle & \leftarrow & \langle f_2, m_2 \rangle
\end{array}$$

The arrows represent the cumulative effects of the constraints and their ranking. Under the assumption that f_1 is preferred to f_2, and m_1 is preferred to m_2, pair $\langle f_1, m_1 \rangle$ is preferred to pair $\langle f_2, m_1 \rangle$ as well as to pair $\langle f_1, m_2 \rangle$. Furthermore, pair $\langle f_2, m_1 \rangle$ is preferred to pair $\langle f_2, m_2 \rangle$, and pair $\langle f_1, m_2 \rangle$ is preferred to pair $\langle f_2, m_2 \rangle$.

Under strong bidirectional optimization, only the pair $\langle f_1, m_1 \rangle$ is a bidirectionally optimal pair. This pair combines the preferred form with the preferred meaning. This is the only pair from which no arrows are leaving. If no arrows are leaving from a pair, this pair is bidirectionally optimal in a strong sense. The arrow notation is taken from game theory. The notion of strong bidirectional optimality is equivalent to the notion of a Nash equilibrium in game theory (Dekker and van Rooy, 2000). Thus the interaction between a speaker and a hearer engaged in a communicative act is in a sense similar to the interaction between two players playing a strategic game.

Under weak bidirectional optimization, an additional super-optimal pair emerges. A form-meaning pair $\langle f, m \rangle$ is called super-optimal if and only if there is no other super-optimal pair $\langle f', m \rangle$ such that $\langle f', m \rangle$ is more harmonic than $\langle f, m \rangle$ and there is no other super-optimal pair $\langle f, m' \rangle$ such that $\langle f, m' \rangle$

is more harmonic than $\langle f, m \rangle$. The reader may verify that according to this definition, there are two super-optimal pairs in Diagram 1.1, namely $\langle f_1, m_1 \rangle$ and $\langle f_2, m_2 \rangle$. Indeed, although f_2 is not an optimal form itself and m_2 is not an optimal meaning, the pair $\langle f_2, m_2 \rangle$ is super-optimal because there is no super-optimal pair that blocks it. The two candidates $\langle f_1, m_2 \rangle$ and $\langle f_2, m_1 \rangle$ are not super-optimal because they are both blocked by the other super-optimal pair $\langle f_1, m_1 \rangle$. As a result, they are not in competition with the pair $\langle f_2, m_2 \rangle$ anymore. The effects of blocking can be visualized by removing arrows from the diagram. In particular, all arrows have to be removed that point to pairs that point to the optimal pair.

Diagram 1.2: Removal of arrows under weak bidirectional optimization

$\langle f_1, m_1 \rangle$ $\leftarrow$ $\langle f_2, \cancel{m_1} \rangle$

  $\uparrow$

$\langle f_1, \cancel{m_2} \rangle$ $\langle f_2, m_2 \rangle$

In Diagram 1.2, then, the two arrows have to be removed that point to the pairs $\langle f_1, m_2 \rangle$ and $\langle f_2, m_1 \rangle$ (the blocked pairs). As a result, no arrows are leaving from the pair in the bottom right corner anymore, so this pair is optimal as well.

This process of weak bidirectional optimization can be illustrated by our earlier example of *refrigerant* versus *refrigerator*. Let *refrigerant* be form f_1 and its meaning m_1, and let *refrigerator* be form f_2 and its meaning m_2. Suppose we have a constraint $*f_2$ (read: No f_2) that prefers f_1 to f_2 (for example, a constraint that prefers forms resulting from restricted rules to forms resulting from more general rules) and a constraint $*m_2$ that prefers m_1 to m_2 (for example, a constraint that prefers restricted meanings to more general meanings). The candidates *<refrigerant*, appliance> and *<refrigerator*, substance> are not super-optimal because they are both blocked by the super-optimal pair *<refrigerant*, substance>. As a result, the suboptimal form f_2 (*refrigerator*) is not blocked entirely, but only with respect to its use for a super-optimal meaning m_1 (the substance). So whereas the pair *<refrigerant*, substance> (i.e., $\langle f_1, m_1 \rangle$) is the best form-meaning pair, the pair *<refrigerator*, appliance> (i.e., $\langle f_2, m_2 \rangle$) also emerges as a bidirectionally optimal pair as a result of partial blocking. In later chapters we will see many instances of sentence interpretation where Horn's division of pragmatic labor plays a role.

The competition between form-meaning pairs under weak bidirectional optimization can be represented in an OT tableau as well:

Tableau 1.4: Weak bidirectional optimization

		$*f_2$	$*m_2$
☞	$\langle f_1, m_1 \rangle$		
	$\langle f_1, m_2 \rangle$		*
	$\langle f_2, m_1 \rangle$	*	
☞	$\langle f_2, m_2 \rangle$	*	*

The four possible form-meaning pairs are given in the leftmost column. All pairs containing the form f_2 violate the markedness constraint on forms $*f_2$. All pairs containing the meaning m_2 violate the markedness constraint on meanings $*m_2$. The relative ranking of the constraints $*f_2$ and $*m_2$ is irrelevant, which is indicated by the dashed line. The first pair satisfies both constraints and hence is a super-optimal pair. This is indicated by the victory sign (☞). As a result, the second and third pair are blocked. Therefore, the fourth pair emerges as a super-optimal pair in the second round of optimization.

1.3.3 Strong bidirectional optimization and multiple optimal solutions

In the previous section, we considered the situation in which markedness constraints were decisive in determining the relative preferences among forms and the relative preferences among meanings. As a result, strong bidirectional optimization gives rise to one optimal pair, and weak bidirectional optimization gives rise to two or more optimal pairs. But the situation can be different when one or more strong faithfulness constraints play a role. In that case, also strong bidirectional optimization may give rise to two optimal pairs. This is relevant because (non-recursive) strong bidirectional optimization is less complex than (recursive) weak bidirectional optimization. To obtain two optimal pairs we do not necessarily have to revert to the more complex mechanism of weak bidirectional optimization. There are two more ways of avoiding total blocking and obtaining two optimal pairs. The almost trivial case is one where we have two dominant faithfulness constraints $*\langle f_2, m_1 \rangle$ (read: No association between form f_2 and meaning m_1) and $*\langle f_1, m_2 \rangle$ (read: No association between form f_1 and meaning m_2). These two constraints have the effect that f_1 is associated with m_1, and f_2 is associated with m_2 (Blutner and Zeevat, to appear), thus giving rise to Horn's division of pragmatic labor.

A somewhat less trivial case is one where we have a single dominant faithfulness constraint in combination with a particular markedness constraint. Consider the following pattern of arrows between the same four pairs:

Diagram 1.3: Strong bidirectional optimization yielding two optimal pairs

$$\begin{array}{ccc}
\langle f_1, m_1 \rangle & \leftarrow & \langle f_2, m_1 \rangle \\
\uparrow & & \\
\langle f_1, m_2 \rangle & \rightarrow & \langle f_2, m_2 \rangle
\end{array}$$

Suppose we have a markedness constraint on forms preferring f_1 to f_2, just as in the earlier example. But now we do not have a markedness constraint on meanings preferring m_1 to m_2, but rather a stronger faithfulness constraint prohibiting the association between f_1 and m_2. In our dance example, this would be equivalent to the restriction that the best female dancer and the next-to-best male dancer do not want to dance with each other, perhaps because they do not like each other or do not know each other. This results in two differences between Diagram 1.1 and Diagram 1.3. First, in Diagram 1.3 there is no arrow going from $\langle f_2, m_2 \rangle$ to $\langle f_2, m_1 \rangle$ or vice versa. Thus f_2 is potentially ambiguous between m_1 and m_2. Secondly, the arrow between $\langle f_1, m_2 \rangle$ and $\langle f_2, m_2 \rangle$ is reversed and hence the pair $\langle f_2, m_2 \rangle$ is preferred to the pair $\langle f_1, m_2 \rangle$. As a result, strong bidirectional optimization also gives rise to two optimal pairs, namely $\langle f_1, m_1 \rangle$ and $\langle f_2, m_2 \rangle$. Both pairs are pairs from which no arrows are leaving. Note that the potential ambiguity between m_1 and m_2 has disappeared as a result of bidirectional optimization: Meaning m_2 must be associated with form f_2. Again, this competition can be represented in an OT tableau:

Tableau 1.5: Strong bidirectional optimization yielding two optimal pairs

	$*\langle f_1,m_2 \rangle$	$*f_2$
☞ $\langle f_1, m_1 \rangle$		
$\langle f_1, m_2 \rangle$	*	
$\langle f_2, m_1 \rangle$		*
☞ $\langle f_2, m_2 \rangle$		*

Because for both the pair $\langle f_1, m_1 \rangle$ and the pair $\langle f_2, m_2 \rangle$ there is no pair with either a better form or a better meaning, these two pairs are optimal pairs in strong bidirectional OT. This is obvious for the pair $\langle f_1, m_1 \rangle$, which satisfies both constraints, but less obvious for the pair $\langle f_2, m_2 \rangle$. However, if this fourth pair is compared to its competing pairs, the second and third pair, it can be seen that the fourth pair is better than the second pair, because the faithfulness constraint $*\langle f_1, m_2 \rangle$ violated by the second pair is stronger than the markedness constraint $*f_2$ violated by the fourth pair. In addition, the fourth pair is equally good as the third pair, because they both violate the markedness constraint $*f_2$ but satisfy the faithfulness constraint $*\langle f_1, m_2 \rangle$. Crucially, the third pair is not better than the fourth pair. Hence, there does not exist a better competitor for $\langle f_2, m_2 \rangle$. In Chapter 5 we will see that the linguistic example of contrastive stress illustrates this pattern of interaction between a markedness constraint on forms and a stronger faithfulness constraint.

The abstract situation depicted in Diagram 1.3 and Tableau 1.5 shows that if we have potential *ambiguity* (i.e., if form f_2 is potentially ambiguous between meaning m_1 and meaning m_2), this ambiguity may disappear under bidirectional optimization. Note that this does not imply that all cases of potential ambiguity disappear under bidirectional optimization. Only if there is an alternative form f_1 which is the preferred way to express one of the two meanings does the potential ambiguity disappear. A similar result can be obtained with a markedness constraint on meanings $*m_2$ in combination with a stronger faithfulness constraint $*<f_2, m_1>$, as the reader can verify. In this case, there is potential *optionality* (i.e., meaning m_2 may be optionally expressed as form f_1 or as form f_2), which disappears under bidirectional optimization.

So if the strongly bidirectional OT system not only contains markedness constraints, but in addition has one or more faithfulness constraints, we create the possibility of ending up with multiple optimal solutions also for strong bidirectional optimization. This is relevant because there may be reasons to prefer strong bidirectional optimization to weak bidirectional optimization, as is pointed out in the next section.

1.3.4 The relation between OT syntax and OT semantics

In this book, we investigate the assumption that speakers and hearers take into account their conversational partner's perspective in communication, although usually not in a conscious fashion. As was shown above, this assumption is able to explain cases of total and partial blocking in language. In the next chapters, we present evidence that the intricate interaction between speaking and understanding not only shapes the forms and meanings within one language, but is also able to explain why languages can differ with respect to their mappings between form and meaning, and how they can differ. Obviously, taking into account someone else's perspective in decision making, on top of your own perspective, is a highly complex task. Indeed, as we will show, children until a rather late age experience problems performing this task.

If production and comprehension are interrelated, an important question to ask is what is the exact relation between production and comprehension. A number of studies have argued against the recursive mechanism of weak bidirectional optimization as an online mechanism of linguistic processing (Beaver and Lee, 2004; Zeevat, 2000). Beaver and Lee's main objection concerns its property of recursion, which allows for an in principle infinite number of rounds of optimization. Because suboptimal candidates can become winners in a second or later round of optimization, 'in Weak OT, everyone is a winner', as Beaver and Lee (2004:126) put it. In other words, weak bidirectional OT's property of recursion results in an overgeneration of form-meaning pairs. However, Blutner, de Hoop and Hendriks (2006:149) suggest that general cognitive limitations on recursion may restrict recursion in bidirectional optimization. These general cognitive limitations would then restrict the application of bidirectional optimization to at most two rounds, in agreement with the bounds that can be observed for higher order epistemic reasoning required for playing strategic games (Hedden and Zhang, 2002). Because it seems possible to explain restrictions on the recursive application of bidirectional optimization by general cognitive limitations, the remainder of this book will appeal to weak bidirectional optimization for the proposed analyses. But note that in at least some of the cases the proposed analysis in terms of the recursive mechanism of weak bidirectional optimization can be reformulated in terms of the non-recursive mechanism of strong bidirectional optimization (see Section 5.5 of Chapter 5).

Although most linguists agree that hearers somehow take into account the alternative forms a speaker could have used (this forms the basis of the well-known Gricean implicatures), there seems to be a general feeling among linguists that speakers are 'lazy' and do not take into account the perspective of their hearers. Zeevat (2000) illustrates this on the basis of a Dutch example like the following:

(9) Wie   ziet   Jan?
    who   sees   Jan
    (i)   'Who sees Jan?'
    (ii)   'Whom does Jan see?'

Meaning (i), where *wie* is interpreted as the subject of the verb, reflects the canonical word order in main clauses in Dutch, which is SVO (Subject-Verb-Object). Meaning (ii), on the other hand, where *wie* is interpreted as the direct object of the verb, reflects a non-canonical OVS word order. According to all known syntactic analyses, meaning (ii) is more marked than meaning (i). Hence, meaning (i) is the optimal meaning. Nevertheless, as Zeevat points out, sentence (9) allows for meaning (ii), although not as the preferred reading. Zeevat argues that this example presents a major problem for symmetric bidirectional optimization models, in which the influence of comprehension on production is the mirror image of the influence of production on comprehension, such as the two versions of bidirectional OT discussed earlier. Because meaning (i) is the optimal meaning, and because there is only one form, this form is predicted to be unambiguously interpreted as (i) in a symmetric bidirectional OT model.

Because this prediction seems to be contradicted by the facts in Dutch, Zeevat argues for an asymmetric version of bidirectional OT. In Zeevat's asymmetric version, a unidirectional OT model for production forms the basic system. In comprehension, the set of candidate meanings is restricted by using results of production as a filter. So production is a unidirectional process, whereas comprehension is a bidirectional process, reflecting the view that speakers do not care about hearers but hearers have to take into account speakers. As a result, ambiguity such as exemplified in (9) is predicted by the model. A completely opposite asymmetric version of bidirectional OT has been proposed by Wilson (2001), who argues that the candidate set for production should be restricted by using results of comprehension (see also Jäger, 2004, for a slightly different proposal).

A drawback of these asymmetric OT models is that they fail to explain certain phenomena that seem to require the interaction between production and comprehension. Zeevat's asymmetric model, for example, fails to account for partial blocking phenomena on the side of the hearer, as well as for word order freezing phenomena and recoverability effects on the side of the speaker. Word order freezing is the phenomenon that in certain circumstances the options for word order variation disappear. For example, in principle both SVO word order (10) and OVS word order (11) are possible in Dutch main clauses, although the SVO word order is the unmarked word order:

(10) Zij ziet hem.
    she sees him
    'She sees him.'

(11) Hem ziet zij niet.
    him sees she not
    'She does not see him.'

The pronouns *zij* and *hem* carry case information and hence disambiguate the grammatical function of the pronouns. When the pronouns are replaced by proper names, however, the word order variation disappears. Sentence (12) can only mean that Marie sees Jan, not that Jan sees Marie.

(12) Marie ziet Jan.
    Marie sees Jan
    'Marie sees Jan.'

Although the syntax of Dutch allows both word order variants (compare (10) and (11)), speakers use sentence (12) only for expressing the meaning that Marie sees Jan, which reflects the canonical word order SVO. This seems to be related to the fact that hearers will interpret (12) as only expressing the canonical word order. So speakers must be aware of the hearer's options, otherwise they would use this sentence for expressing both meanings. Word order freezing therefore yields another argument for symmetric bidirectional optimization (see also Kuhn, 2003; Lee, 2001; Vogel, 2004). But how then should we account for the ambiguity of (9)? According to Bouma (2006, 2008), the ambiguity in (9) can be accounted for in a symmetric bidirectional model if certain constraints are unranked with respect to each other. However, by allowing constraints to be unranked with respect to each other we weaken the assumption of strict dominance among constraints. It is an empirical issue whether this weakening of the grammar is allowed in the light of other properties of the language.

In this section we discussed several possible architectures of a bidirectional optimization model, differing in the way comprehension and production (i.e., OT syntax and OT semantics) are related. We listed several strengths and weaknesses of each of these architectures. Which architecture is the correct one for describing and explaining natural language phenomena cannot be decided on the basis of current work and is a topic for future research. In the following chapters, we will proceed from a symmetric weakly bidirectional OT model of grammar and show how such a model is able to account for a wide range of natural language phenomena. Alternative bidirectional optimization models will only be discussed when relevant.

The next section is concerned with the embedding of OT within cognitive science. Because OT is a formal and functional theory at the same time, it is a natural step to attempt to integrate linguistic results with results obtained in other areas of cognitive science where the focus is on developing formal models for explaining human cognitive behavior.

1.4   OT and cognitive science

An important step in the study of language was the Chomskyan revolution in the late 1950s and early 1960s. In cognitive science, a similar revolution took place during the same period, which is generally referred to as the cognitive revolution. In 1959, Chomsky published an influential critique of B.F. Skinner's *Verbal Behavior*, a book in which Skinner offered a speculative explanation of language in behavioral terms. Chomsky's critique on Skinner and his other work during this period contained several important ideas which have influenced linguistics and cognitive science since. Two ideas are of particular interest for the discussion in this book, because they allow us to distinguish OT from other theories of language: the idea that grammar should be studied as a formal system, and the idea that the grammar is a system of knowledge.

In his book *Syntactic Structures* (1957), Chomsky introduced transformational grammars. Utterances (sequences of words) are taken to have a syntax which can be largely characterised by a formal grammar. This formal grammar accounts for the productivity of language: With a finite set of rules it is possible to generate an infinite number of sentences. The finite set of rules distinguishes sentences that are generated by the grammar from sentences that are not generated by the grammar. As a result, this generative syntactic approach is able to yield precise predictions as to which forms are possible in a given language and which forms are not. This formal approach to syntax was later extended to semantics, and became successful through the work of Richard Montague in the late 1960s. It is now employed in many linguistic frameworks, including model-theoretical semantics, head-driven phrase-structure grammar, lexical-functional grammar, and categorial grammar. As the aim of these formal approaches is to build precise models of (usually subsets of) natural language, they lend themselves for use in natural language applications such as automatic parsers, intelligent search engines and question-answer systems.

A second idea that has influenced both linguistics and cognitive science is the idea that human behavior can only be explained by referring to mentalist notions such as memory, attention, meaning, and knowledge. Many linguists now view the study of language as the study of the knowledge that language users posses. However, these linguists do not usually aim at investigating why language structure is the way it is. Because Chomsky hypothesized that an important part of the grammar must be innate, functionalist explanations are usually rejected in generative syntax (e.g., Newmeyer, 2002; see Bresnan and Aissen, 2002, for a reply). Some other linguistic frameworks do take a functionalist perspective on language (e.g., functional grammar, cognitive linguistics), but generally tend to put much less emphasis on formal analysis.

OT is a formal as well as functional theory and hence combines insights from generative syntax with insights from functionalist theories of language. On the formal side, OT yields precise and testable predictions with respect to possible and impossible forms and meanings. As a result, OT provides a strong and falsifiable theory which lends itself to computational modelling, as can be witnessed by many existing computational OT models in areas such as phonological parsing, pronoun resolution, syntactic parsing, and musical grouping. An asset of OT is its robustness. Not only well-formed sentences but also ill-formed sentences can be given an optimal interpretation. This accounts for the capacity of human hearers to also be able to interpret unacceptable sentences such as *Who do you think that hit John?* As we will see in later chapters, incomplete or conflicting information does not pose a problem for OT models either. Instead, an optimization approach is particularly suited for situations in which a system has to deal with conflicting information.

On the functional side, OT allows for a cognitive or physical grounding of the constraints (cf. Boersma, 1998), although it need not be the case that all constraints must have a functional motivation. For example, many markedness constraints promote economy on the side of the speaker or the hearer (e.g., the constraint DROP-TOPIC that was discussed in section 1.2.2). Furthermore, as in many functionalist theories, similar types of explanation can be given across different modules of the grammar because OT can be applied to phenomena in phonology, morphology, syntax, semantics and pragmatics alike. Because the basic assumptions of OT are such that OT does not require a modular view on the grammar, cross-modular constraint interaction and the interaction of linguistic constraints with non-linguistic constraints can also be explained.

The formal as well as functional approach of OT will be illustrated on the basis of many concrete examples presented in the rest of this book. These examples will demonstrate the explanatory force of OT with respect to the comprehension of words and sentences, cross-linguistic variation in meanings, and the acquisition of meanings in a first language.

1.5   Overview of the rest of the book

This chapter offered a brief introduction into optimization approaches to natural language interpretation. We put forward the view that natural language interpretation can be viewed as a process of optimization over a set of conflicting constraints. The remainder of the book investigates conflicts in interpretation that arise at different linguistic levels: the level of the discourse, the level of the sentence, and the level of word meaning. We start from the highest level, that of the discourse (Chapter 2), and descend to phenomena that are at the interface of discourse and sentence (Chapters 3, 4 and 5), further down to the level of the sentence (Chapters 6 and 7), and end with the lowest level of meaning, namely that of word meaning (Chapter 8).

In Chapter 2, we discuss the rhetorical relations that hold between different clauses in a discourse. It is shown that speakers and writers use their knowledge of how hearers and readers will interpret the utterance to manipulate and persuade their audience. Chapter 3 focuses on word order variation in Dutch. Here it is argued that hearers must optimize bidirectionally and take into account the alternative forms a speaker could have used to arrive at the intended meaning of the sentence. Chapter 4 shows that under this bidirectional analysis of word order scrambling in Dutch, children must be assumed initially not to optimize bidirectionally. Only from the age of 7 or even later do they show the adult pattern of forms and meanings, and start to assign marked meanings to marked forms. Chapter 5 argues that this is not a particularity of the phenomenon under discussion or the language under discussion, but rather seems to be a general pattern in first language acquisition. Assuming that the capacity for bidirectional optimization may take some time to acquire or mature, a straightforward explanation can be provided for the remarkable observation that children's production of a given form may precede their comprehension of the same form by several years. Chapter 6 investigates the phenomenon of negation across languages. It is shown that the stepwise re-ranking of constraints on negation derives the well-known patterns of diachronic language change known as the Jespersen cycle. A similar cross-linguistic perspective is taken in Chapter 7, where the differences among languages in the interpretation of bare nouns such as *jail* (as in *in jail*, as opposed to *in the jail*) are investigated. The resulting bidirectional analysis is able to explain some well-known differences between Germanic languages and Romance languages, which have never been given a systematic explanation before. In Chapter 8, it is shown that such a bidirectional analysis can be extended to the lexicon and is able to explain the different but related meanings of prepositions such as *through* and *around*. Words seem to constrain each other's meaning, resulting in different meaning patterns. Chapter 9, finally, wraps up the discussion.

2   Rhetorical structure

'Let rhetoric be an ability, in each case, to see the available means of persuasion.'

(Aristotle, Pisteis)

2.1   Cause and effect

Since Artistotle's work on rhetoric (Kennedy, 1991), understanding the available means of persuasion is treated as a major part of rhetoric. Persuasion occurs through (the apparent truth of) the argument (*logos*), through (the character of) the speaker (*ēthos*), or through (the emotion of) the hearers (*pathos*). In the present chapter we focus on the first strategy of persuasion and we will argue that in order to persuade their audience, speakers (writers) effectively use their implicit linguistic knowledge of how hearers arrive at the optimal interpretation of a speaker's utterance. We will illustrate this use of bidirectional optimization with an alternation in the order in which a *when*-clause and a main clause are presented and the concomitant interpretations.

Whatever its justice, Parmenion's murder seemed inevitable. As Robin Lane Fox puts it: 'Parmenion, powerful father to a condemned son, was a threat quite unprecedented since Alexander's accession, and it is not in the least surprising that in self-defense Alexander arranged his assassination.' (Robin Lane Fox, *Alexander the Great*, Penguin Books, 1973). The circumstances under which Parmenion was killed, are well-known. An envoy was sent out to offer Parmenion two letters. The first one was from Alexander the Great himself. The second one was sealed as if from Parmenion's condemned son.

(1)   He began to read the letter with pleasure, when they stabbed him.

The relation between the main clause and the *when*-clause in (1) is a temporal relation in accordance with the basic meaning of *when* (cf. de Swart, 1999). Crucially, we do not get the interpretation that the event that the *when*-clause refers to is a consequence of, or otherwise caused or triggered by the event described in the main clause. Nor do we get an interpretation in which the event referred to by the *when*-clause triggers or causes the event in the main clause. The interpretation obtained in (1) is that the events of reading and stabbing are temporally related to each other: he started reading the letter with pleasure

25

and while he was reading they stabbed him. Thus, there is temporal overlap between the state of reading the letter and the stabbing.

According to de Swart (1999) the semantics of *when* is a relation of temporal overlap, but this is a rather 'weak' meaning that is often augmented or overruled by the establishment of a 'stronger' rhetorical relation such as a causal relation. A postponed *when*-clause such as in (1) often gives rise to a special effect in a narration. It is used to 'interrupt' a certain state. The main clause provides the background information for the event in the temporal clause. The effect is that *suddenly* something happens within the context given by the preceding main clause. That is indeed the interpretation obtained in (1): He was reading the letter with pleasure, and *then* – all of a sudden – they stabbed him. Another example is given below:

(2)   He and Massingham were at the door when she suddenly called out imperiously: 'Young man!'

[P.D. James, Death of an expert witness]

De Swart (1999) calls the interpretation of the postponed *when*-clause in examples such as (1) and (2) 'narrative'. It is not always the case that the main clause provides the background state and the *when*-clause the interrupting event in a narration. In fact, the *when*-clause can also be preposed and contain the state which forms the background for the 'sudden' event given by the main clause.

(3)   When they were in the car fastening their seat-belts, Massingham exploded: 'Good God, you'd think Kerrison could find someone more suitable than that old hag to care for his children. She's a slut, a dipsomaniac, and she's half-mad.'

[P.D. James, Death of an expert witness]

Sentences (2) and (3) are alike but with reversed roles for the *when*-clause and the main clause. Both fragments have in common that the first clause provides the state that is interrupted by the event referred to in the second clause. Note that in (3) too we get the interpretation of temporal overlap, which is due to the meaning of *when* (de Swart, 1999). Clearly, the *when*-clause in (3) is used to specify the time at which Massingham exploded and it could even be replaced by a simple time adverbial such as *at 6 o'clock* or *at that moment*. In (1)-(3) the temporal overlap reading is in accordance with the basic meaning of *when* and it is the preferred reading.

The relation called *Background* by Lascarides and Asher (1993) gives an interpretation that is hardly distinguishable from the temporal overlap reading:

(4)   *Background*(a,b): The state described in b is the 'backdrop' or circumstances under which the event in a occurred (no causal connections but the event and state temporally overlap).

However, we claim that it is the *when*-clause itself that provides the meaning of temporal overlap, and in the context of a state that is 'interrupted' by an event, this automatically gives the suggestion of the state describing the situation in which the event occurred. Another example of this reading is given below:

(5)   Olympias was an orphan under her uncle's guardianship, when Philip first met her.

[Robin Lane Fox, *Alexander the Great*]

Whereas Lascarides and Asher (1993) would call this a rhetorical relation of *Background*, we assume that the interpretation that is obtained is the consequence of the basic temporal meaning of *when*.

As pointed out above, the semantics of *when* can be defined as the relation of temporal overlap, but very often, 'stronger' rhetorical relations emerge (de Swart, 1999). In (3), it is hard to imagine (though possible in a certain context) that the situation described by the *when*-clause provides the trigger or causal antecedent for the situation of the main clause. However, a causal interpretation does arise in (6), for example:

(6)   He had such an effect on me that he'd only have to be working close to me in the Laboratory and I'd start shaking. When he was away at a scene of crime it was like heaven. I could work perfectly well then.

[P.D. James, *Death of an expert witness*]

Obviously, the state that the person describes as 'like heaven' is the effect of the situation of the other person being away. It was like heaven *because* he was away. This is a stronger relation than the relation of temporal overlap, although clearly in this example the two states completely overlap in time. So, here we see that the basic interpretation of temporal overlap between the two states is augmented by a causal relation, such that the state given by the *when*-clause is the cause and the state described in the main clause the effect.

In fact, the establishment of a stronger rhetorical relation, such as a causal one, can even cancel out the temporal overlap interpretation.

(7)   When Alexander asked his music-teacher why it mattered if he played one string rather than another, the teacher told him it did not matter at all for a future king, but it did for one who wanted to be a musician.

[Robin Lane Fox, *Alexander the Great*]

In (7) both the preposed *when*-clause and the main clause refer to events, not states, and the optimal interpretation is such that there is no temporal overlap between the two events. In time, the event of asking is followed by the event of answering. Only when the teacher would start his answer before Alexander had finished his question, would there be actual temporal overlap, but this is not very likely. However, whether or not there is temporal overlap or succession does not seem important, because the two events are clearly rhetorically related to each other. There is a clear cause-effect relation: the question triggers the answer. So, the *when*-clause refers to an event, but this event does not have to overlap with the event in the main clause, because there is a causal relation between the two events.

At this point, consider what happens when we prepose the *when*-clause of sentence (1):

(8) #   When they stabbed him, he began to read the letter with pleasure.

Now, a temporal overlap relation is not very plausible: *At 6 o'clock he began to read the letter with pleasure* would be just fine, but to specify the time indirectly as 'when they stabbed him' gives an implausible reading. A causal relation is not plausible either: it is not likely that stabbing him would result in his reading the letter with pleasure. Hence, what we get is an infelicitous sentence, indicated by the symbol '#'.

Crucially, however, it is world knowledge that makes the sentence in (8) infelicitous. When we replace the main clause by another one, as in (9), the sentence becomes fine. The interpretation that immediately arises is a causal one, such that indeed the stabbing is presented as the cause of his death. Again, when there is a cause-effect reading, the temporal overlap reading might disappear. That is, whether or not there is temporal overlap between the two events, or whether the stabbing happens before the dying, seems not important. Both are possible.

(9) When they stabbed him, he died.

Thus, when a stronger rhetorical relation is established between the preposed *when*-clause and the main clause, the temporal overlap interpretation becomes less important, or even disappears. Hinrichs (1981) and Partee (1984) provide the following examples to show that a preposed *when*-event *can* even temporally follow the main event:

(10) When the Smiths threw a party, they invited all their friends.

(11) When Smith spoke, Jones introduced him.

Yet, as Partee (1984) already observes, there is a strong tendency to interpret the *when*-clause event description 'broadly' so that the main clause event occurs within it: throwing a party *includes* planning and sending invitations, and the introduction of the speaker can be counted as *part of* the speaking event. The fact that we automatically construe *spoke* in (11) as 'making a speech' supports this idea. Similar examples (the first one provided by Caroline Féry, p.c., the second one adapted from Moens and Steedman, 1988) are:

(12) When John took a bath, he undressed.

(13) When the council built the bridge, the architect drew up the plans.

Clearly, in all the examples (10)-(13), although the actual temporal order of the events may not match the clause order, it is clear that the *when*-clause provides the trigger or the *rhetorical antecedent* for the event described by the main clause. In (10)-(13) the rhetorical relation between the events is definitely stronger than for example in (3) above, where the *when*-clause just gives the temporal background against which the event described in the main clause happens. In (12) for example, the undressing is *triggered* by the event of taking a bath (and not the other way around), even though the two events take place in reversed temporal order. Thus, the relation established between the two events expressed by the subclause and the main clause is more than the merely 'narrative' relation in (3).

De Swart (1999) argues that in a rhetorical relation, *when*-clauses often provide the rhetorical antecedent (e.g., the cause), but never the rhetorical anaphor (e.g., the effect). Preposing a *when*-clause as in (6) and (7) above evokes a rhetorical relation between the events of the subordinate clause and the main clause: the *when*-clause event functions as the rhetorical 'antecedent', the cause, and the main clause event as the 'anaphor', the effect. The relevant rhetorical relation can be defined as follows (Lascarides and Asher, 1993):

(14) *Result*(a,b): the event or state described in a causes the event or state described in
    b.

The sentences in (1)-(3), on the other hand, seem to lack such a rhetorical relation reading. Instead, we obtain a reading of temporal overlap (de Swart, 1999). As we have already seen, there is not a one to one mapping between the order of the clauses and the type of reading that is preferred. For instance, we can get a causal reading for a postponed *when*-clause as well, as for example in:

(15) He had cried half a day, when his dog fell sick and died.

[Mary Renault, Fire from heaven]

Clearly, the preferred reading of (15) is such that the event described in the *when*-clause provides the rhetorical antecedent or trigger for the event of the main clause: his dog fell sick and died and that caused his crying. Of course, a temporal overlap reading is possible as well, such that his having cried half a day forms the temporal background for the event that his dog fell sick and died, but this is not the reading that comes to mind firstly when reading the sentence in (15).

The possible readings for preposed and postponed *when*-clauses that we have witnessed so far are listed below:

(16) He and Massingham were at the door when she suddenly called out imperiously:
'Young man!'.
Temporal overlap (he and Massingham were at the door ∘ she suddenly called
out) [temporal overlap (= ∘) between the situations represented by the main
clause and the *when*-clause]

(17) When they were in the car fastening their seat-belts, Massingham exploded.
Temporal overlap (they were in the car fastening their seat-belts ∘ Massingham
exploded) [temporal overlap between the situations represented by *when*-clause
and the main clause]

(18) He had cried half a day, when his dog fell sick and died.
Result (his dog fell sick and died, he cried half a day) [the event described by the
when-clause causes the event described by the main clause]

(19) When they stabbed him, he died.
Result (they stabbed him, he died) [the event described by the *when*-clause
causes the event described by the main clause]

To sum up, we never get a causal relation between the two events in which
the event described by the main clause is the rhetorical antecedent (trigger) of
the event described by the *when*-clause (de Swart, 1999). This is independent
of the position of the *when*-clause, i.e., whether it is in preposed or postponed
position. On the other hand, both preposed and postponed *when*-clauses may
express a rhetorical relation such that the *when*-clause event constitutes the
rhetorical antecedent (trigger, cause) for the main clause event (effect). Note
that in the case of these causal readings, there is not necessarily temporal
overlap between the events referred to by the main and the subclause (an
example is (17) where the stabbing may occur *before* the dying). Finally,
both preposed and postponed *when*-clauses allow for a temporal overlap
interpretation.

Obviously, in a temporal overlap interpretation, there *must* be temporal
overlap between the situations provided by the two clauses. This is supported
by the difference in interpretation that emerges between the following two
sequences:

(20) They stabbed him when he died.

(21) They stabbed him. He died.

In (20) a causal reading is highly implausible, as it would say that the dying
caused the stabbing. Thus, what we get in (20) as the optimal interpretation,
is a mere temporal overlap reading, due to the meaning of *when*. On this

reading, the two events temporally overlap: they stabbed him while he was dying. That is, it cannot be the case that the stabbing happens before the dying. In other words, (20) cannot get the same interpretation as (21). In (21) the two independent clauses immediately give rise to the causal interpretation. This goes hand in hand with succession in time: they stabbed him (cause), he died (effect). Even when we interpret the sequence in (21) as merely temporal (no causal relation), we get succession between the two events rather than temporal overlap. The temporal reading of sentences containing *when*-clauses, however, is a reading of temporal overlap and not succession. That is why we have defined this interpretation of *when*-clauses as *Temporal overlap*. We follow de Swart (1999) in her claim that temporal overlap is the basic meaning of *when*, which can however be overruled by a stronger rhetorical relation such as *Result*.

Let us have a closer look at the sentence in (18) above, and the alternative with a preposed *when*-clause. In principle (that is, in the right context), both the causal as well as the temporal reading are possible for both clausal orders, as given below:

(22) He had cried half a day, when his dog fell sick and died.
    (i)   Result (his dog fell sick and died, he cried half a day)
    (ii) Temporal overlap (he cried half a day ∘ his dog fell sick and died)

(23) When his dog fell sick and died, he had cried half a day.
    (i)   Result (his dog fell sick and died, he had cried half a day)
    (ii) Temporal overlap (his dog fell sick and died ∘ he had cried half a day)

Note that the causal reading remains the same for the two clause orders, in accordance with the claim that *when*-clauses like to provide the antecedent in a rhetorical relation but cannot refer to the rhetorical anaphor. The temporal overlap reading in (22) only specifies that the moment at which he had cried half a day overlaps with the event when his dog fell sick and died. As pointed above, this reading naturally arises in a narration when the state of having cried half a day is suddenly interrupted by the following event. In principle, a temporal overlap reading can also be obtained in (23). When there is no cause-effect relation between the death of the dog and the crying, the *when*-clause can be interpreted as an indirect specification of the time, as if it is just another way of saying *at six o'clock*. However, in this configuration and without further context to suggest otherwise, the temporal overlap reading is even less likely in (23) than it is in (22). Whenever a causal reading is possible, both for preposed and for postponed clauses, this comes out as the preferred one.

2.2   Optimal interpretations of *when*-clauses

The interpretation of the sentences in the previous section can be analysed with the help of violable constraints in an Optimality Theoretic fashion. The constraints that play a role in the interpretation of preposed and postponed *when*-clauses can be briefly characterized as follows: (i) a constraint that favors rhetorical (causal) interpretations in discourse, (ii) a constraint on *when*-clauses that they cannot function as the anaphor in a rhetorical relation, (iii) a constraint that states that the interpretation of the *when*-clause must be faithful to its basic meaning of temporal overlap.

It goes without saying that comprehending a discourse involves more than the interpretation of isolated utterances. A major part of our understanding a discourse boils down to our understanding of the rhetorical structure, i.e., the relations among the utterances in the discourse. Our analysis builds on the hypothesis advocated in Hendriks and de Hoop (2001) that the constraints that interact in determining the interpretation of sentences must be soft in nature, i.e., violable and potentially conflicting. This hypothesis can be applied to the interpretation of *when*-clauses, using the insights and analysis developed in de Swart (1999), and de Hoop and de Swart (2000) on the rhetorical characteristics of constructions involving *when*-clauses. First, let us formulate a general pragmatic constraint that favors rhetorical structure in text. The formulation in (24) is adapted from a general constraint called Doap by Williams (1997) (a more detailed discussion of Doap is given in Section 1.3.1) and it resembles a condition dubbed *Maximize discourse coherence* by Asher and Lascarides (1998):

(24) Dorp: Don't overlook rhetorical possibilities. Opportunities to establish a
rhetorical relation must be seized.

The constraint only appreciates textual coherence or rhetorical structure, it does not state which rhetorical relation is suitable at a given moment. A mixture of linguistic information (tense and aspect, word order) and non-linguistic information (world knowledge) decides whether a rhetorical relation is appropriate in a given context and also which rhetorical relation that is going to be. As we have seen above, *when*-clauses in principle allow for two readings, the temporal overlap and the causal one. Following de Hoop and de Swart (2000), we assume that only the causal reading is sufficiently 'strong' to satisfy Dorp. Thus, the temporal overlap reading follows from the semantics of *when* but it violates Dorp in the circumstance that a causal relation could be established. That is why both in (22) and (23) above the temporal reading can only be optimal if the context would somehow indicate that a causal reading is in fact excluded. Otherwise, the causal reading is the optimal interpretation, in accordance with Dorp.

We also observed above that there is an important difference in anaphoric behavior between independent clauses on the one hand and *when*-clauses on the other. Main and independent clauses favor anaphoric readings, whereas *when*-clauses preferably function as the antecedent in a rhetorical relation. Following Lascarides and Asher (1993), de Swart (1999) argues that main and independent clauses seek to establish a rhetorical relation with an earlier sentence in the discourse. A main or independent clause b thus tries to establish a rhetorical relation R with a clause a which is already part of the discourse representation structure built up so far. It is well-known that time adverbials and temporal clauses do not share the anaphoric possibilities of main and independent clauses. We also noted that *when*-clauses cannot be interpreted as the anaphor in a causal relation such as *Result*. This constraint captures the fact that *when*-clauses cannot function as the anaphor b in a rhetorical relation $R(a,b)$ where the event or state represented by b is the result of the event or state expressed by a (de Hoop and de Swart, 2000):

(25) *ANAPHOR: A *when*-clause cannot function as the rhetorical anaphor (e.g., the effect) in a rhetorical (e.g., causal) relation.

We have seen in Section 1.2.1 that when a causal relation is not plausible, we get a basic temporal overlap reading. This was the reading obtained in (1)-(3), for example, where a causal interpretation is highly implausible. We assume that this type of reading is the consequence of the basic meaning of *when*, captured by a faithfulness constraint:

(26) BASIC-INTERPRETATION: Interpret *when* as expressing temporal overlap.

Above we noted that the establishment of a rhetorical relation either cancels out or augments the temporal overlap reading. To keep the analysis straightforward, we assume that the establishment of a rhetorical reading in both cases counts as a violation of the constraint BASIC-INTERPRETATION, because it implies a deviation from the basic meaning of temporal overlap. With these three constraints we can account for the optimal interpretations we get for the sentences (16)-(19). This is illustrated by the tableaux below. Let us start with sentence (19), repeated as (27), which gets a causal interpretation as follows:

(27) When they stabbed him, he died.

Tableau 2.1: Causal interpretation of a sentence with a preposed *when*-clause

when-clause (e_1), main clause (e_2)	*ANAPHOR	DORP	BASIC-I
☞ *Result* (e_1,e_2)			*
Result (e_2,e_1)	*!		*
Temporal overlap ($e_1 \circ e_2$)		*!	

Tableau 2.1 is an OT semantic tableau in which a given form is evaluated against a set of ranked constraints to determine the optimal interpretation. In Tableau 2.1 the input form is the sentence with the *when*-clause (referring to event 1) preceding the main clause (referring to event 2). The candidate output meanings are the following: the first candidate is the rhetorical relation such that the event of the *when*-clause causes the event of the main clause, while in the second candidate interpretation this causal relation is reversed (now, the event of the main clause causes the event in the *when*-clause). The third candidate interpretation involves temporal overlap between the two clauses.

The ranking of the three constraints for English is motivated as follows. So far, we have encountered no examples of *when*-clauses that provide the anaphor in a rhetorical relation, which indicates that we are dealing with a very strong constraint. We therefore assume that *ANAPHOR is undominated (cf. de Hoop and de Swart, 2000). We have seen examples, such as (19) above, where the basic interpretation of *when* (temporal overlap) is clearly violated while the establishment of a rhetorical relation is satisfied. This indicates that DORP must be ranked above BASIC-INTERPRETATON. On the basis of the examples discussed here, we are not able to determine the relative ranking of *ANAPHOR and DORP. The tableau above shows how the causal reading in which the *when*-clause provides the cause and the main clause the effect comes out as the optimal one, since it only violates the lowest ranked constraint. The second candidate where the causal relation is reversed fatally violates the higher ranked constraint *ANAPHOR, while the third candidate fails to establish the obvious causal relation between the stabbing and the dying.

The derivation of sentence (18), repeated below, runs along the same way. The only difference with (27) is that the *when*-clause is in postponed position. However, the optimal reading is again the causal reading. This is illustrated in Tableau 2.2:

(28) He had cried half a day, when his dog fell sick and died.

Tableau 2.2: Causal interpretation of a sentence with a postponed *when*-clause

main clause (e_2), *when*-clause (e_1)	*ANAPHOR	DORP	BASIC-I
☞ *Result* (e_1,e_2)			*
Result (e_2,e_1)	*!		*
Temporal overlap ($e_2 \circ e_1$)		*!	

The constraint violation pattern is similar to the one observed for sentence (27). So, apparently, for the interpretation it does not matter whether a *when*-clause is in preposed or postponed position. When a causal reading is possible, it wins from a temporal overlap reading. And due to the constraint *ANAPHOR, the causal reading is such that the *when*-clause provides the rhetorical antecedent, even if the clausal order is the other way around, as in (28), where the rhetorical anaphor precedes the antecedent.

Let us now look at the examples which are interpreted in a merely temporal way. Sentence (16) is an example of a postponed *when*-clause, which gives rise to a reading of temporal overlap: the event of the *when*-clause 'interrupts' the state of the main clause. Sentence (16) is repeated below as (29), and the derivation of its optimal interpretation is illustrated in Tableau 2.3:

(29) He and Massingham were at the door when she suddenly called out imperiously: 'Young man!'.

Tableau 2.3: Temporal interpretation of a sentence with a postponed *when*-clause

main clause (e_2), *when*-clause (e_1)	*ANAPHOR	DORP	BASIC-I
Result (e_1,e_2)			*!
Result (e_2,e_1)	*!		*
☞ *Temporal overlap* ($e_2 \circ e_1$)			

If there is no (plausible) opportunity to establish a rhetorical relation, then DORP does not get violated by the temporal overlap reading. On the other hand, forcing a causal interpretation would violate BASIC-INTERPRETATION. Therefore, the third candidate, the temporal overlap reading, comes out as optimal. It does not violate any of the three constraints. It goes without saying that the same holds for a sentence like (17), repeated below as (30), where the *when*-clause is in preposed position.

(30) When they were in the car fastening their seat-belts, Massingham exploded.

Tableau 2.4: Temporal interpretation of a sentence with a preposed *when*-clause

when-clause (e_1), main clause (e_2)	*ANAPHOR	DORP	BASIC-I
Result (e_1,e_2)			*!
Result (e_2,e_1)	*!		*
☞ *Temporal overlap* ($e_1 \circ e_2$)			

Again, without further indication from the context a rhetorical relation between the *when*-clause and the main clause is not plausible. Of course, we can come up with a context in which it is expected that a bomb will explode as soon as Massingham fastens his seat-belts, and then a causal relation would become the preferred one again. But without clues for such a scenario, the temporal overlap reading is the most natural one, since it does not violate DORP. Forcing a causal interpretation which is not likely in the context, would violate BASIC-INTERPRETATION.

To sum up, we have seen four scenarios of preposed and postponed *when*-clauses and their optimal interpretations. In all four cases we have derived the optimal interpretation by evaluation of the relevant candidate interpretations against a set of three constraints that have each been independently motivated in the literature.

2.3   The speaker's perspective

If we can get the right interpretations for both clausal orders, then the question arises why there is word order variation at all. That is, many examples where a rhetorical relation is established, have in fact preposed *when*-clauses, while for postponed *when*-clauses the meaning of 'interruption' is quite common. However, we can get a causal interpretation for a postponed *when*-clause as well, and we can get a temporal interpretation for a preposed *when*-clause. So, from the hearer's point of view, there seems to be no reason to use either a preposed or a postponed *when*-clause to express a certain reading. Therefore we will have a look at the data from the speaker's point of view now, in order to find out what drives a speaker to choose one order or the other. The speaker's point of view is actually very simple.

We first need to find out which forms are optimal from an OT syntactic perspective. Of the constraints introduced so far, only *ANAPHOR is a faithfulness constraint that is relevant for the speaker's direction of optimization as well. This constraint is a ban on the interpretation of a *when*-clause as a rhetorical anaphor and thus it can be read as a ban on the expression of a rhetorical anaphor as a *when*-clause as well. The other constraints only deal with the possible interpretations of *when*-clauses, hence they are not relevant from a syntactic point of view. That is, if the speaker wishes to express a rhetorical relation, then DORP is vacuously satisfied by all candidate expressions, whereas if the speaker only wants to express a temporal overlap relation, then DORP is vacuously violated by all candidates. Similarly, if the speaker wants to express a causal relation, then each output containing a *when*-clause will violate BASIC-INTERPRETATION, while every output that contains a *when*-clause will satisfy BASIC-INTERPRETATION when the speaker wishes to express temporal overlap. But if the speaker would only have to deal with the constraint *ANAPHOR, then there would be complete freedom in the choice for a preposed or a postponed *when*-clause. However, a syntactic constraint whose existence has been independently motivated in various domains, is a constraint that favors canonical word order (cf. Grimshaw, 1997). Also, it has been argued that preposed *when*-clauses are topicalized and that the basic word order of a main clause and a subordinate clause in English is the order in which the main clause precedes the *when*-clause. Thus, we get the following constraint:[1]

(31) STAY: The main clause precedes the *when*-clause.

For this investigation into OT syntax, we consider the two interpretations which are relevant here as the input of speaker's optimization. One is the temporal overlap relation between two events, the other is the causal one. To start with the causal meaning: How is this best expressed? We have encountered the two possible orders of main clause and *when*-clause for this reading, while in both cases the *when*-clause functioned as the antecedent. These two candidates should come out as optimal candidates therefore.

Tableau 2.5: Expression of *Result* with a main clause and a *when*-clause

Result (e_1, e_2)	*ANAPHOR	STAY
when-clause (e_1), main clause (e_2)		*!
when-clause (e_2), main clause (e_1)	*!	*
☞? main clause (e_2), *when*-clause (e_1)		
main clause (e_1), *when*-clause (e_2)	*!	

As for the ranking, *ANAPHOR should again be high-ranked in English, as we cannot express the rhetorical anaphor of a causal relation in a *when*-clause. Two candidates are ruled out immediately because they violate this highest ranked constraint. The two remaining candidates are evaluated against STAY, a competition which is won by the third candidate, which satisfies STAY while the other remaining candidate violates it. However, we already know that this outcome cannot be the right one. We have seen that in fact, although a causal relation may be expressed by a postponed *when*-clause as well, many causal relations are expressed via preposed *when*-clauses. If the optimal expression of a causal relation would satisfy STAY, then we would predict that preposed *when*-clauses would not occur at all. Before we try to solve this puzzle, let us first consider what would be the optimal expression of a temporal overlap relation by the speaker. Consider the tableau below.

Tableau 2.6: Expression of *Temporal overlap* with a main clause and a *when*-clause

Temporal overlap $(e_1 \circ e_2)$	*ANAPHOR	STAY
when-clause (e_1), main clause (e_2)		*!
☞ main clause (e_1), *when*-clause (e_2)		

Since there is no rhetorical relation, the *when*-clause does not provide either the antecedent or the anaphor of a rhetorical relation. Hence, the constraint *ANAPHOR is vacuously satisfied by both candidates. Because we are dealing with temporal overlap here and not with succession, we only have to consider two relevant candidates. That is, we assume that we do not have to make a principled distinction between *Temporal overlap* ($e_1 \circ e_2$) and *Temporal overlap* ($e_2 \circ e_1$); dependent on the context, they boil down to the same reading. Clearly, the canonical word order comes out as the optimal one. Hence, again, we would expect to find no examples at all where a temporal overlap reading is expressed by a preposed *when*-clause. But although these examples are not very common indeed, we presented sentence (3) as an example of exactly this temporal overlap reading for a sentence with a preposed *when*-clause.

In sum, we see that on the basis of the two relevant constraints we identified, we cannot derive the right distribution of preposed and postponed *when*-clauses that describe events in the discourse. STAY is a general markedness constraint on word order and although it is lower ranked than *ANAPHOR, it would guarantee basic word order, i.e., a postponed *when*-clause to express a causal as well as a narrative interpretation.

But now we should return to the possible interpretations of preposed and postponed *when*-clauses, and see whether a combination with OT syntax can help us out of the dilemma of the preferred word order. In the next section, we will combine the OT semantics and OT syntactic analyses developed above, in order to solve the problem of the order in which main clauses and *when*-clauses occur.

2.4   A bidirectional analysis

In bidirectional OT, we evaluate form-meaning pairs. Hence, when we compare the causal and temporal readings with the different clause orders, we can evaluate six pairs of form and meaning. One constraint, to wit *ANAPHOR, plays a role in both the OT syntax derivation as well as the OT semantics derivation, while DORP and BASIC-INTERPRETATION are only active in OT semantics and STAY only in OT syntax. In the bidirectional analysis presented below the derivation of the super-optimal pairs of form and meaning is illustrated. As we now compare different meanings *and* different forms in different contexts, the constraint DORP can no longer be evaluated. That is, we must assume that when a causal relation is established between the two clauses, DORP is satisfied, but when no causal relation is established between the two clauses, the context can be such that a causal relation is not plausible, hence there is no 'opportunity to establish' a causal relation, and DORP is still satisfied. Hence, in the bidirectional evaluation of form-meaning pairs, we must assume that DORP does not play a role, i.e., it is vacuously satisfied by all candidate pairs. That is why we leave this constraint out of consideration in the evaluation. As for the ranking of the other constraints, we assume that BASIC-INTERPRETATION and STAY are tied constraints, that is not ranked with respect to each other. As we will see, this gives us the right set of super-optimal pairs of form and meaning.

Tableau 2.7: Bidirectional optimization of two events expressed by a main clause and a *when*-clause

	*ANAPHOR	BASIC-I	STAY
☞ <*when*-clause (e_1), main clause (e_2), *Result* (e_1,e_2)>		*	*
<*when*-clause (e_1), main clause (e_2), *Result* (e_2, e_1)>	*	*	*
<*when*-clause (e_1), main clause (e_2), *Temporal overlap* ($e_1 \circ e_2$)>			*
<main clause (e_2), *when*-clause (e_1), *Result* (e_1,e_2)>		*	
<main clause (e_2), *when*-clause (e_1), *Result* (e_2, e_1)>	*	*	
☞ <main clause (e_2), *when*-clause (e_1), *Temporal overlap* ($e_2 \circ e_1$)>			

In the first round of optimization, one pair of form and meaning comes out as super-optimal, as it does not violate any of the constraints. This is the sixth pair which combines the optimal basic word order with the basic meaning of temporal overlap. This super-optimal pair immediately blocks the other pairs that share either the basic word order (the fourth and fifth pair) or the basic meaning (the third pair) with the super-optimal pair. These three pairs cannot be super-optimal, therefore. The remaining two candidate pairs (the first and second one) differ from the super-optimal pairs in both form (they have a preposed *when*-clause) and meaning (they express a causal reading). Of these two pairs, the second one violates the highest ranked constraint *ANAPHOR, while the first one only violates the two lowest ranked constraints. Thus, the first candidate comes out as super-optimal as well, and it blocks the second candidate. We end up with two bidirectional winners, the postponed *when*-clause is used to express the basic (temporal overlap) meaning, while the preposed *when*-clause is used to express the rhetorical (causal) reading. Now we have solved the puzzle of the distribution of preposed and postponed *when*-clauses. Although unidirectionally, the postponed *when*-clause is the optimal form for both types of readings, from a bidirectional point of view, that is, taking into account both the speaker's and the hearer's options, the preposed *when*-clause is the optimal way to express the rhetorical (causal) reading. This makes the sentences in (16) and (19) with their preferred interpretations the winners from a bidirectional point of view. As argued by de Swart (1999) and de Hoop and de Swart (2000) these are indeed the most common pairs of form and meaning. That is, preposed *when*-clauses are easily interpreted as the antecedent of a rhetorical relation, as in (19), which is repeated below as (32), while postponed *when*-clauses are often used for a 'sudden' event that temporally overlaps (interrupts) the state expressed by the main clause, as in (16), repeated below as (33):

(32) When they stabbed him, he died.

(33) He and Massingham were at the door when she suddenly called out imperiously: 'Young man!'.

The final question that remains to be answered is how we arrive at the form-meaning pairs that we find in the sentences (17) and (18). First, reconsider (18), repeated below for convenience:

(34) He had cried half a day, when his dog fell sick and died.

In (34), the *when*-clause is interpreted as the causal antecedent, although it is in postponed position. Hence, (34) is not bidirectionally optimal. However, we have also witnessed in the previous sections that the sentence is unidirectionally optimal, both from the point of view of the speaker, and from the point of view of the hearer. Thus, the speaker has chosen the syntactically optimal form (the canonical word order) and the hearer will arrive at the right (causal) interpretation, because otherwise DORP would be violated. Definitely, the sentence violates BASIC-INTERPRETATION but we know that this is a low ranked interpretation, so violating it is always better than violating DORP. Therefore, although (34) is not super-optimal, from a unidirectional point of view it does not cause any problems, and hence we do find examples like these as well. Let us now return to the final example, sentence (17), repeated below as (35):

(35) When they were in the car fastening their seat-belts, Massingham exploded.

Sentence (35) is not bidirectionally optimal either, but it only violates one constraint and that is the syntactic constraint STAY which is notoriously a low-ranked constraint that is easily violated, as we have seen. From a unidirectional semantic point of view, (35) is optimal, but not from a syntactic point of view. However, we have not taken into consideration other syntactic constraints that might influence word order. For instance, it is possible that constraints on topicalization and focussing interact with the constraint on canonical word order. Cross-linguistically, temporal adjuncts, and spatio-locational expressions in general, often occupy the first position in a sentence, in order to 'set the scene'. We already noted that the *when*-clause in (35) gets a merely temporal interpretation, and could be replaced by a temporal adverb such as *yesterday* or *at 6 o'clock*. Thus, it might be that another constraint that we have not taken into account in our discussion here, triggers the fronting of the *when*-clause in (35). In the tableau below it is shown that apart from the two bidirectionally optimal pairs of form and meaning, the third and the fourth candidate come out as unidirectionally optimal. The fourth candidate has the optimal form, which it shares with the sixth candidate, while the third candidate has the optimal meaning, which it shares with the sixth candidate. Thus, although the first candidate is bidirectionally optimal as is the sixth one, in a unidirectional competition, it might lose from the third candidate in semantics and from the fourth candidate in syntax. This is shown in the tableau below:

Tableau 2.8: Bidirectional and unidirectional optimization of two events expressed by a main clause and a *when*-clause

		*ANAPHOR	BASIC-I	STAY
☙	<*when*-clause (e_1), main clause (e_2), *Result (e_1,e_2)*>		*	*
	<*when*-clause (e_1), main clause (e_2), *Result (e_2, e_1)*>	*	*	*
(☞)	<*when*-clause (e_1), main clause (e_2), *Temporal overlap ($e_1 \circ e_2$)*>			*
(☞)	<main clause (e_2), *when*-clause (e_1), *Result (e_1,e_2)*>		*	
	<main clause (e_2), *when*-clause (e_1), *Result (e_2, e_1)*>	*	*	
☙	<main clause (e_2), *when*-clause (e_1), *Temporal overlap ($e_2 \circ e_1$)*>			

We conclude that although the sixth and the first candidate are truly bidirectional winners, in real language we expect to find examples of the third and fourth candidates as well. This is indeed the case. However, as argued in the literature, the first and the sixth candidates are the most common. This means that when a speaker wishes to convey a temporal overlap meaning, the use of a postponed *when*-clause will be the best choice, whereas a rhetorical (causal) reading is best expressed by a preposed *when*-clause. In the next section, we will show how this linguistic fact that follows from bidirectional optimization, can be used by speakers to manipulate (persuade) their audience.

2.5   Persuasion through clause order

Parmenion's murder seemed inevitable. Presumably, there was no causal relation whatsoever between the reading the letter with pleasure and the stabbing. However, not all people agree on that. We have seen that when the sequence of events is described as in sentence (1) above, we cannot establish a causal relation at all. The relation between the reading the letter with pleasure and the stabbing can then only be a coincidental, temporal relation. Accordingly, this is usually how the event is described, as for example in (34) or (35):

(36) He began to read it 'with an expression of evident pleasure', when his generals drew their daggers and stabbed him repeatedly.

[Robin Lane Fox, *Alexander the Great*]

(37) He was reading the second 'joyfully, as could be seen from his countenance',
when they struck him down.

[Mary Renault, *The nature of Alexander*]

That is, the reading of the letter expressed by the main clause provides the
state, the background, that is interrupted by the killing event, expressed by the
postponed *when*-clause. As we know now, this is the most common interpretation of a postponed *when*-clause. And this combination of form and meaning is
bidirectionally optimal. In principle, we could get a cause-effect reading such
that the killing would result in the reading of the letter with pleasure. Not only
would the form-meaning pair no longer be bidirectionally optimal, but such
a reading is of course highly implausible according to our world knowledge.
Crucially, a cause-effect reading such that the reading the letter with pleasure
caused the stabbing is not possible at all in (36) and (37), since the stabbing
is described by the *when*-clause and a *when*-clause cannot function as the
rhetorical anaphor in a causal relation. Therefore, we are left with the temporal
overlap reading only. Parmenion was happily reading the letter when suddenly
he got stabbed.

Yet, suppose an author wishes to speculate on a possible causal connection between the reading with pleasure and the killing, in the sense that the
former causes the latter. This can then be done by reformulating the sentence.
A *when*-clause cannot be interpreted as a rhetorical anaphor, hence the killing
event must be expressed by a main clause, whereas the antecedent event of
reading the letter with pleasure is provided by a *when*-clause. Moreover,
in order to exclude a temporal overlap reading, the *when*-clause is best put
in preposed position. This is exactly the rhetorical strategy used by Mary
Renault when she wishes to convince her readers that Parmenion's evident
pleasure while reading the letter actually triggered his murder. Renault's idea
is that Parmenion's smile conveyed his guilty knowledge of the conspiracy
against Alexander the Great. His guilt would justify the murder ordered by
Alexander. So, the letter would be a test case. If Parmenion would show
pleasure, he should be killed. But if he would show something else, he
wouldn't have to be killed.

In the following sentence, Parmenion's reading the letter with pleasure
must be interpreted as a sign that *caused* the stabbing.

(38) It was when Parmenion showed evident pleasure at its contents, and not before,
that he was killed. If he had shown puzzlement, irritation, vague disapproval,
anger, fear, would the daggers have been drawn?

[Mary Renault, *The nature of Alexander*]

Clearly, this speculative interpretation of history is simply achieved by using this particular linguistic construction: a preposed *when*-clause. Note again that the causal relation cannot be attributed to the use of *when* itself: the basic meaning of *when* is temporal overlap between the two events. In fact, this is even emphasized by the contrast with *before* in the subsequent phrase: it was when and not before showing evident pleasure, that Parmenion was killed. In other words, the author only states in words that the temporal relation is one of overlap and not of precedence. However, by preposing the *when*-clause, the rhetorical relation of *Result* is obtained, even without stating this explicitly with a word such as 'because'. Indeed, the author implicitly yet effectively communicates the intended causal relation between reading the letter with pleasure and the stabbing by using a preposed *when*-clause to describe the reading event. The process of bidirectional optimization then leads the hearer to this one and only interpretation: Parmenion's reading the letter with pleasure caused his murder. Thus, via the linguistic mechanism of bidirectional optimization, the author of this sentence forces the reader to understand the *when*-clause as a rhetorical antecedent of a causal relation not by altering the content of the words, but by putting them in a different order.

Notes

1   Note that STAY is a markedness constraint according to the (informal) definition of markedness constraints in Section 1.2.3 of Chapter 1, since it only takes into account the output of optimization.

3 Escape from stress: pronouns in Dutch

3.1 Variation in form versus variation in meaning

This chapter investigates a well-known instantiation of variation of form in Dutch, *viz.* the occurrence of a direct object either to the right or to the left of a sentential adverb, generally captured under the term *scrambling*. We will show that in general there are two structural positions available for direct objects in Dutch. We will argue that an adequate analysis of the phenomenon requires us to link the two forms to different meanings for the objects under consideration. We will show that the two forms do not necessarily correspond to two available meanings in a one to one mapping. Rather, marked forms are used for marked interpretations, and what comes out as 'marked' varies across different types of direct objects. We propose a bidirectional OT analysis to account for the Dutch word order data, in particular with respect to pronominal objects such as *him* and *her*. We illustrate the general idea of bidirectional OT with the link between the marked form (i.e., the position to the right of an adverb) and the marked meaning (i.e., a contrastive meaning) of pronominal objects in Dutch.

In the literature on scrambling in Dutch, the object position to the right of a sentential adverb is called the unscrambled position, the one to the left of the adverb the scrambled position. Hence, (1b) is called the scrambled counterpart of the unscrambled word order in (1a). Sometimes, scrambling is truly optional, as in (1) below, with a definite object. In the sentences under (1) scrambling is optional. That is, the sentences (1a) and (1b) are equally well-formed and without further clues from the context or intonation, there is no clear difference in meaning:

(1) (a) We hebben eerst de kat gevoerd.
           we have first the cat fed

     (b) We hebben de kat eerst gevoerd.
           we have the cat first fed
           'First we fed the cat.'

The paradigm in (1) is an illustration of the fact that *definite* object noun phrases in Dutch scramble freely. There is a tendency that the object to the right of the adverb preferably gets a non-anaphoric reading (such that *de kat* 'the cat' in (1a) refers to a uniquely determined cat, for instance the cat of the speaker, about

which the speaker starts talking 'out of the blue'), while the object to the left
of the adverbs gets an anaphoric reading (one gets the interpretation that a cat
has already been introduced in the discourse and is now being talked about),
but this tendency can easily be overruled (cf. de Hoop, 2000, 2003), also in the
examples in (1). Sentence (1a) can be used in a context where the discussion
is already about the cat, and sentence (1b) can be used 'out of the blue' as well
(hence, without a linguistic antecedent) as long as the speaker and the hearer
both know which unique individual is meant by *de kat* 'the cat'. There is no
clear-cut difference in interpretation between the a- and the b-sentences. Both
sentences fit different contexts. In this respect, definites behave differently
from both indefinites and pronouns. As for indefinites, the scrambled order
is marked (indicated by the sign # before the sentence), and it gives rise to a
special meaning effect. This is illustrated by the following examples:

(2) (a)   We hebben   eerst   een kat   gevoerd.
              we have   first   a   cat   fed

  (b) # We hebben   een   kat eerst   gevoerd.
        we have   a   cat first   fed
       'First we fed a cat.'

Although the orders adverb-before-object, and object-before-adverb in (2)
are both grammatical, the second one, the scrambled word order, is highly
'marked'. Indefinite objects usually occupy the position to the right of the
adverb. So, when they scramble as in (2b), this marked form gives rise to a
marked meaning. That is, while the indefinite object in (2a) gets a neutral,
existential reading (just a cat, some cat, not specified), in (2b) *een kat* 'a cat'
seems to refer to a specific or a certain cat. Following common practice, we will
refer to the first reading of *een kat* 'a cat' as *non-specific* or *non-referential*, and
to the second as *specific* or *referential*. The latter reading is highly marked for
an indefinite object noun phrase, not only because obviously the indefinite form
is not the optimal form for a 'definite' (i.e., specific) reading, but also because
objects in general tend to get a non-specific rather than specific reading. Usually,
a definite or demonstrative form would be chosen to refer to a specific cat. The
indefinite form in combination with the scrambled position thus gives rise to
a marked interpretation, that is, it has a special meaning effect. Also, when a
speaker would like to say something about a specific cat, she could choose to
make the cat the subject rather than the object of the sentence, as in *The cat
had to be fed first*, for example. In the next chapter, we will elaborate upon
the relation between marked forms and marked interpretations of indefinite
noun phrases. In this chapter we will focus on the scrambling behavior of
pronominal objects in Dutch.

Unlike indefinites, pronouns scramble to the left of an adverb almost obligatorily. In (3), it is the *unscrambled* position that is 'marked' for a pronominal object, and again this marked form gives rise to a special meaning effect which leads to a 'marked' (a deictic or contrastive) meaning for a pronoun.

(3) (a) # We hebben eerst hem gevoerd.
        we have first him fed

    (b) We hebben hem eerst gevoerd.
        we have him first fed
        'First we fed him.'

Without doubt, the unmarked reading for pronouns is the anaphoric reading. As in the English translation, the preferred reading of *hem* 'him' in (3b) is an anaphoric one: *him* refers back to a previously mentioned individual in the discourse. Alternatively, *him* can be accented (compare *First we fed HIM*) in which case either a deictic (pointing) or a contrastive (*him*, not *her*) reading is obtained. Under the contrastive reading, the pronoun can still be anaphoric, while deictic readings are non-anaphoric. Both contrastive and deictic readings are marked readings for a pronoun, but deictic readings rarely occur, especially in written language (cf. de Hoop, 2004). In this chapter we abstract away from deictic readings and assume they can be analysed similarly to contrastive readings, since both receive stress and both are marked readings for a pronoun. Thus, we will only deal with the contrastive reading as a marked reading of pronouns and analyse the interplay between scrambling, stress, and interpretation. Before we turn to the analysis of pronouns, however, we will have a closer look at the only truly optional case of scrambling discussed above, the (un)scrambled definite object in (1).

Examination of the examples (1)-(3) reveals that definites behave as if they are in the middle of a scale, where indefinites are at one end and pronouns at the other (cf. Givón, 1983). If we say that pronouns and indefinites are each other's opposite in terms of anaphoricity or topicality, then the scale of interpretation seems to align with the scale of scrambling in Dutch. Indefinites are often the focus (hence non-anaphoric and non-topical) and they prefer to 'stay' in unscrambled position. Pronouns are mostly anaphoric and topical and prefer to scramble. And indeed, definites are often anaphoric, but also quite often non-anaphoric, and accordingly, they feel happy in both positions. Therefore, it is tempting to try to account for the scrambling data in (1)-(3) in terms of topicality and anaphoricity, too. That is, since pronouns are usually topical (or anaphoric) whereas indefinites are usually not, we might wonder whether scrambling (variation in word order of the object and the adverb) in Dutch is actually *triggered* or *driven* by underlying semantic or pragmatic features such as topicality or anaphoricity. Indeed, both analyses have been proposed in the literature.

Choi's (1996) condition NEW requires that a [-new] (i.e., old) element must precede a [+new] (i.e., new) element. However, Choi investigates word order variation among arguments (i.e., the precedence relations among subjects, direct objects and indirect objects), while we are concerned with the relative order of direct objects and adverbs. Therefore, in de Hoop (2000, 2003) Choi's condition is reformulated as follows:

(4)   NEW: Anaphors scramble.

Note that in (4) the term *anaphor* is used rather than *topic*. Both anaphors and topics are often defined in terms of de-accentuation. Yet, not all anaphors are also (sentence or discourse) topics. Besides, it is well-known that objects are less often topics than subjects (which goes hand in hand with the observation that objects are frequently indefinite and not very often pronominal). Still, anaphoric objects in Dutch tend to scramble, even when they are not clear topics. Hence, the notion *anaphor* better captures the Dutch scrambling data than the notion *topic*.

As we pointed out above, definites are in the middle of a scale: they are anaphoric more often than indefinites but less often than pronouns. Definite objects can occur in both scrambled and unscrambled positions in Dutch, usually without any effect on the grammaticality or well-formedness of the sentence. The condition NEW in (4) suggests that this optionality is more apparent than real and that the context determines whether a definite should be in scrambled or unscrambled position, in accordance with the claims made by Choi (1996). However, de Hoop (2003) discusses data from a Dutch children's book and finds several counterexamples to this generalization. She concludes that scrambling of definites is really optional in Dutch, despite the general tendency that anaphoric definites scramble more often than not. This optionality can be illustrated by embedding the example sentences in (1) in a broader context. First, consider a context in which there is no antecedent available for *de kat* 'the cat'.

(5)   We gaan naar de bioscoop, maar…
      (a)   we   hebben   eerst   de   kat   gevoerd.
            we   have   first   the   cat   fed

      (b)   we   hebben   de   kat   eerst   gevoerd.
            we   have   the   cat   first   fed
            'We're going to the cinema, but first we fed the cat.'

When there is no antecedent for *de kat* 'the cat' in the previous discourse, *de kat* gets a non-anaphoric interpretation. Because it is a definite, it must refer uniquely, though, so the implicature is that it refers to the cat of the speaker (or of the persons denoted by *we*), although it can also be the cat of somebody else as long as the speaker *and* the hearer know which cat is meant. However, this reading is obtained in both the a- and the b-sentence. That is, Dutch native speakers agree that replacement of one word order variant by the other is allowed in the above case. The same holds for non-anaphoric definite objects which refer to a unique individual, such as *the sun* or *the queen*, and for non-anaphoric non-specific definites such as *the bus* in expressions like *take the bus* (van der Does and de Hoop, 1998), as shown in the following examples.

(6) (a) We willen   morgen   de koningin zien.
         we want   tomorrow the queen   see

     (b) We willen de koningin   morgen   zien.
         we want the queen   tomorrow see
         'We want to see the queen tomorrow.'

(7) (a) We willen morgen   de bus nemen.
         we want tomorrow the bus take

     (b) We willen de bus morgen   nemen.
         we want the bus tomorrow take
         'We want to take the bus tomorrow.'

Thus, in (5)-(7) we see truly optional scrambling of *non-anaphoric* definites, i.e., definite objects that do not have an antecedent in the previous discourse. Similarly, anaphoric definites can scramble freely. That is, we can make up a context in which the definite noun phrase must get an anaphoric interpretation:

(8) De buren hebben een kat en een hond. Toen wij op ze moesten passen,...
     (a) hebben we eerst de kat gevoerd.
         have   we first   the cat fed

     (b) hebben we de kat eerst gevoerd.
         have   we the cat first   fed
         'The neighbours have a cat and a dog. When we had to look after them, we
         first fed the cat.'

In (8) *de kat* 'the cat' is interpreted anaphorically, i.e., it necessarily refers back to *the cat of the neighbours*, independent of whether it is in unscrambled position as in (8a) or in scrambled position as in (8b). Crucially, because there is a potential antecedent (*een kat* 'a cat' in the preceding sentence), we must assign an anaphoric interpretation. Unlike in (5) above, *de kat* 'the cat' in (8) cannot refer to the cat of the speaker or the cat of the speaker and the other person denoted by *we*. In (8) *the cat* must refer to the cat of the neighbours. Hence, the object gets an anaphoric interpretation independent of its position. But if anaphoric definites as well as non-anaphoric definites freely alternate between the scrambled and the unscrambled position in Dutch, then NEW alone cannot adequately describe scrambling in Dutch. We will argue below that NEW interacts with other constraints, which explains the pattern of optional scrambling.

In the literature it is usually assumed that the unscrambled word order is the unmarked or canonical word order in Dutch. So, if a direct object does not scramble, it satisfies the constraint STAY (Grimshaw, 1997; see also Section 2.3). Here we use a slightly different formulation than Grimshaw's to focus on the phenomenon of scrambling.

(9) STAY: No scrambling.

Obviously, each anaphoric object will give rise to a conflict between the conditions NEW and STAY. Dependent on which of the two constraints is stronger, anaphors will either scramble (NEW >> STAY) or stay in situ (STAY >> NEW). A third possibility is that the constraints are equally strong, in which case we expect optional scrambling. This is how Choi (1996) accounts for certain optional patterns of scrambling. However, NEW and STAY cannot account for the fact that sometimes, non-anaphoric objects scramble as well. If NEW and STAY were the only constraints that govern word order variation in Dutch, non-anaphoric objects would never scramble. This is not the case, however, as we have seen (examples (5b), (6b), (7b)). Hence, a third constraint has to be involved. STAY is a constraint that disfavors scrambled structures in general. However, frequency and well-formedness of scrambling of different types of objects seems to be also a matter of pure form (indefinite, definite, pronoun), irrespective of discourse status (being an anaphor or not). Therefore, we adopt the following constraint (de Hoop, 2000, 2003) that obviously conflicts with STAY:

(10) SCRAMBLING 1 (SC1): Definite objects scramble.

In an OT-syntactic analysis the input is a semantic representation, while the candidate outputs are a set of syntactic structures. The optimal syntactic structure (the winner) is the structure that best satisfies the different constraints.

In OT syntax only optimal structures are grammatical. This means that when the input contains an anaphoric definite in Dutch, both the scrambled and the unscrambled output structure have to be optimal, since they are both well-formed. This can be represented in an OT syntax tableau:

Tableau 3.1: From anaphoric definite to optional scrambling

Anaphoric definite	Sc1	New	Stay
☞ + scrambling			*
☞ - scrambling	*	*	

The input in Tableau 3.1 gives rise to two optimal output structures, a scrambled and an unscrambled structure. To account for this pattern, we have to assume that the three constraints are not ranked with respect to each other in Dutch, or, they are equally strong.

Let us now consider the case of non-anaphoric definites. New, the condition that plays an important part in the scrambling behavior of anaphoric definites, is not activated in the case of non-anaphoric definites. This leaves only the conflicting constraints Stay and Sc1 to affect the scrambling behavior of non-anaphoric definites, as illustrated in Tableau 3.2. Again, both output candidates are winners, since the constraints Sc1 and Stay are not ranked with respect to each other:

Tableau 3.2: From non-anaphoric definite to optional scrambling

Non-anaphoric definite	Sc1	New	Stay
☞ + scrambling			*
☞ - scrambling	*		

Although we are now able to explain why there are two optimal output structures for an input containing an anaphoric definite as well as for an input containing a non-anaphoric definite, this is not yet totally satisfactory. In fact, it would be more satisfactory if we could also account for the fact that we observe a strong tendency to satisfy New. That is, anaphoric definites scramble more often than not. Clearly, the analysis represented in Tableau 3.1 above does not explain this tendency. It only accounts for the observation that both output structures are well-formed in the case of an anaphoric definite. De Hoop (2000, 2003) explains this pattern with the partial ranking model of Anttila and Cho (1998). Under the assumption that constraints are partially ordered instead of totally ordered in natural languages, Anttila and Cho (1998) account for patterns of optionality. They derive statistical predictions and generalizations with respect to grammaticality judgements as well as preferences. When three constraints are not ranked with respect to each other as in our example, this partial hierarchy captures a set of six possible rankings, i.e., six total hierarchies. Subsequently, Anttila and Cho use the following formula:

(11) (a)   An output candidate is predicted by the grammar iff it wins in some tableau.

(b)   If a candidate wins in n tableaux and t is the total number of tableaux, then the candidate's probability of occurrence is n/t.

By (11a), both scrambled and unscrambled anaphoric definites are predicted by the grammar. Furthermore, by (11b) we predict that 2/3 of the anaphoric definites scramble. This means that even if scrambling is in principle free for anaphoric definites, we do scramble them more often than we leave them in situ. In general, it seems easier to scramble non-anaphoric definites than to leave anaphoric ones in situ. This is explained by the fact that NEW does not play a role in the case of non-anaphoric definites. Hence, NEW is vacuously satisfied when the input contains a non-anaphoric definite. Indeed, the model of Anttila and Cho (1998) predicts scrambling of a non-anaphoric definite in 50% of the cases (cf. de Hoop, 2000, 2003).

If indeed definite objects are free to scramble or not, only partly dependent on their anaphoricity, then how come hearers/readers in Dutch never interpret these definites wrongly? Hearers are able to correctly assign anaphoric interpretations to definites in both scrambled and unscrambled position (see example (8) above). Similarly, non-anaphoric definites are interpreted correctly, again irrespective of scrambling (example (5)-(7) above). This can be explained by distinguishing productive from interpretive optimization.

Word order conditions such as Sc1 and STAY are not relevant conditions in OT semantics, since they are violated or satisfied already at input level, hence they cannot affect the candidate outputs (anaphoric or non-anaphoric readings) for a certain input. NEW is important, because in interpretive optimization it is violated whenever an unscrambled definite gets an anaphoric interpretation. However, there is another constraint involved here which obviously outranks NEW. This stronger constraint favors anaphoric interpretations and it was called DOAP by Williams (1997).

(12) DOAP: Don't Overlook Anaphoric Possibilities. Opportunities to anaphorize text must be seized.

DOAP is a general pragmatic constraint that is satisfied whenever a noun phrase is interpreted anaphorically. In the previous chapter, we proposed a similar constraint, DORP, in the domain of rhetorical structure. While DORP favors the establishment of rhetorical relations between situations in the discourse, DOAP favors the establishment of coreference relations between discourse referents. In other words, when there is a potentially anaphoric noun phrase and a potential linguistic antecedent, then DOAP requires a referential link between the antecedent and the anaphor. DOAP, being an interpretive constraint, applies to noun phrases independently of their syntactic position (scrambled or unscrambled). Thus, we obtain the anaphoric interpretation as the optimal (hence, the only) interpretation for the definite in (13) below, whether it has scrambled or not.

(13) Gisteren moesten we op de kat van de buren passen. We wilden naar de bioscoop gaan, maar…

    (a) we moesten eerst de kat voeren.
         we had-to first the cat feed

    (b) we moesten de kat eerst voeren.
         we had-to the cat first feed
         'Yesterday, we had to look after the cat of our neighbours. We wanted to go to the cinema, but first we had to feed the cat.'

In (13) it is impossible to interpret *de kat* 'the cat' as referring to an individual other than the cat of the neighbours, for instance the cat of the speaker. This equally holds for the scrambled object in (13b) as well as the unscrambled one in (13a), which proves that DOAP must be stronger than NEW. The optimal anaphoric interpretation of (13a) violates NEW, but this is not a fatal violation: NEW must be violated in (13a) in order to satisfy DOAP. The other (non-anaphoric) interpretation would violate DOAP. Because there is a better candidate interpretation available, the interpretation that violates DOAP is not available for (13a) (the cat of the neighbours and the 'unscrambled cat' have to be one and the same cat). This is illustrated in Tableaux 3.3 and 3.4.

Tableau 3.3: From scrambled object to anaphoric interpretation

Linguistic antecedent + scrambled definite	DOAP	NEW
☞ anaphoric interpretation		
non-anaphoric interpretation	*!	

Tableau 3.4: From unscrambled object to anaphoric interpretation

Linguistic antecedent + unscrambled definite	DOAP	NEW
☞ anaphoric interpretation		*
non-anaphoric interpretation	*!	

In this section we discussed the OT analysis for the optional scrambling of definite objects in Dutch, proposed by de Hoop (2000, 2003). By distinguishing between productive and interpretive optimization, it explains why optional scrambling does not affect the interpretation of definites.

However, while the analysis can account for the scrambling behavior of definite objects in Dutch, it does not account for the scrambling behavior of indefinite noun phrases and pronouns. That is, it does not account for the link observed above between marked forms and marked meanings in the distribution of indefinite and pronominal objects. If we assume a word order constraint such as 'Pronouns scramble' then we can account for the fact that this constraint is hardly ever violated if we assume that this constraint is stronger than STAY, but the problem is that we should then predict obligatory scrambling of pronouns. However, as pointed out above, we do find cases where pronouns stay in situ, but where this induces a 'special meaning effect'. The same but reverse holds for indefinites. A word order constraint that states that indefinite noun phrases do not scramble, in addition to STAY, would predict no scrambling for indefinite objects at all. The question arises how we can explain the fact that unscrambled pronouns and scrambled indefinites do exist and moreover, that they give rise to a certain interpretation. We claim that a bidirectional approach as also taken in the previous chapter can solve this problem. In this chapter we will develop a bidirectional perspective as well in order to account for the scrambling behavior of pronominal objects in Dutch. In the next chapter we will present a bidirectional analysis of the scrambling characteristics of indefinite objects in Dutch, in relation to children's late acquisition of marked meanings for marked forms.

3.2   Super-optimal pronominal objects in Dutch

In the present section we will present the basic picture of a bidirectional OT perspective on scrambled pronouns in Dutch, that will be further refined in Section 3.3 below. Reconsider the core facts, presented in example (3) of the previous section, repeated below as (14). Pronouns usually scramble, so for pronouns the word order in (14b) is the unmarked one.

(14) (a) # We hebben eerst hem   gevoerd.
           we have   first him   fed

   (b)   We hebben hem   eerst gevoerd.
           we have   him   first fed
           'First we fed him.'

The unmarked reading that goes with the unmarked (scrambled) position of the pronominal object in (14b) is the anaphoric reading, i.e., *hem* 'him' seems to refer back to an individual previously introduced in the discourse. When the pronoun occupies the marked (unscrambled) position, this induces a shift in meaning. The reading that arises for the pronoun in the unscrambled position in (14a) is a deictic (non-anaphoric) or a contrastive reading, which are both marked (less frequent) interpretations for pronouns (see Chapter 9 for a discussion of the different perspectives on markedness). These readings are the direct result of accenting the pronoun. The unscrambled object position is typically the position where the main sentence stress falls in Dutch, because this is the most embedded position of the sentence (Neeleman and Reinhart, 1998, following Cinque, 1993). On the deictic reading, this stress can be accompanied by pointing or by a movement of the head. On the contrastive reading, the stress signals a rhetorical relation of Contrast in the discourse (see Chapter 2 for some other examples of rhetorical relations that can be established in discourse) between the individual denoted by the pronoun and another individual in the discourse (de Hoop, 2004). So, without further clues, the unmarked order for the pronominal object in (14b) is associated with an unmarked interpretation, while in (14a), the marked position induces a 'special effect', that is, a marked reading for the pronoun, either deictic or contrastive. De Hoop (2004) found around 50 examples of stressed pronouns (indicated by the use of italics) in the novel *Fire from heaven* by Mary Renault, of which only one or two were examples of deictic pronouns. The other occurrences were all interpreted as contrastive, but not deictic, readings. This might be related to a difference between oral and written language, but it might also be that the rhetorical relation of Contrast is more frequent in discourse than deixis. Because we will only present examples from written language in our discussion of scrambled pronouns in the next section, we will ignore the deictic reading of pronouns in our analysis. Yet, the deictic reading is also a marked reading for pronouns, and it also comes with stress. Therefore, we believe our analysis could be easily extended to capture this type of marked meaning for pronominal objects as well.

A bidirectional OT approach makes it possible to account for the fact that marked (sub-optimal) forms are used for marked (sub-optimal) meanings, in this case the use of the unscrambled position for a contrastive pronominal object. This is illustrated in Tableau 3.5. In this bidirectional OT tableau, the optimal form is simply the result of an undefined constraint F and the optimal meaning of an undefined constraint M. In the remainder of this chapter, we will investigate what actual constraints on form and meaning determine the super-optimal form-meaning pairs.

Tableau 3.5: Super-optimal form-meaning pairs of pronominal objects

Pronominal object	F	M
☞ <[scrambled], non-contrastive>		
<[unscrambled], non-contrastive>	*	
<[scrambled], contrastive>		*
☞ <[unscrambled], contrastive>	*	*

The unmarked form and unmarked meaning would be the optimal outcomes of unidirectional optimization, from meaning to form and *vice versa*. However, it is quite clear that a unidirectional approach (either productive or interpretive optimization) could never account for the occurrence of sub-optimal forms in combination with sub-optimal meanings in such a natural way. The bidirectional OT approach straightforwardly accounts for this general pattern. The same holds for the general pattern of combining forms and meanings of indefinite objects in Dutch which will be the subject of the next chapter.

At this point, we will examine how the marked forms and meanings come about. In the remainder of this chapter we will investigate the potentially conflicting constraints that play a role in determining the optimal form of pronominal objects. Because form does not only involve position but also stress, we will see that even the unscrambled position can be the optimal form for pronouns under certain conditions. As for the optimal *reading* of pronouns, we will simply assume a constraint that penalizes contrastive readings for pronouns. In this chapter the bidirectional analysis focuses on the structural aspects, that is the variation in marked and unmarked forms for pronouns. The next chapter, on the other hand, focuses more on the interpretive aspects, that is, the variation in marked and unmarked readings of indefinites.

3.3   More super-optimal pronominal objects in Dutch

The bidirectional tableau presented in the previous section predicts that pronouns usually scramble (as this is the unmarked form) and get a non-contrastive interpretation, whereas an unscrambled pronoun is a marked form that is used to express a marked (contrastive) reading. The use of an unscrambled pronoun (marked form) for a contrastive reading (marked meaning) is exemplified by the following example. In this chapter, examples written in italics are examples taken from the book *Kees de jongen* by Theo Thijssen (Amsterdam, 1939 edition).[1]

(15) 'Afgelopen', zei oom schor, en Kees hoorde hem snikken. 'Ach God', zei tante. En Kees hoorde ook haar snikken.

' 'It's over', said uncle hoarsely, and Kees heard him sob. 'Oh God', said aunt. And Kees heard her sob as well.'

In (15) a rhetorical relation of Contrast is established between two situations: Kees heard *him* (his uncle) sob and Kees heard *her* (his aunt) sob. The pronoun *haar* is in unscrambled position (to the right of the particle *ook* 'too') and it gets accented. A similar example is given in (16).

(16) Hij keek haar na uit z'n bed. Ze bleef even stil staan. Haar hoofd, beschenen door het lampje, kwam net boven de trapopening uit. Ze tilde 't lampje hoog boven zich uit, dat het licht ook hem weer bescheen.
'He watched her from his bed. She stood still for a moment. Her head, lighted by the lamp, reached just above the opening of the stair. She raised the lamp high above her, so that the light also shined on him again.'

Again, the pronoun *hem* 'him' is to the right of *ook* 'too', and it gets accentuated due to a contrastive reading: first, the light shines on *her*, then the light shines on *him*. Clearly, in these cases the marked (unscrambled) form goes with the marked (contrastive) meaning. Two constraints, one on forms and one on meanings, could account for this markedness pattern in a bidirectional perspective. Let us formulate the following constraints:

(17) SCRAMBLING 2 (Sc2): Pronouns scramble.

(18) *CONTRAST: Pronouns refer anaphorically and non-contrastively.

The constraint SCRAMBLING 2 (Sc2) is similar to SCRAMBLING 1 (Sc1) ('Definite objects scramble') proposed above, but it applies to pronouns instead of definites (de Hoop, 2000, 2003). The constraint *CONTRAST penalizes a contrastive reading on a pronoun (de Hoop, 2004). This might eventually turn out to be a more general constraint that not only applies to pronouns, but here it is formulated with respect to pronouns only.

Tableau 3.6: Super-optimal form-meaning pairs of pronominal objects

	Pronominal object	Sc2	*CONTRAST
☞	<[scrambled], non-contrastive>		
	<[unscrambled], non-contrastive>	*	
	<[scrambled], contrastive>		*
☞	<[unscrambled], contrastive>	*	*

Tableau 3.6 provides us with two super-optimal form-meaning pairs of pronominal objects, one that assigns a non-contrastive interpretation to a scrambled pronoun and one that assigns a contrastive interpretation to an unscrambled pronoun. The other two form-meaning pairs are not super-optimal, hence they should not occur. But pronouns do not have to stay in situ to get a contrastive

reading. For example, when the pronoun does scramble, as in (15') below, we still get the (same) contrastive reading.

(15') 'Afgelopen', zei oom schor, en Kees hoorde hem snikken. 'Ach God', zei tante. En Kees hoorde haar ook snikken.
' 'It's over', said uncle hoarsely, and Kees heard him sob. 'Oh God', said aunt. And Kees heard her sob as well.'

Indeed, although Tableau 3.6 might capture the general pattern, it turns out to be too simple to deal with the complete set of data in Dutch. That is, we do find examples of the two other candidate pairs of form and meaning as well, those which are not super-optimal in Tableau 3.6. An example of a scrambled pronoun with a contrastive reading is presented in (19), and an example of an unscrambled pronoun with a non-contrastive reading in (20) below.

(19) Maar niemand wat geven, en háár alleen wel wat?
'But to give no one anything, and only *her* something?'

In (19) the pronoun *her* scrambled to the left of the focus adverb *alleen*, but it does get a contrastive reading. That is, a relation of Contrast is established between two situations: to give *no one* anything, and to give *her* something. Incidentally, the accents on *haar, háár,* 'her', signal the contrastive stress. One might expect that this extra clue is required because the pronoun is in scrambled position. However, in the following example the author uses an accent to indicate contrastive stress on a pronoun in unscrambled position.

(20) En in-eens, daar kreeg de dolheid ook hèm goed te pakken; hij rende rond, en greep, greep maar; af en toe had-ie twee, drie mutsen tegelijk in z'n handen, hij strooide ze in 't rond.
'And at once, the craziness also really got to *him*; he ran around and grabbed, just grabbed, every once and a while he had two, three caps in his hands at the same time, he scattered them around.'

The context in which this example is used is the following: the boys of the school are engaged in a game of grabbing caps from the girls. The *him,* Kees, first does not play along, but then, all of a sudden he does. Thus, a relation of Contrast is established between two situations: the other boys getting crazy, and then also Kees getting crazy. So, both in (19) and (20) there is a clear contrastive reading available for the stressed pronoun, independent of whether the pronoun is in scrambled position (as in (19)) or in unscrambled position (as in (20)). The example in (19) is at odds with the predictions of the bidirectional analysis presented so far. It is an instantiation of the third candidate form-meaning pair in Tableau 3.6 which does not come out as super-optimal, and thus it should not occur. Likewise, the example in (21) represents a non-super-optimal pair, in this case the second candidate in Tableau 3.6 above.

(21) Zou Rosa Overbeek natuurlijk hem opstoken: 'Laat je je dàt doen? Je bent gek, het is gemeen.'
'Then Rosa Overbeek had to provoke him of course: 'Are you going to let that be done to you? You're crazy, it's mean.' '

As observed by van Balen and de Hoop (2005), (21) is an example of pronoun *hem* 'him' which occurs in unscrambled position (to the right of the sentential adverb *natuurlijk* 'of course'), yet which does not get accented and which does not get a contrastive reading either (there is no relation of Contrast established in the discourse). Van Balen and De Hoop found a number of examples like this and they argue that in all these examples it seems to be the case that the adverb gets stressed and not the pronoun.

To conclude, Tableau 3.6 does not yet give an adequate picture of the possible form-meaning pairs of pronominal objects in Dutch. Apart from the two super-optimal form-meaning pairs, we also find examples of the other two form-meaning pairs, the combination of a scrambled pronoun and a contrastive reading (unmarked form – marked meaning) and the combination of an unscrambled pronoun and a non-contrastive reading (marked form – unmarked meaning). The next step is to solve the puzzle presented by these findings, in order to present a more fine-grained analysis that does make the right predictions concerning the different super-optimal pairs of form and meaning, taking into account stress as a partly independent feature of the form as well.

Above it was pointed out that there is no one to one mapping between position and stress. Not all scrambled pronouns are de-accentuated and not all unscrambled pronouns receive stress. However, one other generalization does hold: contrastively stressed pronouns get a contrastive interpretation and vice versa. Therefore, a one to one mapping can be established between form and meaning after all. However, the crucial feature of the form is not the structural position the pronoun sits in (scrambled or unscrambled) but whether or not the pronoun bears stress (de-accentuated versus accentuated). One clear advantage of OT over grammatical models that work with inviolable constraints is that OT is cross-modular. Hence, constraints from different modules (syntax and phonology, for example) can indeed interact.

Neeleman and Reinhart (1998) argue that the scrambled and unscrambled structures for objects in Dutch differ with respect to stress. Following Cinque (1993) they assume that main stress (assigned by the nuclear stress rule) falls on the object in unscrambled position, but on the verb when the object is in scrambled position. They assume that both positions (scrambled and unscrambled) are base-generated positions, so objects do not actually scramble (move) to get de-stressed. However, economy considerations guarantee that the scrambled structure will be used when the verb needs to be stressed, whereas the unscrambled structure will be used when the object needs to be stressed.

According to Neeleman and Reinhart (1998), scrambling an object pronoun has the same effect as de-stressing of the pronoun in English. They even claim that scrambling is obligatory for pronominal objects because de-stressing a pronoun cannot apply when the pronoun is to the right of an adverb. They argue that since in principle the use of a scrambled structure is completely free (as both orders are base-generated), scrambling is less costly than applying a special stress shift operation. Hence, they predict that unstressed pronouns cannot occur in unscrambled positions in Dutch. However, we have already presented the example in (21) above as a counterexample to this generalization and more examples are found as well (van Balen and de Hoop, 2005):

(22) 'Stil', zei tante Jeanne, 'omdat, omdat je pa... omdat moe nou jullie helemaal niet om d'r heen kan hebben, jou ook niet.'
' 'Quiet', said aunt Jeanne, 'because, because your dad... because your mom can't have you(.PL) around her right now, not even you(.SG).' '

In (22), the pronoun is in unscrambled position, i.e., to the right of the adverb *nou* 'right now', yet it is unstressed and does not get a contrastive reading. In the story, the father of Kees is very ill and about to die, and the aunt tells Kees that his mother cannot have her children around her at this moment, not even Kees. Definitely, there is no contrastive reading available for *jullie* 'you(-pl)' (as there is no one in the context that the mother can have around her right now) and the pronoun remains unstressed, although it is in unscrambled position. One more example is provided in (23).

(23) Maar deze mevrouw was een edele dame, en als ze ooit hem nodig had... Maar hoe zou ze hem ooit nodig hebben? Kon je niet weten.
'But this lady was a noble woman, and if she ever needed him... But when would she ever need him? You never know.'

In the first sentence, the pronoun is to the right of the adverb, *ooit hem* 'ever him', while in the second sentence it is to the left, *hem ooit* 'him ever'. Both times the pronoun is unstressed and does not get a contrastive reading in the context of the story. In the first sentence, the pronoun is in unscrambled position, however.

To sum up, Neeleman and Reinhart (1998) argue that an unstressed pronoun *must* be in scrambled position in Dutch, as they assume an absolute relation between scrambled order and de-accentuation of the object. However, we have seen instances of unstressed pronouns in unscrambled position as well as of stressed pronouns in scrambled position. Therefore, we conclude that the link between scrambling and stress is not as tight as Neeleman and Reinhart (1998) believe. We have seen no examples, however, in which the link between contrastive stress and contrastive reading was missing. Notoriously, pronouns are not likely to carry stress (German, Pierrehumbert and Kaufmann, 2006). Therefore, we assume that the marked form for a pronominal object is the stressed form (rather than the unscrambled form), and that the constraint that requires the pronoun to remain unstressed is thus stronger than the constraint that requires the pronoun to scramble. The ranking of the two constraints is given in (26).

(24) *STRESS: No stress on pronouns.

(25) SCRAMBLING 2 (SC2): Pronouns scramble.

(26) *STRESS >> SC2

Obviously, the two constraints on the form of pronouns happen to coincide most of the time, which is why Neeleman and Reinhart assume a direct connection between the two. However, if there is a constraint that says that pronouns scramble and if it is true that in scrambled position pronouns are unstressed, then how can unstressed pronouns ever be in unscrambled position? There must be another, conflicting, constraint that favors the unscrambled position for pronouns. Otherwise, all unstressed pronouns would end up in scrambled position. There is of course yet another constraint that plays a role in the scrambling behavior of pronouns, namely STAY, which applies to all sorts of objects. Neeleman and Reinhart (1998) extensively argue that scrambling and non-scrambling structures are equally economical as they are both base-generated structures, hence they cannot appeal to a constraint such as STAY that would explain that even for pronouns there is a conflicting constraint that requires them to stay in unscrambled position. Unlike Neeleman and Reinhart (1998), we assume that STAY *is* violated in the case of scrambling a pronominal object. However, this constraint must be either low-ranked with respect to the other constraints, or, alternatively, it is not very effective because it is usually overruled by a stronger constraint. We claim that the latter is the case. In general, *STRESS and SC2 go hand in hand, and that is why STAY hardly plays a role at all for pronouns. However, when *STRESS can be satisfied without satisfaction of SC2, then STAY may enter the picture. However, STAY cannot be stronger than SC2 as that would lead to unstressed unscrambled pronouns all over the place. In fact, although the examples we presented in (21)-(23) are perfectly grammatical, they are quite rare. Hence, we propose the following ranking of the three constraints on the form of pronominal objects in Dutch:

(27) *STRESS >> {SC2, STAY}

This ranking predicts that pronouns are usually unstressed, which is in accordance with their main (anaphoric) function (Bresnan, 2001). Scrambling is an easy way to satisfy *STRESS, as also argued by Neeleman and Reinhart (1998). The two constraints SC2 and STAY are necessarily in conflict. This means that satisfaction of SC2 in order to satisfy *STRESS must always result in a violation of STAY. However, if there is an alternative way of satisfying *STRESS without satisfying SC2, then STAY can sometimes determine the winning form as well since STAY and SC2 are tied constraints. In that particular case, we witness an unstressed pronoun in unscrambled position. In the next section we will argue that there is indeed an alternative way of satisfying *STRESS.

At this point, we can derive all four super-optimal form-meaning pairs. We assume that STAY (don't scramble) is equally strong as SC2 (pronouns scramble) but because SC2 usually goes hand in hand with *STRESS, we hardly ever see the effect of this general constraint on word order. But if, for some reason, *STRESS is satisfied independently of the satisfaction of SC2, then this may result in a winner that satisfies STAY and violates SC2 instead of the other way around. It is of course this super-optimal form-meaning pair (an unstressed pronoun in unscrambled position) that won the competition in the examples (21)-(23). Thus, not only a scrambled unstressed pronoun can be the winner of unidirectional optimization (and thus be the unmarked form), also an unscrambled unstressed pronoun can be optimal (and thus unmarked). Similarly, a stressed pronoun in unscrambled position is a marked form, but a stressed pronoun in scrambled position is an equally marked form. The first one violates *STRESS as well as SC2, while the second one violates *STRESS as well as STAY. Both forms are marked (in the sense that they violate these constraints, but also because stressed pronouns are overall more infrequent than unstressed ones), hence both can form a super-optimal form-meaning pair with the marked, contrastive, reading. This is in accordance with what we actually find in Dutch, as pointed out above. That is, although the unscrambled position almost always results in the stressing (and thus, a contrastive reading) of the pronoun, a pronoun in scrambled position can just as well get stress and a contrastive reading. In other words, the pronoun does not have to be in unscrambled position to get stressed. Tableau 3.7 shows the derivation of exactly four super-optimal form-meaning pairs that we can find in Dutch.

Tableau 3.7: Super-optimal form-meaning pairs of pronominal objects

Pronominal object	*STRESS	SC2	STAY	*CONTRAST
☞ <[- stress; scrambled], non-contrastive>			*	
<[+ stress; scrambled], non-contrastive>	*		*	
☞ <[- stress; unscrambled], non-contrastive>		*		
<[+ stress; unscrambled], non-contrastive>	*	*		
<[- stress; scrambled], contrastive>			*	*
☞ <[+ stress; scrambled], contrastive>	*		*	*
<[- stress; unscrambled], contrastive>		*		*
☞ <[+ stress; unscrambled], contrastive>	*	*		*

Because the constraints STAY and SC2 are tied constraints, i.e., not ranked with respect to each other, the first and the third candidate form-meaning pairs are both (equally) optimal, hence super-optimal. These two pairs assign an unstressed pronoun a non-contrastive interpretation, but the position of the unstressed pronoun differs: the pronoun is in scrambled position in candidate 1 and in unscrambled position in candidate 3. Subsequently, all other pairs that have either an unstressed pronoun or a non-contrastive interpretation are blocked by the first two super-optimal pairs. The remaining pairs are those which link a stressed pronoun to a contrastive interpretation. The sixth and eighth candidate pairs violate the highest constraint on forms and the constraint on meaning, but they are not blocked by the other super-optimal pairs which make them super-optimal themselves. These two super-optimal pairs differ in the position of the pronoun, scrambled or unscrambled, but because of the tie between STAY and SC2, they are equally super-optimal as well.

Let us repeat some of the Dutch examples that correspond to the four super-optimal form meaning pairs. The first pair links an unstressed, scrambled pronoun to a non-contrastive interpretation.

(28) Maar hoe   zou   ze hem   ooit   nodig hebben?
     but how   would she him   ever   need have
     'But when would she ever need him?'

The second pair combines an unstressed, unscrambled pronoun with a non-contrastive interpretation:

(29) ... en   als ze ooit hem   nodig had...
          and if she ever him   need had
     '... and if she ever needed him ...'

The third super-optimal pair represents a stressed, scrambled pronoun with a contrastive reading:

(30) Maar niemand wat   geven, en háár alleen wel wat?
     but   nobody   something give   and *he* only   AFF something
     'But to give no one anything, and only *her* something?'

Finally, the fourth super-optimal pair combines a stressed, unscrambled pronoun with a contrastive reading:

(31) ... daar kreeg de dolheid   ook   hèm   goed te pakken...
         there got the craziness also *him* well to get
     '... the craziness also really got to him...'

Thus, all four possible pairs of form and meaning that we encounter for Dutch pronominal objects, are derivable from the three constraints on form combined with the relevant constraint on meaning. A remaining question that needs to be answered concerns the second super-optimal form-meaning pair. Usually, pronouns scramble in order to escape from stress assignment, and if they do not, they get stressed (with a concomitant contrastive reading). We assumed that when there is an alternative escape from stress possible, pronouns do not have to scramble anymore. By staying in unscrambled position, they can satisfy the ban on scrambling. The question is of course what this alternative escape route can be. This question will be answered in the next section.

3.4 Escape from stress

Reconsider the crucial examples of unscrambled unstressed pronouns in (21)-(23), repeated below for convenience.

(32) Zou Rosa Overbeek natuurlijk hem opstoken: 'Laat je je dàt doen? Je bent gek, het is gemeen.'
     'Then Rosa Overbeek had to provoke him of course: 'Are you going to let that be done to you? You're crazy, it's mean.' '

(33) 'Stil', zei tante Jeanne, 'omdat, omdat je pa... omdat moe nou jullie helemaal niet om d'r heen kan hebben, jou ook niet.'
     ' 'Quiet', said aunt Jeanne, 'because, because your dad... because your mom can't have you(.PL) around her right now, not even you(.SG).' '

(34) Maar deze mevrouw was een edele dame, en als ze ooit hem nodig had... Maar hoe zou ze hem ooit nodig hebben? Kon je niet weten.
     'But this lady was a noble woman, and if she ever needed him... But when would she ever need him? You never know.'

Van Balen and de Hoop (2005) observe that the fact that the pronouns in (32)-(34) do not get stressed seems to be related to the fact that the adverbs the pronouns are adjacent to, do get stressed. Of course, the sentences come from a written and not an oral text, but when we pronounce these sentences, it seems natural to stress the adverbs. This also makes sense in the context of the story. Below we indicate the stress on the adverbs by using capital letters.

(35) Zou   Rosa Overbeek NATUURLIJK   hem   opstoken...
     would Rosa Overbeek of course   him   provoke...
     'Then Rosa Overbeek had to provoke him of course...'

This modal construction is used to express the fantasy of Kees, a 12-year old boy, who is constantly day-dreaming about situations that might happen in which he is always the hero. Also, note that Kees has a crush on Rosa Overbeek, a girl in his class. In that context, stress on the adverb becomes very natural: *of course* Rosa should stand by him in his fantasy.

The example in (33) was already explained above. Here, the adverb *nou* 'now' is stressed since *right now* is really a very bad moment for the mother to have the children around her (as the father is about to die):

(36) ... omdat   moe   NOU jullie helemaal nietom d'r heen   kan hebben
       because mom   now   you.PL at all   not around her round can have
     '... because your mom can't have you around her right now'

In the third example again stress on the adverb seems natural. Kees starts day-dreaming about his heroic deeds in the future: if she *ever* needed him, then...

(37) ... en   als ze   OOIT hem   nodig had...
       and if   she ever him   need had
     '... and if she ever needed him...'

Féry (2005) argues that some types of topicalization are motivated by the need to separate two accents which would be adjacent in the alternative word order. Two adjacent accents of equal strengths are not allowed (Selkirk, 1984). In OT this condition is known as *CLASH (Hayes, 1995; Elenbaas and Kager, 1999; Féry, 2005).

(38) *CLASH: Equally strong accents are not adjacent.

Scrambling is one way to avoid accent on a pronoun. However, if a pronoun is adjacent to an element that carries main stress, then the pronoun will not be accented, in order to avoid a violation of *CLASH. Thus, stressing the adverb results in destressing the pronoun, just like scrambling does. So, when the adverb is stressed, *CLASH allows the adjacent pronoun to stay in unscrambled position without getting stressed. As a result, the scrambled order is not the absolute winner anymore. Scrambling an unstressed pronoun would still satisfy Sc2 but violate STAY, whereas for the unscrambled order this would be the other way around (STAY would be satisfied and Sc2 violated).

3.5 Conclusion

In this chapter we accounted for the interplay between position, stress and meaning of pronominal objects in Dutch. We offered a bidirectional OT analysis that goes beyond the simple picture of one marked form linked to one marked meaning, and one unmarked form linked to one unmarked meaning. In fact, as we hope to have shown, different forms (scrambled and unscrambled) can come out as unmarked when they are unstressed and different forms (scrambled and unscrambled) can come out as marked when they are stressed. As before, the marked forms correspond to a marked meaning, which is the contrastive reading for pronouns, while the unmarked forms correspond to unmarked (anaphoric, non-contrastive) readings for pronouns.

Notes

1   Thanks to Jennifer Spenader for translating these examples for us.

4 Children's late mastery of marked interpretations

4.1 Children's interpretations of indefinites

In the previous chapter, we have witnessed how differences in word order in Dutch may go hand in hand with differences in interpretation. One question we wish to raise in the present chapter is how children acquire these form-meaning pairs. In particular, we investigate children's interpretation of indefinite noun phrases in Dutch in different positions in the sentence. Just as we have seen for pronominal objects in the previous chapter, the interpretation of sentences containing indefinite objects (and also indefinite subjects) shows a sensitivity to word order (that is, their position in the sentence). When do children acquire this sensitivity?

The basic word order of a language, i.e., the main order of the subject, the object and the verb (for instance S-O-V or S-V-O) is acquired very early, as it is evident in children's language before age 3 (Meisel, 1992). By age 4, relatively complex syntactic structures such as passive constructions are already known to most children (Borer and Wexler, 1987; Thornton, 1995). In the domain of word order variation, such as scrambling (see the previous chapter), several studies on the acquisition of object scrambling show that children are capable of producing scrambled structures already at a young age as well. For instance, Eisenbeiss (1994) and Schaeffer (1997) show that children aged 2 to 5 frequently scramble definite objects, and Schaeffer (1997) also showed that 4-year old children are capable of scrambling indefinite objects. Unsworth (2005) presents data of a group of 5-year-old children, who all produce scrambled structures. Nearly all definite objects produced by these children appear in the scrambled position, as do the majority of indefinite objects in a context designed to elicit referential interpretations.

Strikingly, however, when it comes to interpreting these word order varieties, the pattern changes. Krämer (2000) showed in several experiments that Dutch children even until the age of 7 have problems in assigning the correct (adultlike) interpretation of scrambled indefinite objects in Dutch. This goes against the generally held assumption in the field of first language acquisition that children first learn to comprehend certain structures before they are able to correctly produce them. In fact, we find that children who can use and understand indefinites and who have acquired the syntactic structures involved, yet do not distinguish the different interpretations of indefinites in an adultlike manner.

For children aged roughly between 4 and 7, the syntactic structure in which the indefinite noun phrase appears does not have the effect it has for adults. We argue that the children's lack of sensitivity to these word order effects reflects a general developmental pattern, by which indefinite objects tend to be interpreted non-referentially, independent of context and word order, while indefinite subjects tend to be interpreted referentially. The question that we focus on in this chapter is why adults are sensitive to these syntactic effects, and why children are not, even though children this age have generally acquired most of adult syntax.

To the student of child language acquisition, the most striking aspect concerning children's indefinite interpretations is the late age of acquisition. The youngest age for which the errors have been reported is four years. In a number of studies, there is a decline in error rate, or at least an indication of a decline, by age seven (Klein, 1996; Krämer, 2000). Other studies report no decline by this age (Krämer, 2000) and even frequent occurrence of the errors at ages 9 and 11 (Termeer, 2002; Unsworth, 2005).

The discrepancy between what children know at an early age and the surprisingly late errors in indefinite interpretations leads to the question of the nature of children's errors. It would seem that, unlike what is commonly assumed, there is something about children's grammars that is not adultlike by age 5. What is this aspect of grammar that still needs to develop? We will come back to this matter in Section 4.4. First, we will present and discuss the relevant data in previous accounts in the literature.

4.2   Indefinite noun phrase interpretations in Dutch

Notoriously, indefinite noun phrases can take different readings. In a sentence such as *He's reading a book*, the indefinite object *a book* can get either a 'referential' reading (paraphrasable as 'a certain book') or a 'non-referential' reading (one book or another, no specific book). In Dutch, as in several other languages, an indefinite object takes on the referential interpretation if it appears to the left of an adverb intervening between the object and the verb, as in (1a), and the non-referential reading when it occurs immediately adjacent to the verb, as in (1b). This phenomenon was also discussed in the previous chapter. Recall that we call the object position to the left of the adverb the scrambled position, while the other position is referred to as the unscrambled one.

(1) (a) De vrouw   heeft   een kat zachtjes geaaid.
          the woman   has   a   cat softly   stroked
          'The woman softly stroked a (particular) cat.'

   (b) De vrouw   heeft   zachtjes een kat geaaid.
          the woman   has   softly   a   cat stroked
          'The woman softly stroked a cat.'

Different authors have labeled the two readings differently, for instance 'specific' or 'non-specific', but in this chapter we will use the terms 'referential' and 'non-referential' for the two interpretations of indefinite noun phrases.

A similar interpretive difference can be found for subjects. Here, the referential reading typically occurs in the canonical, sentence-initial, subject position, as in (2a), while the non-referential reading occurs in an existential construction (where the existence/happening of an event is described in a 'There is/are…' sentence), as in (2b). The association of the sentence-initial subject position with a referential reading is discussed in Milsark (1977) for English. The association is similar, but stronger, in Dutch.

(2) (a) Een meisje   klimt   op de   schommel.
          A   girl   climbs   on the swing
          'A (particular) girl is climbing on the swing.'

   (b) Er   klimt   een   meisje op de   schommel.
          there climbs   a   girl   on the swing
          'A girl is climbing on the swing.'

In examples (1) and (2), the distinction between the referential and non-referential readings of the indefinites is intuitive, but somewhat hard to capture. To bring about clearly distinct readings, we can use the relative scope of the indefinite object and an adverb of frequency as a diagnostic. This proves useful, as we will see below, to assess children's interpretations. Compare (3 a, b). In (3a) we say that the frequency adverb 'twice' is *in the scope of* the indefinite object (that is, the adverb is to the right of the object), while in (3b) the indefinite object is *in the scope* of the adverb (that is, the object is to the right of the adverb):

(3) (a) De vrouw   heeft   een kat twee   keer   geaaid.
          the woman   has   a   cat twice   stroked
          'The woman stroked a cat twice.' (one and the same cat)

   (b) De vrouw   heeft   twee   keer   een kat geaaid.
          the woman   has   twice   a   cat stroked
          'The woman stroked a cat twice.' (likely: two different cats)

In these sentences the two word orders mirror the preferred 'scope readings'. On the one hand, in (3a) *een kat* 'a cat' precedes *twee keer* 'twice' and the reading we get is that there is a (certain) cat (hence, a referential reading) which the woman stroked twice. On the other hand, in (3b) *twee keer* 'twice' precedes *een kat* 'a cat' and the preferred reading is that there were two 'stroking-events' which each involved a cat (hence, a non-referential cat), so it is most likely that the woman in fact stroked two different cats (although, incidentally, she might have stroked the same cat twice at two different occasions).

(4) (a) Een   meisje klimt   twee keer   op de schommel.
          a   girl   climbs   twice   on the swing
          'A girl is climbing on the swing twice' (one and the same girl)

     (b) Er   klimt   twee keer   een meisje op de schommel.
          there climbs twice   a   girl   on the swing
          'A girl is climbing on the swing twice.' (likely: two different girls)[1]

In (4) the alternation is between a canonical sentence and an existential ('there is…') sentence. In the first one, the word order is such that the subject *een meisje* 'a girl' precedes *twee keer* 'twice', and again this gives rise to the reading where a (certain) girl (that is, the referential reading) is climbing on the swing twice. The other reading is obtained in the existential sentence in (4b) where *twee keer* 'twice' precedes *een meisje* 'a girl'. Here, we get the preferred reading that there are two 'climbing-events' involving a girl each (that is, the non-referential reading). So, the most natural reading is that there are two different girls climbing on the swing (one after the other).

4.3   Children's interpretations of indefinites

4.3.1 Indefinite objects

Definite and indefinite determiners are used by children as early as age 2, and whenever indefinite forms are used, they tend to be used correctly (Maratsos, 1974; Karmiloff-Smith, 1979; Zehler and Brewer, 1982).[2]

The second component of grammatical knowledge required for the interpretation of indefinites consists of the meanings that indefinites may take. The question is whether the children of the relevant ages are able to assign both referential and non-referential meanings. Referential interpretations of pronouns and definite descriptions are abundant by age 3, and so are non-referential interpretations of indefinites (Maratsos, 1974; Karmiloff-Smith,

1979). Thus, there is in principle no problem in understanding or using noun phrases referentially and non-referentially.

Krämer (2000), however, tested the influence of scrambling on the interpretation of indefinite objects in Dutch children between 4;0 and 8;0, using sentences like those in (5):

(5) (a) Je   mag   twee   keer   een   potje   omdraaien.
          you may two   time   a   pot   around-turn
          'You may turn a pot around twice.'

     (b) Je   mag   een   potje   twee   keer   omdraaien.
          you may a   pot   two   time   around-turn
          'You may turn a pot around twice.'

Children as well as adults obtain a non-referential reading for the unscrambled indefinite in (5). In the act out task in which the children and adults are asked to perform the 'act' described in this sentence, that means that they turn two pots. For most children below age 7, however, the scrambled indefinites are also interpreted non-referentially, whereas adults always interpret the scrambled indefinites referentially. So, adults always turn one pot twice when they hear (5b) while children generally turn two pots.

Krämer (2000) found similar responses for sentences containing an indefinite object and negation, as in (6):

(6) (a) Het meisje   heeft   geen   appel geplukt.
          the girl   has   not. a apple picked
          'The girl did not pick an apple.' (did not pick any apples)

     (b) Het meisje   heeft   een appel   niet geplukt.
          the girl   has   an apple   not picked
          'The girl did not pick a(n) (particular) apple.'

Most children aged 4 to 7 rejected the referential reading for both sentence types, whereas all adults accepted this reading for sentence (6b).

Interestingly, this finding of children disfavoring the referential interpretation of indefinite objects seems to reflect a universal tendency. For English and Kannada, a Dravidian language (spoken in India), it was also found that children aged 4 and older would only accept non-referential readings for indefinite objects. Numeral noun phrases such as *two guys* also allow for two interpretation, a referential or a non-referential one. The interpretation of sentences like (7) and (8) was investigated in Lidz and Musolino (2002):

(7) Donald didn't find two guys.

(8) Huduganu eraDu ungra karedis-al-illa.
Ernie two ring buy.NEG.INF
'Ernie didn't buy two rings.'

In (7) and (8) two readings are possible. The non-referential reading of the object in (7) is obtained when the sentence describes the situation when it is not the case that Donald found two guys. This non-referential reading of the object in (7) and (8) was accepted by nearly all adults, and 81% (English) and 75% (Kannada) of the children. In contrast, whereas nearly all adults also accepted the referential reading of the object (e.g., there are two guys that Donald didn't find), only 33% (English) and 23% (Kannada) of 4-year-old children accepted the referential reading.[3]

The differential preferences of adults and children for referential and non-referential interpretations of indefinite objects do not seem to be restricted to sentences involving scope ambiguities. Foley, Lust, Battin, Koehne and White (2000) asked children to act out sentences like (9):

(9) Bert touches an apple, and Oscar does, too.

Children aged 4 to 7 preferred to act out this sentence by having Bert and Oscar each touch their own apple (as above, this corresponds to a non-referential reading of an apple). Adults, however, preferred the referential reading on which Bert and Oscar touch the same apple (so, there is only one apple involved).

4.3.2 Indefinite subjects

Whereas for indefinite objects, children prefer non-referential interpretations, the situation for indefinite subjects is opposite. Children generally prefer referential subject interpretations, when adults have the same preference, but as we will see below, even when adults prefer non-referential interpretations.

The interpretation of indefinite subjects has not been as widely researched as that of objects, but cross-linguistic data is available at least for sentence-initial subjects. Musolino (1998) and Lidz and Musolino (2006) report on the interpretation of canonical sentences in English and Kannada. Musolino found that 100% of English adults, and 74% of 4 to 7-year old children accepted a referential reading of sentence (10).

(10) Some horses won't jump over the fence.

A referential reading can be paraphrased as 'For some (of the) horses it is the case that they won't jump over the fence' while a non-referential can be paraphrased as 'It is not the case that (it will happen that) some horses will jump over the fence'. Lidz and Musolino found that 95% of 4-year-old Kannada children would accept a referential reading of (11), as did adults, whereas only 12.5% would accept a non-referential reading.

(11) EraDu   chitte   paTNa-kke   hoog-al-illa.
     Two   butterfly   city.DAT   go.INF.NEG
     'Two butterflies didn't go to the city.'

Klein (1996) found that Dutch children aged 4–7 in the majority of cases accepted the referential reading for the subject in standard subject position, in sentences like (12):

(12) Een   meisje   gleed   twee   keer   uit.
     A   girl   slipped two   time   out
     'A girl slipped twice.'

Termeer (2002) found similar results for older children, aged 8 to 10. Interestingly, her results for the existential sentence in (13) are different:

(13) Er   ging   twee   keer   een jongen   van de   glijbaan af.
     there went   two   time   a   boy   of the   slide off
     'Twice, there went a boy down the slide.'

Only 32% of the children between age 8;7 and 10;4 get an adult-like non-referential reading (two events involving one boy each) for the embedded indefinite subject in (13).

In sum, whereas we find a pattern of children preferring non-referential interpretations for indefinite objects, even when adults will assign referential interpretations, for indefinite subjects, children actually prefer referential inter-pretations, even when adults assign non-referential interpretations. Children even display these preferences when the syntactic configuration of the sentences excludes these readings for adults, as has been shown for Dutch. For children, scrambling does not lead to referential objects and the existential construction does not lead to non-referential subjects.

A host of studies present findings that support the picture that we sketched above (Boysson-Bardiès and Bacri, 1977; Klein, 1996; Musolino, 1998; Krämer, 2000; Foley et al., 2000; Su, 2001; Lidz and Musolino, 2002; Lidz and Musolino, 2006; Termeer, 2002; Unsworth, 2005), but there are exceptions. Gualmini (2002) and Miller and Schmitt (2004) show that, in certain contexts, children of the relevant ages are able to obtain adultlike readings. Krämer (2000) and Philip and Termeer (2002) report child interpretations that deviate both from the adults, and from the general pattern of child errors.

In what follows, we will mainly be concerned with explaining the general pattern of findings, but we believe that an account of children's interpretations of indefinites must be able to accommodate also the more exceptional findings. In fact, we believe that these 'exceptions to the rule' can contribute valuable information about the factors that play a role in both child and adult interpretation of indefinites. Hence we will return to them in Section 4.8.

4.4 Previous accounts

Several accounts have been proposed of the findings laid out above. The following section briefly reviews these accounts. None of them, however, are able to explain the pattern of errors that was found.

4.4.1 Lidz and Musolino (2002)

Lidz and Musolino (2002) consider children's deviating interpretations not so much as a preference for non-referential (indefinite) readings, but as the result of a deviant application of syntactic scope. For children, the scope properties of an indefinite noun phrase would be determined entirely by its syntactic position with respect to the adverb. If the indefinite c-commands the operator, it takes wide scope with respect to the operator, whereas if the indefinite is c-commanded by the operator, it takes narrow scope.[4] The narrow-scope reading roughly corresponds to what we have called the non-referential reading, while the wide-scope reading corresponds to the reading that we referred to as the referential one. Such a mechanism would explain why English-speaking 4-year olds prefer narrow-scope readings of the indefinites in sentences like (7) and why Kannada-speaking 4-year olds do the same for sentences like (8), repeated below as (14) and (15).

(14) Donald didn't find two guys.

(15) Huduganu eraDu ungra karedis-al-illa.
     Ernie   two   ring   buy.NEG.INF
     'Ernie didn't buy two rings.'

According to Lidz and Musolino's analysis, although the word order of the adverb and the indefinite object differs in these languages, in both English and Kannada the adverb c-commands the indefinite object. Lidz and Musolino's proposal also captures the wide-scope readings of sentence-initial indefinite subjects, as these always c-command the adverb. However, the proposal fails to account for the Dutch child data, as all of the Dutch studies employed scrambled indefinite objects, which c-command the adverb. In spite of this, Dutch children have narrow-scope (non-referential) readings of these objects, just like English and Kannada children. In other words, word order (and therefore, c-command in Lidz and Musolino's approach) does not influence the Dutch children who prefer a non-referential (narrow-scope) reading for indefinite objects irrespective of their position relative to the adverb.

4.4.2 Krämer (2000)

Krämer (2000) proposes the Non-Integration Hypothesis in order to account for the fact that children preferably interpret indefinite objects as non-referential, independent of their position. The assumption underlying this explanation is that referential indefinites require a discourse process called 'accommodation' that involves linking to information presented previously in the discourse. According to Krämer's hypothesis, children experience difficulty in entertaining interpretations which require that such a discourse relation be established, and therefore interpret indefinites in their more basic, non-referential, interpretation. However, while this hypothesis would explain the data regarding indefinite objects, it clearly does not capture children's preference for referential interpretations of indefinite subjects.

4.4.3 Gualmini (2002)

Gualmini (2002), focusing on the studies by Musolino and colleagues, argues that children's deviant interpretations are in fact an experimental artefact, due to infelicitous use of negation in the experiments. Gualmini argues that a proposition can be negated felicitously only if there is an expectation of the contrary, i.e., that the non-negated proposition will hold. He supports his argument by experimental results. In Gualmini's experiment, for a sentence such as *The firefighter didn't find two dwarves*, a strong expectation is set up of the firefighter finding the dwarves. In the scenario, the firefighter looks very hard for the dwarves. The expectation is reinforced repeatedly by mentioning the dwarves that he still needs to find but doesn't manage to find, because they did such a good job hiding. Indeed, Gualmini found that 90% of the children correctly accepted the test sentence after this scenario, providing evidence of their ability to entertain referential readings.

However, the child language phenomenon that we would like to explain cannot be explained away as an artefact due to infelicitous negation. Klein

(1996), Foley et al. (2000), Krämer (2000) and Unsworth (2005) report similar results for sentences that did not involve negation but adverbial phrases such as *twice*. Furthermore, Gualmini's finding does not explain the subject-object asymmetry, nor does it account for children's preference for non-referential interpretations of indefinite objects in those experiments that do employ negation. While an infelicitous experimental context could lead to errors in numerous ways, one does not expect it to lead to a consistent pattern of erroneous responses that holds across experiments, experimental methods, and across languages. We must thus conclude that the pattern of findings presented in Section 4.3 cannot be explained away as an experimental artefact. In the next section we will present our bidirectional OT analysis of the data, following de Hoop and Krämer (2006).

4.5   Knowledge of the grammar versus use of the grammar

Previous accounts fail to capture the overall pattern of findings: Children are adult-like in their interpretation of referential indefinite subjects and in their interpretation of non-referential indefinite objects. They differ from adults when they have to interpret non-referential indefinite subjects and when they have to interpret referential indefinite objects. We believe that the answer to this problem lies not in children's acquisition of the grammar as such. They do not lack the requisite knowledge of the grammar. We propose that children's interpretations differ from those of adults because they use their knowledge in a different way.

As a first step in explaining the pattern of children's interpretations, it is important to note that the children's interpretations of indefinite objects and subjects in fact conform to the general pattern of adult interpretations that we find cross-linguistically. In the languages of the world, subjects outrank objects in referentiality: they tend to be referential, definite, topical, animate, high-prominent in the discourse, while objects tend to be non-referential, indefinite, inanimate, low-prominent in the discourse, instead (a.o. Comrie, 1989; Aissen, 2003; Lee, 2003). However, adults are able to assign a non-referential reading to indefinite subjects and a referential reading to indefinite objects when required. We propose that it is children's failure to depart from the general pattern which leads to their non-adultlike interpretations of the sentences we have given above.

Now, why do children fail in this respect, specifically, how is it possible that children as 'old' as nine years ignore the effects of word order? In the analysis that we lay out below, the deviant interpretations are caused by children's difficulty in applying bidirectional optimization. In Section 4.6 we will analyze the adult pattern and we will provide a bidirectional Optimality Theoretic account of this pattern. In Section 4.7, we describe how our account straightforwardly explains why children deviate from the adult pattern in exactly the way they do.

4.6   Form and meaning of indefinites

Dutch indefinite object NPs may appear either in scrambled or unscrambled position, as was illustrated in (1a) and (1b), repeated below in (16).

(16) (a) De vrouw   heeft   een kat zachtjes geaaid.
          the woman has   a   cat softly   stroked
          'The woman softly stroked a (particular) cat.'

     (b) De vrouw   heeft   zachtjes een kat geaaid.
          the woman has   softly   a   cat stroked
          'The woman softly stroked a cat.'

If we define markedness in terms of frequency, the syntactic form in (16a) is clearly more marked than the form in (16b), as the most frequent position for indefinite objects is the unscrambled position. As the markedness principle leads us to expect, the preferred reading of scrambled indefinite objects is indeed the more marked (less frequent) referential reading, whereas the preferred reading of the unscrambled indefinite object is the unmarked non-referential reading. As we have seen in the previous chapter, the scrambled position is not the marked (less frequent) position for all objects. For pronouns, the scrambled position is almost always used for the unmarked anaphoric reading, while the unscrambled position generally leads to the marked contrastive reading.

   Dutch, like English, also has multiple positions available for indefinite subjects. As illustrated in (2) above, repeated below in (17), indefinite subjects can occur either in standard subject position, or post-verbally in an existential sentence.

(17) (a) Een   meisje klimt   op de schommel.
          a   girl   climbs   on the swing
          'A (particular) girl is climbing on the swing.'

     (b) Er   klimt   een meisje op de schommel.
          there climbs a   girl   on the swing
          'A girl is climbing on the swing.'

Since the existential construction is more complex (hence, less economical) than canonical sentences, we consider (17a), in which the subject appears in standard subject position, the unmarked case, and (17b) the marked case. Note that we find a conflict of interpretation concerning the meaning of the indefinite subjects. That is, an indefinite subject is subject to two conflicting constraints: because it is a subject, it would favor a referential reading, but because it is an indefinite noun phrase, it would favor an indefinite (non-referential) reading. Note also that such a conflict does not arise for indefinite objects. There, the two constraints go hand in hand: because the indefinite object is an object, it favors a non-referential reading, and because it is an indefinite noun phrase, it favors a non-referential reading, too. In accordance with the cross-linguistic pattern, Dutch subjects generally receive a referential reading, while indefinites generally receive a non-referential reading. We assume therefore that the first condition is stronger than the second condition, such that the unmarked reading for indefinite subjects is referential. This unmarked reading is then associated with the unmarked form (standard subject position), and the marked, non-referential reading is associated with the marked form (embedded subject position).

In conclusion, the subject-object asymmetry in connection with the markedness principle adequately describes the adult pattern of the interpretation of indefinite noun phrases in relation to their position in the sentence. On the one hand, the unmarked reading for an indefinite object noun phrase is the non-referential reading (triggered both by the indefiniteness of the noun phrase and the fact that it is the object). On the other hand, the unmarked reading for an indefinite subject is the referential reading (in accordance with the subject-object asymmetry, but thereby violating the indefiniteness condition). Furthermore, the unmarked position for an indefinite object is the unscrambled position, and the unmarked position for an indefinite subject is the standard subject position. Thus, the markedness principle correctly derives the fact that adults link the scrambled position to the referential reading of indefinite objects and the embedded subject position to the non-referential reading of indefinite subjects.

At this point, we will address the question of how the markedness principle comes to play a role in adult grammar, showing that principles of language use are at the root of adults' interpretations of indefinites. We will present our bidirectional Optimality Theoretic analysis to explain in what sense exactly children's interpretations deviate from adults' interpretations.

In our analysis of indefinite subjects and objects, we will use constraints that are based on existing generalisations found in the linguistic literature mentioned, although for convenience, we use simplified formulations of these generalisations. We will use the following constraints on meaning and form in our analysis:

(18) Subj/Ref-Obj/non-ref (Sron): Subjects outrank objects in referentiality, i.e., subjects get a referential interpretation, while objects get a non-referential interpretation.

(19) Indef/Non-Ref (In): Indefinite noun phrases get a non-referential interpretation.

(20) Scrambling (Scr): Indefinite objects do not scramble.

(21) Subj/stand (Ss): Subjects are in standard subject position.

These four constraints will give us the unmarked meanings of indefinite subjects and objects as the optimal candidates from an OT-semantic point of view, and the unmarked forms from an OT-syntactic point of view. These constraints, however, cannot account for the marked meanings or the marked forms.

Two kinds of factors are instrumental in provoking a marked meaning, namely marked forms but also contextual factors. Thus, we find that marked meanings of unmarked forms can be triggered by contextual factors – a fact which can be captured in the non-modular OT model as interaction of contextual and prosodic constraints with the constraints proposed above. Take, for instance, the English equivalent of example (1), given as (22) below.

(22) The woman softly stroked a cat.

English does not have more than one form for transitive sentences containing an indefinite object. If the context includes mention of the existence of a particular cat, or even an expectation that a particular cat might end up being stroked, this will bring about the marked, referential reading of the indefinite object. If the context contains no such information, the unmarked reading will prevail. For English subjects, a marked form does exist: the existential construction. Nevertheless, contextual constraints may trigger marked readings of the unmarked form. Note, for example, that the English translation of both Dutch sentence forms in (2) above is a canonical sentence.

We cannot simply say that context 'overrules' syntactic information. On the contrary, whenever a marked form is used, it can only have a marked meaning, even if contextual information seems better compatible with the unmarked meaning. Dutch scrambled indefinite objects must have a marked, referential reading, while Dutch and English indefinite subjects in existential sentences must have a marked, non-referential reading. How do these unmarked and marked form-meaning pairs arise? Again, bidirectional OT (Blutner, 2000) provides us with a straightforward explanation. Recall that bidirectional OT provides us with two super-optimal form-meaning pairs, in accordance with the markedness principle: the unmarked form with the unmarked meaning, and the marked form with the marked meaning.

We evaluate form-meaning pairs against the four constraints given above (see (18)-(21)). The super-optimal pairs are indicated with the symbol ✌ in the tableaux.

Tableau 4.1: Indefinite objects in Dutch

		Sron	In	Scr
✌	<- scrambling, non-referential>			
	<- scrambling, referential>	*	*	
	<+ scrambling, non-referential>			*
✌	<+ scrambling, referential>	*	*	*

In the tableau above we see that although the indefinite object that combines a referential meaning with a scrambled word order violates all three constraints that seem to be relevant, it does represent a super-optimal pair, simply because there is no super-optimal pair available that has either a better form or a better meaning. The only other super-optimal pair has both a better form and a better meaning and therefore it cannot block the 'marked' super-optimal pair. Thus, the bidirectional OT approach straightforwardly accounts for the scrambling phenomenon of indefinite objects in Dutch.

A similar analysis can be provided for the possible forms and meanings of indefinite subjects, as illustrated below.

Tableau 4.2: Indefinite subjects in Dutch

		Sron	In	Ss
✌	<standard, referential>		*	
	<standard, non-referential>	*		
	<existential, referential>		*	*
✌	<existential, non-referential>	*		*

Because the constraint Sron (subjects get a referential reading) outranks In (indefinites get a non-referential reading), the meaning that satisfies Sron and violates In is the optimal (unmarked) meaning, while the meaning that violates Sron but satisfies In is less harmonic (marked). One super-optimal pair links the unmarked meaning to the unmarked position (the standard subject position) while the other super-optimal pair links the marked meaning to the marked position (the embedded subject position in an existential sentence).

We find that a bidirectional OT analysis straightforwardly explains the adult pattern of the interpretation of both indefinite objects and indefinite subjects. Adults are able to evaluate form-meaning pairs. Not only can they find the optimal form for a certain meaning or the optimal meaning of a certain form, they are also capable of determining as a second super-optimal pair the combination of a form that is sub-optimal from a unidirectional syntactic perspective and a meaning that is sub-optimal from a unidirectional semantic perspective.

4.7   A role for pragmatic development in the acquisition of word order

We are now in a position to specify in what sense the children's interpretations differ from the adults'. We find that children deviate from adults' interpretations when they are required to arrive at a 'marked' meaning for a marked form. Our proposal is that children fail to optimize bidirectionally (de Hoop and Krämer, 2006). For children, the optimal interpretation of an indefinite object is the interpretation that is optimal from a unidirectional OT semantics point of view, hence, the non-referential interpretation. The same holds for the optimal interpretation of indefinite subjects, which is the referential interpretation. Thus, everything else being equal, children's optimal interpretation of a marked form will be the same as their optimal interpretation of an unmarked form.

Our analysis of children's interpretations is thus primarily a pragmatic one: children may have an adult-like grammar, but they do not apply the pragmatically motivated process of bidirectional optimization to this grammar. This view explains why mastery of the syntax of object scrambling and existential structures does not automatically lead to adultlike interpretations. This leads us to the question of what could be the source of children's difficulty with bidirectional optimization. Consider the 'reasoning' that is involved in applying bidirectional optimization. When two forms and two meanings are available, the hearer must take into account that the speaker has two choices, and that the speaker, in selecting the form, will take into account the hearer's awareness of this fact. It is only because the speaker can count on the hearer's awareness of this fact, and again on the hearer's realizing that the speaker will count on the hearer's awareness, etcetera, that the speaker can manage to effect a shift away from the unmarked meaning through the use of a marked form. Thus, for a hearer to apply bidirectional optimization, he must take into account not only the speaker's perspective, but also the fact that the speaker's perspective includes an estimation of the hearer's perspective. This may require more cognitive resources than the children have available (cf. Chapter 5).

Note that our analysis does not predict a radical difference between child and adult grammars as such. We do not predict that children are unable to assign referential interpretations to indefinite objects, or non-referential interpretations to indefinite subjects. On the contrary, we assume that children are sensitive to the same factors that determine adults' interpretations. We expect that children become increasingly sensitive to factors that determine when they should deviate from the unmarked, and when they should not. Eventually, what the children need to learn, is to deviate from the unmarked on the mere basis of the speaker's use of one linguistic form rather than another. In the next section we discuss some exceptional findings, that do not conform to the generalization sketched in Section 4.3. These findings show that children are sensitive to the same factors as adults, even though this does not always result in adultlike interpretations.

4.8   Further findings

A few studies have found child interpretations that do not conform to the general pattern of deviant findings. The nature of the findings is twofold. On the one hand, Krämer (2000) and Philip and Termeer (2002) present cases in which children deviate from the general pattern while adults do not, resulting in non-adultlike responses. In our model, these findings are captured by cross-modular constraint interaction. On the other hand, Gualmini (2002) and Miller and Schmitt (2004) show that children can be lured into deviating from the general pattern in the same manner as adults. The same factors that play a role in adults' interpretations are also at work in children's interpretation, while the exact balancing of the factors still needs to be acquired. Interestingly, the child language studies discussed below allow us to observe factors that remain below the surface in adult interpretation.

4.8.1 Cross-modular constraint interaction

One of the experiments reported in Krämer (2000) involves children's interpretations of indefinite subjects, in sentences like (23):

(23) Een knikker mag   twee keer   rollen (- en dat mag jij laten zien).
     a   marble   may   two   time   roll
     'A marble can roll twice (- now you go ahead and show me).'

The experiment was comparable to the experiment involving scrambled indefinite objects reported on in Section 4.3.1. Krämer found that 57% of 4- to 7-year old children allowed or preferred a non-referential interpretation also for the indefinite subjects, contra the general pattern in which children interpret subject NPs referentially. What could it be that sets this study apart from the other studies? When we compare this experiment to the experiments reporting referential subject interpretations, we find that only in this experiment the subjects are inanimate, not previously introduced in the discourse, not agents, and not showing any intentions. In all of the other studies, the subject referents were animate protagonists of a story, and they had been introduced previously. The subjects in the exceptional experiment simply have too many properties that do not sit comfortably with referentiality. This finding shows that children are sensitive to the properties involved in the subject-object asymmetry, and relatively insensitive to the form of the sentence.

Philip and Termeer (2002) present the results of an experiment investigating children's interpretation of a sentence with a sentence-initial indefinite subject and a universally quantified object, as in (24):

(24) Een   hond   heeft   ieder   bot   begraven.
     a   dog   has   every   bone   buried
     'A dog buried every bone.'

Fifty-seven percent of the 5- and 6-year old children preferred a reading on which the quantified object took scope over the subject (each bone was buried by a dog), hence a non-referential reading of the indefinite subject, contra the general pattern. This is not surprising if we take into account the fact that strongly quantified noun phrases generally take wide scope. Thus we find once more that the children are sensitive to the quantificational and referential properties of the given noun phrases, but do not heed the cue that the word order offers them.

4.8.2 Contextual cues

Two studies (Gualmini, 2002; Miller and Schmitt, 2004) show that certain modifications of the context promote children's ability to assign marked, referential, readings to indefinite objects. The findings show that children may be sensitive to contextual cues leading to marked readings, provided that these cues are pressed home harder than is needed for adults.

The story context in Gualmini (2002) raises both the prominence and the relevance of the objects. For the sentence *The firefighter didn't find two dwarfs*, the story first makes explicit that it is the firefighter's goal, and the pivotal point of the story, that he find the dwarfs. The scenario combines raising the relevance of the objects (dwarfs that are not found) with repeated explicit reference to the object NPs.

Schmitt and Miller's experimental set-up contained two elements that we believe to be of importance. First and foremost, the referents of the objects had a strong conceptual link to preceding discourse, such as a drawer that was part of a previously introduced chest of drawers. The conceptual link facilitated the referential reading of the indefinite in the discourse. Secondly, the test stories in a number of cases heightened the relevance of the referential reading of the object, as in the sentence *Kelly didn't paint an egg.* In the story, the little girl Kelly is told by her mother to paint all of the easter eggs before she goes to play outside. The outcome of the story, in which there is an egg which Kelly did not paint, makes clear that Kelly did not listen to her mother.

Nearly all children in the experiment accepted the test sentence, showing that 4-year-old children are capable of obtaining referential readings of indefinite objects, given the right context. It is likely that the focus on whether the girl complied with her mother's wish or not plays a role here. The one egg that has not been painted becomes highly prominent, because it is the object that enables the witness to determine that Kelly did not do as she was told – a situation which is clearly relevant to children. A similar effect of relevance, in a highly similar scenario, was found for children's comprehension of scalar implicatures by Feeney, Scrafton, Duckworth and Handley (2004).

4.9 Conclusion

The topic of this chapter, children's interpretations of indefinites, constitutes a problem in the study of child language acquisition. Why do children often fail to obtain adult-like interpretations of indefinites, why do they acquire them at such a late age, and why do the errors pattern the way they do?

The bidirectional Optimality Theoretic approach to word order variation in Dutch allows us to answer these questions. We have shown that children's interpretations of indefinites conform to a particular pattern: generally, children interpret indefinite objects non-referentially, and indefinite subjects referentially. This pattern corresponds to a cross-linguistic pattern by which subjects outrank objects in referentiality. While adults will deviate from this pattern when needed, children aged 4 to 11 often fail to do so. Children differ from adults in that they will less easily deviate from the unmarked.

Adults, who optimize bidirectionally, will assign a marked, suboptimal, meaning, to a marked, suboptimal, form. Children, who optimize unidirectionally, will assign the unmarked meaning to both the marked and the unmarked form, as this meaning violates the fewest constraints. The cause for children's failure to employ bidirectional optimization may lie in the cognitive demands of bidirectional optimization, which forces the language user to simultaneously take both hearer and speaker perspective into account. The role of cognitive limitations in the development of bidirectional optimization will be taken up again in Chapter 5, which argues that a range of phenomena in child language acquisition can be explained as a failure to optimize bidirectionally.

On our account, the differences between the child and adult grammar are small. Although some factors, such as animacy or prominence, may weigh slightly heavier in the child's grammar, children and adults are sensitive to the same factors. The difference between adults and children lies not in the grammar, but in how it is used.

Notes

1   Note that the order 'Er klimt een meisje twee keer op de schommel' is also possible, in which case the indefinite subject takes wide scope again.

2   For studies reporting on a restricted phenomenon of overgeneralization of the definite determiner, see Maratsos, 1974; Karmiloff-Smith, 1979; Schafer and de Villiers, 2000; Schaeffer and Matthewson, 2005.

3   Several studies suggest that the tendency does not hold, or to a much weaker extent, for Spanish and Chinese (Miller and Schmitt, 2005; Su, 2001). Yang (2008), however, also investigates Chinese children's interpretations of indefinite objects, and finds that Mandarin children, just like Dutch, English and Kannada children, start out with an overall preference for a non-referential reading of indefinite objects.

4   'C-command' is a structural relation, that can be roughly defined in terms of positions in a syntactic tree: X c-commands Y iff Y is dominated by the node in the tree that strictly dominates X, but Y is not dominated by X.

5 Speaking versus understanding in language acquisition

5.1 Introduction

Previous chapters of this book have paid considerable attention to bidirectional Optimality Theory, stressing the importance of bidirectionality in natural language interpretation. In Chapter 4, we suggested that children deviate from adults with respect to the interpretation of indefinite noun phrases because they fail to optimize bidirectionally. As a result, they experience problems interpreting marked forms such as post-verbally occurring indefinite subjects and scrambled indefinite objects. In the present chapter, we ask the question whether this failure to optimize bidirectionally is an example of a more general pattern that can also be observed in other areas of language comprehension. A second question we aim to answer here is whether this hypothesized failure to optimize bidirectionally has similar consequences for children's *production* of marked forms. That is, do children also experience problems producing marked forms?

In Section 5.2, we will present several phenomena in child language acquisition providing suggestive evidence that children's failure to optimize bidirectionally with indefinites is in fact part of a general pattern in child language. For each of the phenomena we present, a bidirectional analysis leads to a correct, adult-like interpretation, and for each of them, we find that children deviate from the adult interpretation until a relatively late age. The deviations can be accounted for by assuming that children's interpretations are computed unidirectionally, rather than bidirectionally. We will briefly review the role of bidirectionality in children's interpretation of indefinites, which was discussed in the previous chapter, and in children's interpretation of pronouns and scalar implicatures. In Sections 5.3, 5.4 and 5.5, we will present an in-depth analysis of the role of bidirectionality in the interpretation and production of contrastive stress. This then leads to a discussion of the effects of cognitive limitations on bidirectionality (Section 5.6), which we argue to work in two ways: First, they restrict the number of possible form-meaning pairings in a given language, thus co-determining the grammar of any given language. Secondly, for language learners, such cognitive limitations play an even greater role, leading to the absence of bidirectionality and causing differences between children's and adults' interpretations. As a result, children's production of a given form may precede their comprehension of the same form by several years, something which is difficult to explain in a rule-based grammar in which knowledge of a given rule implies the use of this rule in comprehension and production alike.

This view of language acquisition may help to elucidate the nature of bidirectionality: Is it primarily a mechanism of language change, or is it also an online mechanism of language interpretation? Blutner and Zeevat (2004b) suggest that bidirectional optimization must be seen purely in an evolutionary perspective. When two forms and two meanings are available, language users will pair an unmarked form to an unmarked meaning, and a marked form to a marked meaning. This pairing is the result of applying pragmatic principles of language use: A speaker knows that a hearer will pair the marked meaning to the marked form, because the hearer knows that the speaker also has an unmarked form available, which she would have used, had she intended the unmarked meaning. Eventually, these form-meaning pairs fossilize, until one form is used exclusively for the one, and the other form, for the other meaning. In this manner, a pragmatic principle may be responsible for (part of) the form-meaning relations that make up a given language. On Blutner and Zeevat's evolutionary view of bidirectionality, form-meaning pairs that have been determined by bidirectional optimization constitute fixed relations to a learner who sets out acquiring the language. No learner, indeed no user of the language, needs to perform a bidirectional computation for any form-meaning pair she encounters. The evidence discussed in this chapter, however, suggests that bidirectionality is not merely an evolutionary mechanism. Some form-meaning pairings have not been fossilized or automatized, but must be computed anew in a given situation.

The proposed view of bidirectionality as a partly online mechanism of natural language interpretation raises the question of whether bidirectionality is a property of an individual's linguistic performance from the onset of language acquisition, or whether it is acquired or instantiated at some later time. We believe that the latter is the case. Whenever a bidirectional pair has to be computed online in a given situation, it is necessary for the hearer to realize which options were available to the speaker, and also to realize that the speaker's eventual choice is co-determined by the speaker's assumption that the hearer is able to share her perspective. It is to be expected that such online computation requires considerable cognitive resources, such that it may exceed children's capabilities.

5.2   Lack of bidirectionality in language acquisition

5.2.1 Indefinite noun phrases

Children's interpretation of indefinite object and subject noun phrases has already been discussed in Chapter 4. Dutch unscrambled object noun phrases, as in (1a), are interpreted non-referentially, whereas scrambled object noun phrases, as in (1b), are interpreted referentially.

(1) (a) Je mag twee keer een potje omdraaien.
          you may two   time a   pot   around-turn
          'You may turn a pot around twice.' (turn two potentially different pots)

     (b) Je mag een potje twee keer omdraaien.
          you may a   pot   two   time around-turn
          'You may turn a pot around twice.' (turn one and the same pot twice)

According to the analysis of indefinites proposed in Chapter 4, (1b) violates constraints on meaning which determine that objects are interpreted non-referentially, and that indefinites are interpreted non-referentially. In addition, (1b) violates a constraint on form, which dictates that object noun phrases do not scramble. Sentence (1a), in contrast, does not violate either form or meaning constraints. Hence, an adult hearer, interpreting (1b) bidirectionally, will assign this form the marked, referential interpretation, as he is aware that the speaker would have chosen the unmarked form (1a), had she intended the unmarked, non-referential, meaning. Children, aged 4 to, roughly, 11 (Unsworth, 2005) assign the non-referential interpretation to both (1a) and (1b). From a unidirectional perspective, this is the preferred interpretation, as it does not violate either of the meaning constraints. Accordingly, our proposal is that children apply unidirectional rather than bidirectional optimization to sentences like (1a) and (1b). A similar analysis was provided in Chapter 4 for children's errors in the interpretation of indefinite subject noun phrases.

5.2.2 Pronouns

Delays in comprehension have also been observed in other areas of interpretation. Hendriks and Spenader (2004, 2006) discuss a well-known delay in the correct interpretation of object pronouns. According to their analysis, object pronouns are ambiguous and can in principle either refer back to the subject of the same finite verb, or refer to some other individual mentioned earlier. Consider the following sequence of sentences:

(2)   (a)   Here are Bert and Ernie.
        (b)   Bert is washing him.

On Hendriks and Spenader's analysis, coreference between the pronominal object *him* and the subject *Bert* in (2b) is blocked by bidirectional optimization. The hearer must draw the conclusion that coreference is not possible between *him* and *Bert* because, if the speaker had wanted to express coreference, the speaker would have used the reflexive *himself* rather than the pronoun *him*. It has been widely documented (see, e.g., Chien and Wexler, 1990; Grimshaw and Rosen, 1990) that children until at least 6;6 years of age allow coreference in these cases, displaying the so-called Pronoun Interpretation Problem. This problem receives an explanation if children until about the age of 6 or 7 lack the ability to reason about the speaker's alternatives. Indeed, Hendriks and Spenader argue that children apply unidirectional optimization, whereas the adult pattern arises as a result of bidirectional optimization.

5.2.3 Scalar implicatures

We predict that delays in comprehension occur during language development in exactly those cases where comprehension involves reasoning about the speaker's alternatives. One of the phenomena that have been argued to require reasoning about alternative forms is scalar implicatures. In the following sentence, the word *some* has been used, which is the weaker form on an implicational scale which also includes the stronger form *all*.

(3)   Some of the boys went to the party.

The literal meaning of this sentence is that at least two of the boys went to the party. Therefore, this sentence is compatible with a situation in which in fact all of the boys went to the party. However, adults will generally reason that if the speaker would have wanted to express the fact that all of the boys went to the party, then the speaker would have used the stronger form *all*. Since the speaker did not use this stronger form, the hearer may conclude that the speaker does not have evidence for this stronger meaning and hence will interpret (3) as meaning that not all of the boys went to the party. Young children often display little sensitivity to this type of pragmatic implicature (Noveck, 2001; Papafragou and Musolino, 2003). More often than adults, children allow for the literal meaning according to which it may very well be the case that all boys went to the party. This supports the view that young children experience difficulty when they are required to optimize bidirectionally.

5.3   Contrastive stress and focus

In this section, we discuss children's performance with respect to contrastive stress. Previous studies have shown that children seem to experience serious difficulties comprehending contrastive stress, yet show no difficulties in their production of contrastive stress. Section 5.4 below presents a unidirectional OT analysis of children's production and comprehension of contrastive stress, accounting for the observed asymmetry between comprehension and production. As will be argued in Section 5.5, adults' production and comprehension of contrastive stress requires bidirectional optimization.

A well-known property of the focus-sensitive operator *only* is that the truth conditions it gives rise to can vary with the placement of stress. Most theories of *only* agree that the operator *only* is somehow related to the focus of the utterance. One of the few syntactic restrictions on *only* seems to be that *only* must c-command the phrase in focus.[1] A different placement of stress can result in a different interpretation of focus. For example, if stress is placed on the direct object, as in (4), the meaning could be paraphrased as: the only thing Tigger threw to Piglet was a chair. In this case, the focus is on the direct object *a chair*. The sentence is false if Tigger also threw something else to Piglet, for example a table. On the other hand, if stress is placed on the indirect object, as in (5), the sentence can still be true in this situation. Here, the focus is either on the indirect object *Piglet* (the narrow focus reading: 'the only one Tigger threw a chair to is Piglet') or on the entire verb phrase *threw a chair to Piglet* (the wide focus reading: 'the only thing Tigger did was throw a chair to Piglet'). That is, (5) shows focal ambiguity.

(4)   Tigger only threw a CHAIR to Piglet.

(5)   Tigger only threw a chair to PIGLET.

The focus with which *only* associates, and which is marked by main stress, is believed to give rise to a set of alternatives (Rooth, 1985). Informally speaking, the operator *only* has the effect that of this set of alternatives, the alternative mentioned by the sentence is the only alternative for which the property expressed by the rest of the sentence holds. So in (4), the set of alternatives is the set {a chair, a table, a ball, …}, and *only* indicates that the property of being thrown to Piglet only holds for a chair, and not for any of the other alternatives. Similarly, under a narrow focus interpretation the set of alternatives in (5) is

{Piglet, Winnie, Eeyore, ...}, and under a wide focus interpretation the set of alternatives is {throw a chair to Piglet, throw a table to Winnie, dance, ...}, and *only* indicates that other alternatives than the one mentioned in the sentence do not hold.

The crucial difference between the two sentences is that stress falls on the default, unmarked, position in (5), whereas stress falls on a special, marked, position in (4). Szendröi (2004), in a truth value judgment task investigating 28 Dutch children age 4;1 to 6;10, found that children's performance in a story context is more or less adult-like (to be precize 84.8%) on sentences like (5), while it is around chance (namely 52.5%) on sentences like (4). Examples of the Dutch sentences used by Szendröi (2004) in her experiment are the following:

(6) Hij heeft alleen een STOEL naar   Knorretje gegooid.
     he   has   only a   chair   to   Piglet   thrown
     'He only threw a CHAIR to Piglet.'

(7) Hij heeft alleen een stoel   naar   KNORRETJE gegooid.
     he   has   only a   chair   to   Piglet   thrown
     'He only threw a chair to PIGLET.'

Like adults, children allow both a narrow focus interpretation and a wide focus interpretation for sentence (7). But unlike the adults, for sentence (6) the children allow a wide focus interpretation in addition to the narrow focus interpretation: They also allow the reading of (6) that the only thing Tigger did was throw a chair to Piglet. Similar results were found for English by Gennari, Gualmini, Crain, Meroni and Maciukaite (2001), Gualmini, Maciukaite and Crain (2003), and Halbert, Crain, Shankweiler and Woodams (1995). Children's problems with the interpretation of marked stress are not particular to focus selection but also occur in other contexts of contrastive stress, for example with stressed pronouns (McDaniel and Maxfield, 1992). Another set of problems children display with stress, but which should be distinguished from the cases under discussion in this chapter, involves the non-adult selection of the direct object as the focus when *only* is a modifier of the subject (as in: *Only the bird is holding a flag.*). Many children seem to allow association of the focus-sensitive operator with the direct object *a flag* in these cases, violating the condition that *only* must c-command the phrase in focus (Crain, Philip, Drozd, Roeper and Matsuoka, 1992; Drozd and van Loosbroek, 1998). Children's incorrect association with the direct object when *only* precedes the subject presumably has a different source than children's association with the object when *only* is a verb phrase modifier, perhaps reflecting children's incomplete acquisition of the c-command condition on focus.

The results with respect to children's comprehension of (4)/(6) and (5)/ (7) indicate that, for English and Dutch children, sentences (4) and (6) are just as ambiguous as sentences (5) and (7). For adults, on the other hand, only sentences (5) and (7) are ambiguous between a narrow focus reading and a wide focus reading. Sentences (4) and (6) are non-ambiguous for adults and always receive a narrow focus reading. So an important question is why sentences with marked stress are ambiguous for children but not for adults.

Children's inability to correctly comprehend marked stress is not reflected in their production of marked stress. In an experiment by Hornby and Hass (1970), children between the ages of 3;8 and 4;6 were shown pictures and asked to describe them. The pictures were presented in pairs differing in only one element. Children stressed the contrastive element 80% of the times in their description of the second picture. This suggests that children's prosodic production is more or less adultlike. In their review of acquisition experiments investigating prosodic competence, Cutler and Swinney (1987) conclude that, with respect to prosody in general, young children's productive skills appear to outstrip their receptive skills. This seems to go against the general pattern in child language that correct comprehension of a given form precedes the correct production of this form. Cutler and Swinney explain this observation by assuming (following Bolinger), that accenting in fact is a primitive physiological reaction associated with speaker excitation. Thus, in children's correct production of contrastive stress, no linguistic intention or underlying meaning representation need be involved – children's knowledge of the principles determining stress placement in production is only apparent. The stress pattern they produce merely is the effect of a non-intentional physiological reaction. However, this explanation is unsatisfactory, both from a theoretical and an empirical point of view. A theoretical problem is posed by the question how children would ever learn that there are rules or constraints determining stress placement. As they seem to be able to place stress correctly in the supposed absence of such knowledge, what kind of input would trigger an adultlike motivation for stress placement? Also, more recent evidence shows that two-year old children are already able to correctly mark the focus with which focus particles associate by means of contrastive accent (Nederstigt, 2001), a finding which is not compatible with a view of accent placement as a primitive physiological reaction. We therefore conclude that the discrepancy between children's production and comprehension of contrastive stress is real, and needs to be explained.

At first sight, it is a challenge to explain this asymmetry between comprehension and production in child language from the properties of the grammar. If children are able to produce a given form, then certainly these forms must belong to their competence grammar and it is then expected that these children are able to correctly comprehend these forms as well. In the next section, it is shown that OT is able to provide an explanation for this remarkable asymmetry.

5.4   Children's production and interpretation of contrastive stress

In this section, we present an OT analysis of children's production and comprehension of contrastive stress, based on the analysis of Hendriks, Hendrickx, Looije and Pals (2005), which provides an explanation for the observed asymmetry between comprehension and production. The proposed OT analysis resembles Reinhart's (2004) processing account but places the computation of, and comparison among, alternative forms and meanings within the grammar. The difference between children and adults lies in the way in which they perform this comparison. Children compare alternative forms and meanings through unidirectional optimization, whereas adults compare alternative forms and meanings through bidirectional optimization.

As will be shown below, the following violable constraints on comprehension and production suffice to explain the child language data as well as the adult data:

(8)   BINDFOCUS: The focus must be in the c-command domain of the focus particle *only*.

(9)   MARKFOCUS: The focus must contain the word carrying main stress.

(10)   NUCLEARSTRESS: The main stress must fall on the most deeply embedded constituent in the sentence.

The constraint BINDFOCUS expresses the well-known syntactic requirement that the focus a focus particle associates with must be contained in its c-command domain. It establishes a relation between a particular form (the position of *only*) and a particular meaning (the selected focus). However, for the sake of simplicity we keep the position of the focus particle constant in our analysis, and only consider sentences where the focus particle is a verb phrase modifier, intervening between the subject and the verb phrase. It is conceivable that this constraint plays a role in production too, and helps to determine the optimal position of the focus particle given a particular focus structure as the input. But in all examples below the position of *only* will be the position immediately preceding the verb phrase. As a result, BINDFOCUS has an effect in comprehension only.

The constraint MARKFOCUS expresses the observation that semantic focus is somehow marked by main stress on one of its segments. Since it is a faithfulness constraint relating aspects of form (i.e., stress) to aspects of meaning (i.e., focus), this constraint is relevant for comprehension as well as for production.

The constraint NUCLEARSTRESS, finally, is the violable version of the Nuclear Stress Rule (cf. Chomsky and Halle, 1968; Cinque, 1993; Reinhart, 2004, among others) which was already mentioned in Section 3.3 of Chapter 3. It restricts the placement of the main stress of a sentence, irrespective of the potential meaning of the sentence. Aloni, Butler and Hindsill (2007) employ this constraint in their bidirectional OT account of free focus. Free focus is the focus occurring in the absence of a focus particle or other overt operator, which contrasts with the bound focus occurring in the presence of *only*. The constraint NUCLEARSTRESS thus restricts the placement of main stress in the presence of free focus as well as bound focus. Because NUCLEARSTRESS restricts the placement of the main stress of a sentence irrespective of its potential meaning, it is a markedness constraint on forms.

As we will show, the interaction between these three constraints explains the child language data discussed in the previous section as well as the correct adult pattern. The key difference between our explanation of the child language data and our explanation of the adult pattern is the type of optimization. Using only these constraints, children's production data can be described by unidirectional optimization from meaning to form. Similarly, children's comprehension data can be described by unidirectional optimization from form to meaning. As will be shown in the next section, the same constraints predict the adult pattern of production and comprehension when bidirectional optimization is used. Thus we argue that children begin with unidirectional optimization. In order to arrive at the correct adult interpretation for marked stress, children must start to optimize bidirectionally. In other terms, children must start to take into account not only their own alternatives in production and comprehension, but also the alternatives available to their hypothetical partner in conversation.

First consider the situation in which a speaker wishes to produce a sentence in which focus is on the entire verb phrase. For example, the speaker wants to express the fact that the only thing Tigger did was throw a chair to Piglet, and that he did not do anything else. Because BINDFOCUS acts as a markedness constraint on meanings here, and the meaning is given, only MARKFOCUS and NUCLEARSTRESS are relevant for distinguishing between candidate forms. This is illustrated by the following OT tableau:

Tableau 5.1: OT production of focus on the verb phrase

Focus on verb phrase	BINDFOCUS	MARKFOCUS	NUCLEARSTRESS
stress on subject		*!	*
stress on verb			*!
stress on direct object			*!
☞ stress on indirect object			

In Tableau 5.1, the input for optimization is the intended meaning for the sentence that is to be produced. Because we limit ourselves to aspects of meaning and form relevant to the present discussion, the input consists of the intended focus. The candidate outputs differ in the placement of main stress. Main stress can fall on the subject, the main verb, the direct object, the indirect object, etcetera. We assume the constraint MARKFOCUS to be stronger than NUCLEARSTRESS, because otherwise stress would be incorrectly predicted to always fall on the same, unmarked, position. The first candidate, according to which stress is placed on the subject, violates the constraint MARKFOCUS because stress is placed outside the focused verb phrase. Furthermore, the first three candidates violate NUCLEARSTRESS because the most deeply embedded constituent in a transitive construction such as (4) and (5) is the indirect object. Only if stress is placed on the indirect object, as in the fourth candidate, is this constraint satisfied. Consequently, the fourth candidate is the optimal form because this candidate satisfies both constraints. The sentence that is produced in the situation sketched above thus is: *Tigger only threw a chair to PIGLET* (i.e., sentence (5)).

Now consider the situation in which a speaker wishes to place focus on the indirect object (Tableau 5.2). For example, the speaker wants to express the fact that the only one to whom Tigger threw a chair was Piglet, and to no one else. The same constraints apply, and the same candidate outputs are relevant. However, because the input differs, the behavior of the candidates with respect to the faithfulness constraint MARKFOCUS, which establishes a relation between forms and meanings, differs. The first three candidates now violate MARKFOCUS and NUCLEARSTRESS, but because the fourth candidate satisfies both constraints, again the fourth candidate is the optimal form for the given meaning:

Tableau 5.2: OT production of indirect object focus

Focus on indirect object	BINDFOCUS	MARKFOCUS	NUCLEARSTRESS
stress on subject		*!	*
stress on verb		*!	*
stress on direct object		*!	*
☞ stress on indirect object			

This again yields a sentence like (5) as the optimal output, provided that *only* is a verb phrase modifier. Of course, if not only the position of main stress but also the position of *only* is taken to be subject to optimization, the sentence *Tigger threw a chair only to PIGLET* would be a possible output as well, also satisfying all three constraints. However, since sentence (5) seems to be strongly preferred in this case, additional constraints must be involved in the placement of *only*.

A third situation (Tableau 5.3) is the situation in which a speaker wishes to express focus on the direct object. This situation arises if the speaker wants to express the fact that the only thing Tigger threw to Piglet was a chair, and nothing else. Again, only stress on the indirect object satisfies the constraint NUCLEARSTRESS. But in this case, stress on the indirect object violates the stronger constraint MARKFOCUS, because the focused direct object does not contain the word carrying stress. As a result, the third candidate, carrying stress on the direct object, now is the optimal form. In this case, sentences such as (4) are produced: *Tigger only threw a CHAIR to Piglet*. Notice that in this case also the optimal candidate violates one of the constraints. However, because in OT constraint violation is not always fatal, this candidate nevertheless is the optimal form. Hence, it is the form that will be produced to express the input meaning.

Tableau 5.3: OT production of direct object focus

Focus on direct object	BINDFOCUS	MARKFOCUS	NUCLEARSTRESS
stress on subject		*!	*
stress on verb		*!	*
☞ stress on direct object			*
stress on indirect object		*!	

In the three situations exemplified by Tableaux 5.1, 5.2 and 5.3, OT produces the correct form for a given meaning. Thus, if we assume that children have knowledge of the constraints and their ranking, OT predicts the correct results for children's production of marked and unmarked stress.

Now let us look at comprehension. Comprehension proceeds in the opposite direction from production. Rather than starting with a meaning as the input, and selecting the optimal form for this meaning, optimization starts with a form, and selects the optimal meaning for this form. In comprehension, the constraint NUCLEARSTRESS is not relevant, since this is a constraint on forms only, and the form is given here. As a result, this constraint does not distinguish between possible outputs. The constraint MARKFOCUS, which played a role in production too, and the constraint BINDFOCUS interact to yield the optimal focus selection for a given form.

The first situation we consider is the situation in which a speaker chooses to place stress on the indirect object. An example is sentence (5), repeated below:

(11) Tigger only threw a chair to PIGLET.

Here, stress is placed on an unmarked position, resulting in satisfaction of the constraint NUCLEARSTRESS by all candidate meanings. In effect, this constraint does not distinguish between potential meanings in comprehension.

Tableau 5.4: OT interpretation of stress on indirect object

Stress on indirect object	BINDFOCUS	MARKFOCUS	NUCLEARSTRESS
focus on subject	*!	*	
focus on direct object		*!	
☞ focus on indirect object			
☞ focus on verb phrase			
focus on sentence	*!		

As can be seen from Tableau 5.4, if a hearer is confronted with a sentence such as (11), OT predicts that this results in two optimal meanings, namely the meaning according to which focus falls on the indirect object (narrow focus) and the meaning according to which focus falls on the entire verb phrase (wide focus). Both of these meanings satisfy BINDFOCUS and MARKFOCUS. This corresponds to the interpretations selected by both children and adults. Focus on the subject and on the entire sentence violate BINDFOCUS, and focus on the direct object violates MARKFOCUS, which yields these candidates suboptimal.

Now consider the situation in which a speaker utters sentence (4), repeated below.

(12) Tigger only threw a CHAIR to Piglet.

In this case, stress is placed on a marked position, namely on the direct object. As a result, all candidate forms violate the constraint NUCLEARSTRESS.

Tableau 5.5: OT interpretation of stress on direct object

Stress on direct object	BINDFOCUS	MARKFOCUS	NUCLEARSTRESS
focus on subject	*!	*	*
☞ focus on direct object			*
focus on indirect object		*!	*
☞ focus on verb phrase			*
focus on sentence	*!		*

Again, two meanings are selected as the optimal meaning, namely the meaning according to which focus falls on the direct object (narrow focus) and the meaning according to which focus falls on the verb phrase (wide focus). This corresponds to children's responses to sentences like (12), but differs from adults' responses. So the interaction among violable constraints described in this section yields an explanation for children's production *and* comprehension of marked and unmarked stress. It is correctly predicted that children show no difficulties in the production of marked as well as unmarked stress. Also, children are predicted to not experience any difficulties in the comprehension of unmarked stress. Only with respect to the comprehension of marked stress, children's behavior is predicted to be non-adultlike.

For children, sentence (12) is ambiguous. This follows from the fact that both the verb phrase focus meaning and the direct object focus meaning satisfy BINDFOCUS and MARKFOCUS. Because NUCLEARSTRESS does not distinguish between candidate meanings, these two meanings are both optimal and hence are possible meanings for sentence (12). But if both meanings are in principle possible for sentence (12), why isn't sentence (12) ambiguous for adults? This question will be addressed in the next section.

5.5   Adults' production and interpretation of contrastive stress

To account for the non-ambiguity of sentence (12), we argue that a bidirectional perspective should be taken. In bidirectional OT, optimal pairs can block other pairs with the same form but a less harmonic meaning, or with the same meaning but a less harmonic form (Blutner, 2000). Bidirectional optimization of the interpretation of bound focus and the placement of main stress is illustrated in Tableau 5.6:

Tableau 5.6: Bidirectional OT tableau of focus and stress

			BINDFOCUS	MARKFOCUS	NUCLEARSTRESS
	1.	<stress on direct object, focus on subject>	*	*	*
☞	2.	<stress on direct object, focus on direct object>			*
	3.	<stress on direct object, focus on indirect object>		*	*
	4.	<stress on direct object, focus on verb phrase>			*
	5.	<stress on direct object, focus on sentence>	*		*
	6.	<stress on indirect object, focus on subject>	*	*	
	7.	<stress on indirect object, focus on direct object>		*	
☞	8.	<stress on indirect object, focus on indirect object>			
☞	9.	<stress on indirect object, focus on verb phrase>			
	10.	<stress on indirect object, focus on sentence>	*		

In the leftmost column, all relevant pairs of possible forms and meanings are listed. The pairs are evaluated with respect to the same set of constraints under the same ranking as in unidirectional OT. Two of the pairs that are listed in Tableau 5.6 satisfy all constraints, namely the pairs <stress on indirect object, focus on indirect object> (candidate 8) and <stress on indirect object, focus on verb phrase> (candidate 9). As a result, these pairs are super-optimal and hence are possible form-meaning pairs in English. Subsequently, all other pairs that have either stress on the indirect object or focus on the indirect object or verb phrase are blocked by the first two super-optimal pairs. Of the remaining pairs, the pair <stress on direct object, focus on direct object> (candidate 2) satisfies the constraints best and hence emerges as a super-optimal pair too. Thus weak bidirectional optimization gives rise to the adult pattern of forms and meanings.

Note that candidate 2 also is an optimal pair under strong bidirectional optimization. This follows from the definition of strong bidirectional optimization given in Chapter 1 and repeated below:

(13) Strong bidirectional optimization (adapted from Blutner, 2000):
A form-meaning pair <f, m> is bidirectionally optimal iff:
(a)   there is no other pair <f', m> such that <f', m> is more harmonic than <f,m>.
(b)   there is no other pair <f, m'> such that <f, m'> is more harmonic than <f,m>.

For candidate 2, there is another pair with either the same form or the same meaning that is *equally* harmonic, namely the pair <stress on direct object, focus on verb phrase> (candidate 4). Candidate 2 and candidate 4 both violate the constraint NUCLEARSTRESS and satisfy the two stronger constraints. But crucially, there is no pair with either the same form or the same meaning that is *more* harmonic than candidate 2. Candidates 8 and 9 are more harmonic than candidate 2 because they satisfy all three constraints, whereas candidate 2 violates one of the constraints. However, these two candidates have both another form and another meaning and hence do not compete with candidate 2. So for candidate 2 there is no other pair with either a better form or a better meaning. As a result, candidate 2 also is a bidirectionally optimal pair according to the definition of strong bidirectional optimization in (13). Because candidates 2, 8 and 9 are bidirectionally optimal, the pair <stress on direct object, focus on verb phrase> (candidate 4), and in fact all other pairs in Tableau 5.6, are blocked. For candidate 4, there is a pair with a better form, namely candidate 9. This pair thus blocks candidate 4. According to the definition in (13) then, candidate 4 is not a bidirectionally optimal pair.

Thus, the result of both weak and strong bidirectional optimization is that the adult pattern emerges. Stress on the indirect object (i.e., unmarked or default stress) is ambiguous between a narrow focus and a wide focus interpretation, because candidates 8 and 9 are both optimal. Stress on the direct object (i.e., marked or shifted stress), on the other hand, only has the narrow focus interpretation because the optimal candidate 9 blocks the wide focus interpretation for a sentence with stress on the direct object (candidate 4).

Note that although the meanings under consideration (the different options for focus) are equally unmarked according to our constraints, we still get a blocking effect in interpretation. This is due to the form constraint NUCLEARSTRESS, which, for a given meaning, prefers stress on the indirect object to stress on the direct object. So a wide focus interpretation should be expressed by placing stress on the indirect object rather than on the direct object. As a result of this formal preference and the bidirectional perspective, the wide focus interpretation is blocked for a sentence with stress on the direct object, and the narrow focus interpretation is the only remaining interpretation for this sentence. No difference in markedness between the wide focus interpretation and the narrow focus interpretation needs to be postulated to obtain this result. In fact, with respect to the constraints under consideration, the relevant forms are completely ambiguous between the two meanings.

Concluding, the child language data seem to be described best by unidirectional optimization, whereas the adult data seem to be described best by bidirectional optimization. Because adult hearers realize that a wide focus interpretation can best be expressed by a sentence with unmarked stress, this meaning is blocked for a sentence with marked stress. As a result, for adults sentences with marked stress generally only have the narrow focus interpretation. For children, on the other hand, sentences with marked stress can be interpreted in the same way as sentences with unmarked stress. So the comprehension of contrastive stress is yet another example of the general pattern that children deviate from adults with respect to the interpretation of marked forms. With respect to the *production* of marked forms, the optimal output of unidirectional optimization and bidirectional optimization are identical. Consequently, it is predicted that children show no difficulties with respect to the production of bound focus, and hence show no production delay. This prediction seems to be borne out by children's production data discussed in Section 5.2.

Bidirectional OT thus yields detailed predictions with respect to language acquisition, and is able to predict the occurrence of delays in comprehension while at the same time predicting the production of the same forms to be adult-like. This follows from the property of OT that production and comprehension are modeled as opposite directions of optimization (from meaning to form, and from form to meaning, respectively). Because OT incorporates markedness constraints, which do not have any effects in the opposite direction of optimization, under unidirectional optimization production and comprehension can give rise to different form-meaning associations. Such mismatches between production and comprehension may disappear under bidirectional optimization. This then explains how comprehension delays are resolved during the course of language acquisition.

5.6   Cognitive demands of bidirectionality

5.6.1 Cognitive bounds on bidirectional optimization

According to the proposed OT explanation of the comprehension delays discussed in Chapter 4 as well as in the present chapter, there is a certain stage in children's language development at which, apart from the optimization strategy, all other aspects of the grammar are adultlike. That is, children who fail to comprehend indefinite subjects or objects, contrastive stress, object pronouns or scalar implicatures correctly, but who produce the corresponding forms correctly, are assumed to already have acquired the constraints and their relative ranking. The only difference with adults at that stage is that children are not yet able to optimize bidirectionally. This account of the difference between children's and adults' interpretation assumes that bidirectional optimization starts out as an online mechanism of language interpretation. Only with sufficient experience may some, though perhaps not all, bidirectional computations become automatized (see Hendriks, van Rijn and Valkenier, 2007, for a cognitive model simulating this developmental process).

This view differs from that of Blutner and Zeevat (2004b), which holds that the type of bidirectional optimization that causes marked forms to be paired with marked meanings is not an online mechanism used by speakers and hearers to determine the optimal form or meaning, respectively, during sentence processing. Rather, bidirectional optimization must be an entirely off-line process resulting from language change. As they put it, bidirectional optimization is a diachronic law allowing for additional solutions which 'are due to the ability and flexibility of self-organization in language change [...] before the learning mechanism has fully realized the equilibrium between productive and interpretive optimization'.

Considering bidirectional optimization as an off-line process, as Blutner and Zeevat propose, solves some of the problems that were pointed out by Beaver and Lee (2004) in their discussion of optimization strategies. In particular, Beaver and Lee show that if the process of bidirectional optimization is allowed to occur unboundedly, also non-existing form-meaning pairs will arise. They conclude that bidirectional optimization will have to be restricted to two rounds of optimization at most to yield the correct results for natural language. For that reason, they reject bidirectional optimization as an online mechanism of linguistic competence. Rather, bidirectional optimization must be an off-line description of form-meaning relations resulting from some other process.

However, the view that bidirectional optimization is an (occasionally) online process not only explains the child language data discussed in this chapter and the previous one, but also offers a solution to the problem sketched by Beaver and Lee. The number of rounds of optimization may be bounded by general performance restrictions on recursion (Blutner, de Hoop and Hendriks, 2006). Weak bidirectional optimization is a recursive process. Recursive processes in natural language are known to be subject to cognitive restrictions such as working memory limitation. For example, recursive center embedding as in *The boy the girl the dog bit saw left* is generally considered to result in an unmanageable form. Therefore, the observation that bidirectional optimization tends to be restricted to two rounds of optimization may be an effect of these cognitive bounds on recursion. Consequently, we can view bidirectional optimization as a mechanism describing human linguistic competence while acknowledging that the recursion allowed for by this mechanism is limited by performance factors.

The advantage of the online view is that the restriction to maximally two rounds of optimization follows from general restrictions on human language processing, and no other grammar-internal mechanisms providing such a restriction need to be stipulated. This does not mean that bidirectional optimization plays no role in language change whatsoever. In the next chapter, we will discuss the role of bidirectional optimization in the diachronic variation of negation across languages.

5.6.2 Acquisition of bidirectional optimization

If there indeed is an online mechanism of bidirectional optimization, which accounts for many aspects of pragmatic interpretation, then it must be acquired or instantiated quite late during acquisition, perhaps even later than 6 or 7 years old. It follows from our proposal that aspects of interpretation that depend on bidirectional optimization are acquired relatively late, as the ability to optimize bidirectionally is predicted to be contingent on the child's knowledge of the constraints and their relative ranking. As a result, the correct meaning for the marked form is predicted to emerge only after the child has shown knowledge of the constraints governing the unmarked form and its interpretation.

However, the question arises what exactly triggers the move from unidirectional to bidirectional optimization at this late age. One possibility is the availability of sufficient working memory capacity (cf. Reinhart, 2004), a proposal which forces us to consider what it is about bidirectional optimization that may be particularly taxing to children's working memory. Three core properties of bidirectional optimization come to mind immediately: (1) recursion, (2) its relation to the development of social cognition, and (3) the amount of processing required. As to the first property, recall that weak bidirectional optimization is a recursive process. Only if children have sufficient working memory capacity to optimize from a given form to a particular meaning, to keep the initial input form active, and to optimize from the resulting optimal meaning to possible forms in order to check whether the optimal form for that meaning is the same as the initial form, will they be able to optimize bidirectionally. Otherwise, their optimal outputs will be determined by unidirectional optimization. However, this property only holds for weak bidirectional optimization. In this chapter, it was shown that the non-recursive version of strong bidirectional optimization may be sufficient for the interpretation of contrastive stress. Since children also experience problems in comprehending contrastive stress, problems with recursion may not completely explain children's difficulty with bidirectional optimization.

The second property of bidirectionality which may yield considerable cognitive difficulties for children is the fact that bidirectional optimization requires the coordination of two opposite perspectives: the speaker's perspective and the hearer's perspective. At the root of the mechanism of bidirectional optimization lies the assumption that the hearer takes into account which options the speaker has for expressing a given meaning, and that the hearer has some understanding of what makes the speaker choose a certain form. The latter assumption requires that the hearer takes into account that any choice the speaker makes is co-determined by the speaker's belief that the hearer will indeed be aware of these options. This means, first of all, that bidirectional optimization may require a child hearer to have a first-order or perhaps even second-order Theory of Mind, and to be able to compute the implications of a recursive Theory of Mind. A child has a first-order Theory of Mind if it is capable of taking into account another person's beliefs, and a second-order Theory of Mind if it is capable of taking into account another person's beliefs about the minds of others (including its own mind). Secondly, if bidirectional optimization requires the hearer to take into account the speaker's choices, this means that the child must be able to draw on this part of social cognition when performing the bidirectional computation that is required for the processing of language, which is arguably not in the same cognitive domain as its linguistic competence.

A third possible explanation for why bidirectional optimization is instantiated relatively late during acquisition relates to children's lower speed of cognitive processing (Hendriks, van Rijn and Valkenier, 2007; Valkenier, 2006). This explanation is based on the assumption that language comprehension and production, as all cognitive processes, are bound in time. Children's application of constraints will initially be slow and effortful. With experience this process will become faster and faster. If bidirectional optimization is the serial application of unidirectional optimization from form to meaning and unidirectional optimization from meaning to form, bidirectional optimization requires more time than unidirectional optimization. It is then predicted that children will initially start with unidirectional optimization, simply because there is not enough time left to optimize in the opposite direction as well. Only when the unidirectional process can be performed fast enough will children be able to optimize bidirectionally.

In the next section, we explore the second explanation for children's difficulties with bidirectional optimization, namely their problems in applying second-order Theory of Mind. Section 5.6.3 elaborates on the third explanation for children's comprehension errors, and compares the predictions of the bidirectional optimization account with respect to adult sentence processing to the alternative account of Reinhart (2004, 2006).

5.6.3 Bidirectional optimization and Theory of Mind

For a language user, applying bidirectional optimization requires an insight in the intentions and decisions of the other participant to the conversation, and therefore, a Theory of Mind. Not only should the language user know the expressive options of the language, but she should also understand why the speaker (or hearer) decides for one, rather than another option. In this chapter and the previous one, we have proposed that a failure to apply bidirectional optimization lies at the root of several delays in language acquisition. Bidirectionality then becomes a key notion in explaining the development of grammar, in the individual who still needs to acquire bidirectional optimization and perhaps also the development of a grammar in an entire language community.

Theory of Mind has enjoyed the attention of students of language acquisition for some time. Bloom (2000) and Tomasello (2003) point out how social cognition may be instrumental in, or indeed largely responsible for, the acquisition of language, in particular reference and labelling. We add to this a different proposal: That social cognition plays a key role in determining the grammar itself.

When considering the relation between language and Theory of Mind, we must distinguish two ways in which Theory of Mind can be approached. On the first approach, Theory of Mind is undivided and generalizable: One either has a Theory of Mind, or one does not. For instance, an individual is said to have a Theory of Mind if she passes a False Belief test, for which an understanding of others' knowledge or views is required. On such a view of Theory of Mind, one might argue that Theory of Mind development is not likely to be implicated in the various language acquisition delays discussed in this chapter and the previous one. These delays disappear at different ages, in many cases well after the age at which children regularly pass False Belief tasks (typically from age 4 on), hence 'acquisition' of a first-order Theory of Mind cannot be the cause of acquisition of these grammatical phenomena.

It is becoming increasingly clear, however, that this notion of Theory of Mind is too simplistic. Whether Theory of Mind is displayed strongly depends on the nature of the task. For instance, it has been fairly standardly assumed since 1983 that the False Belief task (Wimmer and Perner, 1983) indexes Theory of Mind. In this task, an individual needs to decide where someone will, mistakenly, look for a hidden object. Recently, however, it was found that 15-month old children already show an awareness of Theory of Mind. In this task (Onishi and Baillargeon, 2005) children did not need to make a decision, but rather their looking times were measured, showing that the children distinguished between a person looking in a place where the child knows the object is hidden, or in a place where the person in question believes the object to be hidden. Another striking discrepancy between two tasks was found by Flobbe (2006) (see also Flobbe, Verbrugge, Hendriks and Krämer, 2008). Flobbe showed that children who successfully passed a second-order False Belief task ('she knows that he believes...') are for the most part unable to apply second-order Theory of Mind in a strategic game ('my opponent will not make a certain move, because he knows that I will then make a move which will curb his plans'). In fact, many of these children were unable even to apply first-order Theory of Mind in the game ('my opponent will make a certain move, because it is advantageous to him'). These findings show the relevance of the following question: How is Theory of Mind integrated with other areas of knowledge, so as to meet different task demands? Language provides an excellent arena for studying this question. Further investigation of the relation between social cognition and bidirectional optimization will contribute both to our understanding of language, and the nature of Theory of Mind.

5.6.4 Processing of bidirectional optimization

Although the dependence of bidirectional optimization on Theory of Mind may explain children's difficulties in applying bidirectional optimization, it is also conceivable that Theory of Mind is a necessary but not a sufficient condition for applying bidirectional optimization. It may be the case that children, in addition to having a well-developed Theory of Mind, also must possess cognitive capacities such as sufficient processing speed or a sufficiently large working memory to be able to carry out the process of bidirectional optimization.

An alternative account of several of the delays in comprehension that we have discussed above is Reinhart's (2004, 2006). Reinhart's account proceeds from the assumption that children possess the relevant knowledge in comprehension but lack sufficient working memory capacity to carry out the required computations. Reinhart's processing account is based on the process of reference-set computation, which is a computation performed by the parser rather than by the grammar. Reference-set computation involves constructing, for a given derivation, a reference set consisting of pairs of derivation and interpretation. On the basis of this reference set, it can be determined whether a more economical derivation is available for the interpretation. If this is true, the given derivation is blocked. Reinhart's account differs from ours in several respects – for a comparison, we refer the reader to Hendriks and Spenader (2006). Crucially, however, the two accounts make different predictions with respect to when exactly processing difficulties are to be expected. Let us consider again the case of marked and unmarked stress. According to Reinhart, reference-set computations are required by the parser only when interpreting marked stress, resulting in additional processing costs both in adults and in children. Because children have limited working memory capacity, they cannot carry out the required reference-set computation. Although adults have a larger working memory capacity, nevertheless these extra processing costs should be detectable when comprehending sentences with marked stress. Because comprehending sentences with unmarked stress does not require reference-set computation, Reinhart predicts that adults will find sentences with marked stress more difficult to process than sentences with unmarked stress.

On the account presented here, on the other hand, marked stress is not expected to be more difficult to process for adults than unmarked stress. We showed that both marked and unmarked forms and meanings are involved in the computation of bidirectionally optimal form-meaning pairs. In fact, if ambiguity yields some processing difficulties, as we may expect, then sentences with unmarked stress are expected to be more difficult, since these sentences are ambiguous. Sentences with marked stress are not ambiguous due to the blocking effect caused by bidirectional optimization. Indeed, in an eye-tracking experiment, Gennari, Meroni and Crain (2005) found that marked stress in fact facilitates sentence comprehension for adults. This confirms the predictions made by the bidirectional OT model of contrastive stress, and contradicts the predictions of Reinhart's model of reference-set computation.

The difference between Reinhart's processing proposal and the view that we advocate here is not only technical in nature, reflecting a distinction between two different linguistic frameworks. The difference also reflects a different view on the kind of processing limitations that may be involved in language interpretation. In Reinhart's view, the difficulty which results in children's deviant interpretations concerns a kind of processing that is specific to the linguistic system. In our view, in contrast, processing may be affected by more general cognitive restrictions, or even by the cognitive load of applying principles to language processing that originate in other cognitive domains. Thus, the present proposal reflects a view on human cognition which, while recognizing that there are distinct domains of human cognition, allows for extensive cross-modularity.

5.7 Conclusions

In this chapter we discussed several phenomena suggesting that children go through a stage in language development in which they simply try to find the best form for a given meaning, or the best meaning for a given form. We focused on the interpretation of contrastive stress, but argued that acquiring the correct meaning of indefinites (discussed in Chapter 4), pronouns and scalar implicatures proceeds along similar lines. In contrast to young children, adults also take into account their conversational partner's perspective in comprehension and production. So, as a hearer, they also consider the alternative forms the speaker has available, and use this information to determine the optimal meaning. This difference in optimization strategy between children and adults gives rise to comprehension delays as observed in acquisition experiments. Thus, the remarkable pattern is explained that correct production may sometimes precede correct comprehension by several years. The presence of these acquisition delays in comprehension suggests that bidirectional optimization must be learned or instantiated during language development and therefore cannot be purely a mechanism of language change.

Notes

1   'C-command' is a structural relation, that can be roughly defined in terms of positions in a syntactic tree: X c-commands Y iff Y is dominated by the node in the tree that strictly dominates X, but Y is not dominated by X.

6 Patterns of negation in natural language

6.1 Markedness of negation

All human systems of communication have an expression for negation (Horn, 1989). We take it to be a universal feature of human cognition that languages are able to express the meaning ¬p ('not p', where p stands for any proposition) as well as p. In first-order logic, ¬p and p have the same status, and ¬ ¬p is equivalent to p. But if we look at the way in which languages express negation and affirmation, we observe an asymmetry between the expression of a proposition p and its negative counterpart ¬p. Negation is always marked, but affirmation usually is not. That is, negation is always morphologically or syntactically visible or more complex, whereas affirmation takes the 'zero' expression or the simpler expression. The affirmative-negative pair in (1) provides an illustration. The English sentence (1a) expresses an affirmative statement, but does not contain a marker of affirmation. Sentence (1b) owes its character as a negative statement to the presence of *not*, which overtly marks negation.

(1)   (a) It is raining.
        (b) It is *not* raining.

The complexity in expression is related to the semantic markedness of negation in natural language. Horn (1984) proposes a division of pragmatic labor according to which unmarked forms pair up with unmarked meanings and marked forms pair up with marked meanings (cf. Chapter 1). Haspelmath (2006) takes frequency asymmetries in meanings to be the source of asymmetries in form. Negative meanings are relatively infrequent compared to affirmative meanings, so this would immediately explain why the negative expression in (1b) is marked (longer, more complex) than its affirmative counterpart in (1a). Zeevat and Jäger (2002), Jäger (2004) and Mattausch (2004, 2007) model Horn's division of pragmatic labor by means of an evolutionary bidirectional learning algorithm. It would lead too far to present the details of the evolutionary approach in this chapter, but the basic idea is that the Horn pattern emerges as an instance of optimal communication between speaker and hearer.[1] At a somewhat abstract level, Mattausch models Horn's division of pragmatic labor in terms of a competition between two forms (a marked and an unmarked form), and two meanings (a frequent meaning a and an infrequent meaning b). Four bias constraints govern the relation between forms and meanings:

(2)   Bias constraints:
   $*_{M,\alpha}$: The (marked) form m is not related to the meaning α.
   $*_{M,\beta}$: The (marked) form m is not related to the meaning β.
   $*_{U,\alpha}$: The (unmarked) form u is not related to the meaning α.
   $*_{U,\beta}$: The (unmarked) form u is not related to the meaning β.

The bias constraints in (2) mitigate against all possible form-meaning combinations, so it depends on the relative strength of the constraints which form-meaning pairs are more harmonic than others. Besides the bias constraints, Mattausch defines a markedness constraint *MARK, which avoids the use of the marked form m. *MARK models a general notion of economy, a preference of simpler forms over more complex ones. The ranking of *MARK with respect to the bias constraints reflects the balance of economy considerations with faithful correspondence relations between forms and meanings in the process of optimal communication. The network furthermore has a learning algorithm. In the initial training corpus, a model is used in which all four bias constraints are ranked equally high. Due to learning effects, the rankings can shift, and the association between forms and meanings shifts along with the rankings. Learning is driven by frequency distributions in the corpus. In the initial training corpus, there is a frequency asymmetry between meanings α and β, α occurring say 90% of the time, and β 10% of the time. There is an even distribution of marked and unmarked forms over the meanings α and β, so that the choice of a marked or an unmarked form for the frequent or infrequent meaning is entirely open. Learning is iterated over several generations. The input to the next generation is the corpus that constitutes the output of the previous generation. The iterated learning algorithm provides the evolutionary setting of the grammar. After a number of generations, we obtain a system in which the frequent meaning α is preferably associated with the unmarked form u, and the infrequent meaning β associates with the marked form m. If we have a frequent meaning α and an infrequent meaning β, iterated learning over multiple generations leads to a stable ranking of $\{*_{U,\beta}; *_{M,\alpha}\} \gg *\text{MARK} \gg \{*_{U,\alpha}; *_{M,\beta}\}$, as in Figure 6.1, where the vertical axis indicates the relative strength of the constraints with respect to each other.

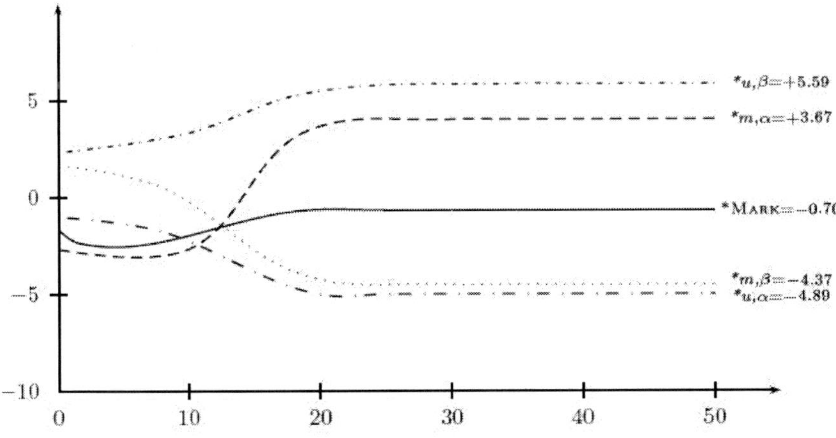

Figure 6.1: Bidirectional iterated learning (generations 1–50) (from Mattausch, 2007)

The ranking $\{*\text{U},\beta; *\text{M},\alpha\} \gg *\text{MARK} \gg \{*\text{U},\alpha; *\text{M},\beta\}$ describes a grammar in which marked forms are motivated for marked meanings only. Bidirectional iterated learning thus derives Horn's division of pragmatic labor as the optimal communication strategy that arises under evolutionary pressure.

The general, abstract approach sketched here can be used to explain various grammaticalization patterns. One of them is the markedness of negation in natural language. If we apply the model to negation, the frequent meaning a in the model is affirmation, and the infrequent meaning b is negation. In principle, the two meanings of affirmation and negation can pair up with two possible forms, an unmarked and a marked form. This could be a sentence with 'zero' marking such as (1a), and a sentence containing an overt marker such as (1b). Below, we will define a markedness constraint for negation. For now, we focus on the bias constraints relevant to the expression and interpretation of negation:

(3)   Bias constraints involving negation:
   $*\text{M,AFF}$: The (marked) form m is not related to the meaning affirmation.
   $*\text{M,NEG}$: The (marked) form m is not related to the meaning negation.
   $*\text{U,AFF}$: The (unmarked) form u is not related to the meaning affirmation.
   $*\text{U,NEG}$: The (unmarked) form u is not related to the meaning negation.

The application of the bidirectional OT learning algorithm in combination with iterated learning in an evolutionary setting reinforces the asymmetry between affirmation and negation. After a number of generations, the system will stabilize on the ranking $\{*\text{U,NEG}, *\text{M,AFF}\} \gg *\text{MARK} \gg \{*\text{U,AFF}, *\text{M,NEG}\}$. Under this ranking, affirmation is expressed by unmarked forms, and sentences containing no marking (1a) will be interpreted as affirmative. The expression of a negative meaning requires the insertion of a special marker, and negative sentences containing a marker of negation (1b) will be interpreted as negative.

We can rewrite Mattausch's result in terms of the faithfulness and markedness constraints we have used in this book so far. The bias constraints *U,NEG and *M,AFF require the unmarked form not to be related to negation, and the marked form not to be related to affirmation. These constraints can be captured by the faithfulness constraint FNEG (Faith negation):

(4) FNEG: Be faithful to negation, i.e., reflect the non-affirmative nature of the input in the output.

Within the generation perspective (OT syntax), FNEG requires negation in the meaning (input) to be reflected in the output (form), and this is in line with *U,NEG. In the interpretation perspective (OT semantics), FNEG requires a formal expression of negation to be interpreted as contributing a semantic negation, as expressed by *M,AFF.

The bias constraints *U,AFF and *M,NEG require the unmarked form not to be related to affirmation, and the marked form not to be related to negation. These constraints can be captured by the faithfulness constraint FAFF (Faith Affirmation).

(5) FAFF: Be faithful to affirmation, i.e., reflect the affirmative nature of the input in the output.

In OT terms, FNEG and FAFF are faithfulness constraints, i.e., constraints which aim at a faithful reflection of features of the input in the output.[2] Given the results of the evolutionary learning process, we obtain the ranking FNEG >> *MARK >> FAFF for all languages. However, if FAFF is always ranked below *MARK, the constraint is in fact inoperative, and we might as well leave it out of the system. This illustrates that faithfulness constraints in linguistic applications of OT tend to target marked, rather than unmarked expressions. In the remainder of this chapter, we will use FNEG, but ignore FAFF, because it does not do any work for the analysis.

The abstract model Jäger and Mattausch propose uses a markedness constraint *MARK that must be adapted to the phenomenon under consideration. The instance of the constraint that plays a role in negative statements is *NEG:

(6) *NEG: Avoid negation in the output.

The use of *NEG in OT syntax is in line with the asymmetric bidirectional model developed by Jäger and Mattausch. Here we present an extension of their approach, and use *NEG in OT semantics as well, where it treats negative meanings as marked, so we build a symmetric model. *NEG is obviously in conflict with FNEG: FNEG requires a reflection in the output of negative features we find in the input, whereas *NEG blocks negation in the output. Such conflicting constraints are characteristic of OT style analyses. The conflict is resolved by the ranking of constraints in terms of strength.

If we rank FNEG higher than *NEG, making it a stronger, more important constraint, we can derive the fact that negative meanings are formally expressed:

Tableau 6.1: Generation of negative sentences

¬p	FNEG	*NEG
S	*!	
☞ not S		*

Which item functions as the marker of propositional negation in a language, and satisfies FNEG is a lexical and not a grammatical matter. In English, this is *not*, in other languages, propositional negation is lexicalized by some other word. All the sentences in (7) express a negative proposition, and contain a linguistic marker of negation (in italics), which is glossed as SN:[3]

(7) (a) John is *not* sick.   [English]

   (b) *Ou* petetai Sokrates.   [Ancient Greek]
       SN   flies   Sokrates
       'Socrates doesn't fly.'

   (c) On *ne* igraet.   [Russian]
       he SN   plays
       'He doesn't play.'

   (d) Juan *no* ha llamado a   su   madre. [Spanish]
       Juan SN   has called   to   his mother
       'Juan hasn't called his mother.'

   (e) János *nem* dohányz-ik.   [Hungarian]
       János SN   smoke.3SG
       'János doesn't smoke.'

The ranking FNEG >> *NEG reflects the accepted view that negative statements are cross-linguistically more marked in form than their affirmative counterparts (Payne, 1985; Horn, 1989; Haspelmath, 1997). There are no languages in which *NEG outranks FNEG, so negation is rightfully claimed to be a universal category (Dahl, 1979). In OT terms, it is unusual to postulate that one constraint always needs to be at the top of the ranking and can never be violated. In this particular case, we do not expect cross-linguistic variation, because all languages adopt an optimal communication strategy under evolutionary pressure.[4]

Jäger (2004) and Mattausch (2004, 2007) use an asymmetric version of bidirectional optimization in which forms are disqualified as candidates if they are not optimally recoverable as the intended meaning and at least one other form is. In the remainder of this chapter, we want to build a symmetric version of bidirectional OT, in which the OT semantics mirrors the OT syntax directly. This will be used to model the optimal interpretation of sentences containing multiple markers of negation. We can do this, because the two constraints FNEG and *NEG are neutral as to what they take to be the input and what the output. They were deliberately phrased in this way, so that they could be used in both OT syntax and OT semantics. FNEG is satisfied in OT semantics if a form marked as negative is mapped onto a negative meaning. *NEG is satisfied in OT semantics if the meaning representation does not involve a negation. Under the same constraint ranking FNEG >> *NEG we adopted in OT syntax, we obtain the interpretation of expressions containing an overt marker of negation as in Tableau 6.2.

Tableau 6.2: Interpretation of propositional negation

not S	FNEG	*NEG
p	*!	
☞ ¬p		*

The input in Tableau 6.2 is a form, and the output candidates evaluated by the grammar are meanings. If FNEG outranks *NEG, we obtain a negative meaning as the optimal interpretation of negative sentences like those in (7) above. This is obviously the desired outcome. Note that the ranking of FNEG above *NEG implies that the semantics of negation cannot be ignored, but does not determine whether every 'bit' of negative meaning that we find in a sentence contributes its own negation. The discussion of double negation and negative concord in Sections 6.2.3 and 6.4 below will show that we need to rank *NEG with respect to an additional semantic constraint to account for these distinctions.

6.2   The position of negation in the sentence

The outcome of the optimization procedure in Section 6.1 is that all natural languages have ways to express propositional negation. The question that arises is how natural languages realize propositional negation, and how they integrate the expression of negation into the syntax. Section 6.2 develops a typology of expressions of propositional negation in natural language.

6.2.1 Preverbal and post-verbal negation

The most common ways that languages realize negation are as (i) a marker of sentential negation, glossed as SN in examples (7) above, (ii) a negative morpheme that appears as a prefix or a suffix on the verb (or an argument of the verb), as in (8a), from Zeijlstra (2004) and (8b), from Morimoto (2001), or (iii) a negative verb as in (8c), from Payne (1985) and (8d), from Mitchell (2006).[5]

(8) (a) Milan   *ne*volá.   [Czech]
          Milan   SN.call
          'Milan doesn't call.'

     (b) Taroo-wa asagohan-o   tabe-na-katta.   [Japanese]
          Taroo.TOP breakfast.ACC   ate.SN.PAST
          'Taroo didn't eat breakfast.'

     (c) Nuŋan   *ə-ŋkī-n*   baka-ra.   [Evenki]
          he   NEG.PAST.3SG   find.PART
          'He didn't find.'

     (d) E-n   lue.   [Finnish]
          NEG.1SG   read
          'I don't read.'

In the remainder of this chapter, we will only be concerned with the expression of negation by means of a negative particle (1b, 7) or a negative morpheme (8a,b), and we will leave negative verbs aside (8c,d).

If a negation marker is used to convey negation, it needs to be integrated in the syntactic structure of the sentence. The main issue discussed in the literature concerns the position of negation with respect to the verb. In (9) and (10), we give examples of negation in preverbal and post-verbal position respectively:[6]

(9) (a) Maria   *non*   parla molto.   [Italian]
          Maria   SN   talks   much.
          'Maria doesn't talk much.'

     (b) *Nid* oedd   Sioned yn   gweithio. [formal Welsh]
          SN   be.IMPF.3SG Sioned PROG work
          'Sioned was not working.'

     (c) Ɂəli   *ma:*   ra:ħ   lidda: ˁirə.   [Baghdad Arabic]
          Ali   SN   went to the   office
          'Ali didn't go to the office.'

(d) A   vaga   koŋ   *ba* bɛnɛ.   [Koromfe]
    ART dog.SG DET.NONHUMAN.SG SN   come.PAST
    'The dog did not come.'

(e) Mary does *not* talk much.   [English]

(10) (a) Maria   a   parla *nen*   tant.   [Piedmontese]
       Maria   CL   talks SN   much
       'Maria doesn't talk much.'

(b) Maria   spricht *nicht* viel.   [German]
    Maria   talks   SN   much
    'Maria doesn't talk much.'

(c) Maria   praat *niet* veel.   [Dutch]
    Maria   talks SN   much.
    'Maria doesn't talk much.'

(d) Mi-zɔk   wi   ndɔng *na*.   [Gbaya Kaka]
    1SG.see person that   SN
    'I do not see those people.'

In most languages, negation either precedes or follows the finite verb. In English, negation follows the auxiliary (1b, 7a), but precedes the main verb (1b, 9e). This motivates the construction of *do*-support illustrated in (9e). The patterns of preverbal and post-verbal negation were first described by Jespersen (1917, 1924, 1933). Jespersen identifies a strong tendency 'to place the negative first, or at any rate as soon as possible, very often immediately before the particular word to be negated (generally the verb)' (Jespersen, 1917:4). Horn (1989:292–293) dubs the term NEGFIRST for this tendency. NEGFIRST is motivated by communicative efficiency, i.e., to 'put the negative word or element as early as possible, so as to leave no doubt in the mind of the hearer as to the purport of what is said' (Jespersen, 1924:297), quoted by Horn (1989:293). See Corblin and Tovena (2003) for discussion of NEGFIRST in Romance.

Although many languages have a preverbal marker of sentential negation, the examples in (10) indicate that NEGFIRST is not an absolute rule. According to Jespersen, NEGFIRST is opposed by another strong tendency, which we label as FOCUSLAST. FOCUSLAST reflects that given information comes early in the sentence, and new or significant information comes last in the sentence. FOCUSLAST is not specific to negation, but is a pragmatic strategy or an instance of information structure that mainly operates at the discourse level. In languages in which word order is not strict, principles of information structure often interact with grammatical structure. If negation is part of the new information expressed by the sentence, we would expect it to show up late, rather than early in the sentence. FocusLast for negation is then motivated by the idea that the negative force is stronger if the negator comes later in the linear order (Mazzon, 2004:97). Frequently, the post-verbal negation is the result of a diachronic development where post-verbal adverbials that originally served as emphatic reinforcements of the negation gradually took over the negative force of the sentence, while maintaining their post-verbal position (10a,b,c).

We will come back to the diachronic development commonly referred to as the 'Jespersen cycle' in Section 6.3 below. For now, we adopt a synchronic approach in a typological perspective. Given that NegFirst and FocusLast are both strong tendencies, but not hard rules, they work best as violable constraints that can be ranked with respect to each other and to other constraints. We can then state that languages with preverbal negation have grammars in which NegFirst is a highly ranked constraint and languages that do not have preverbal negation have grammars in which NegFirst is ranked low. Similarly, if a language has a grammar with a high ranking for FocusLast, it can push the marker of sentential negation to a later, in particular a post-verbal position in the sentence. We propose the following formulations for the two constraints in OT:

(11) NegFirst: Negation precedes the finite verb.

(12) FocusLast: New information comes last in the sentence.[7]

If we allow both rankings NegFirst >> FocusLast and FocusLast >> NegFirst, we can propose the following tableaux for the two positions of the negation marker with respect to the verb:[8]

Tableau 6.3: Preverbal negation (Italian, Spanish, formal Welsh, ...) (first version)

¬p	FNeg	NegFirst	FocusLast
(S) V (O)	*!		
☞ (S) sn V (O)			*
(S) V sn (O)		*!	

Tableau 6.4: Post-verbal negation (Piedmontese, German, Dutch, ...) (first version)

¬p	FNeg	FocusLast	NegFirst
(S) V (O)	*!		
(S) sn V (O)		*!	
☞ (S) V sn (O)			*

Whether we find preverbal or post-verbal negation in a particular language is then due to the ranking of the two constraints FocusLast and NegFirst below

FNEG. However, the situation becomes slightly more complex if we take the economy constraint *NEG into consideration as well, so Tableaux 6.3 and 6.4 are to be considered preliminary representations of the grammar.

6.2.2 Adding discontinuous negation

In Tableaux 6.3 and 6.4, we limited ourselves to the competition between NEGFIRST and FOCUSLAST. This set-up suggests that we have to choose between negation in preverbal or post-verbal position. However, we also find languages that display so-called discontinuous negation. Discontinuous negation combines a preverbal and a post-verbal expression, as in the following examples:[9]

(13) (a) *Ne*   bið he *na* geriht.   [Old English]
      SN   is   he   SN   righted
      'He is not/never set right (=forgiven).'

   (b) Elle *ne* vient *pas*.   [written French]
      She   SN   comes   SN

   (c) U   *n* li   sent *nent*.   [Cairese Piedmontese]
      3.CL   SN   him   hears   SN
      'He can't hear him.'

   (d) Igl bab *na* lavoura *betg*.   [Surmeiran]
      the father SN   works   SN
      'The father doesn't work.'

   (e) *Ni* soniodd   Sioned *ddim* am   y   digwyddiad. [formal Welsh]
      SN   mention.PAST.3SG Sioned SN   about the event
      'Sioned did not talk about the event.'

   (f) *Doedd*   Gwyn *ddim* yn   cysgu. [informal Welsh]
      NEG.be.IMPF.3SG   Gwyn SN   PROG sleep
      'Gwyn was not sleeping.'

   (g) baba wo-shìi nai   tapa   *u*.   [Kanakuru]
      father SN.he   drink tobacco SN
      'My father does not smoke tobacco.'

   (h) nyè-*mé*-yì d☐éàvĕ-á   mè *ò*.   [Ewe]
      1SG.SN.go KV forest.DEF in   SN
      'I am not going into the forest.'

We characterize these cases as discontinuous negation, because there is only one negation in the semantics, that is, all the sentences in (13) express a proposition of the form ¬p, with p an atomic proposition. However, negation is expressed by two 'bits' of form that do not constitute a unit in the sentence. Typically, one 'bit' precedes the verb and the other one follows it. Syntactically, we have double negation, but semantically, we have just a single negation. Example (13a) is from Mazzon (2004:27), who indicates that discontinuous negation was a rather unstable phenomenon in the late Old English and Early Middle English period. The written French example in (13b) illustrates the semantic 'bleaching' of preverbal *ne* to a co-negative, where the expressive force of negation is borne by the post-verbal negator *pas*, not by *ne* (cf. Godard, 2004, and references therein). Formal Welsh reflects an older stage of the language in which the post-verbal *ddim* is optional (13e). In informal Welsh, the preverbal particle has disappeared, but it survives in incorporated form on some verbs, such as *oedd-doedd* (13f). Although the verb appears in a negative form, it is unable to express semantic negation, and the presence of the post-verbal adverb *ddim* is obligatory, as stated by Borsley and Jones (2005).

We do not find discontinuous negation in many languages, and when we find it, it is usually not very stable diachronically (Haspelmath, 1997).[10] Modern English and standard modern Dutch do not have a discontinuous negation anymore. In spoken French, preverbal *ne* is frequently dropped. In colloquial Welsh, the special negative form of the verb is limited to a small number of lexical verbs. Reasons of economy are behind the rarity of discontinuous negation. Syntactically, discontinuous negation is of course rather costly: why use two markers to express a single negation, if one could do the job? In terms of the constraint system adopted here, discontinuous negation violates the markedness constraint *NEG twice, whereas the examples in (9) and (10) only violate this constraint once. Ranking *NEG above one of the faithfulness constraints governing position (NEGFIRST, FOCUSLAST) forces a choice between preverbal and post-verbal negation. The motivation for discontinuous negation is a desire to satisfy the two faithfulness constraints NEGFIRST and FOCUSLAST, at the expense of the markedness constraint *NEG. In the OT system, we can account for discontinuous negation by ranking both NEGFIRST and FOCUSLAST higher than *NEG (Tableau 6.7). Systems with preverbal or post-verbal negation are captured by the ranking of *NEG between the constraints NEGFIRST and FOCUSLAST. Tableaux 6.5 and 6.6 are then the revised versions of Tableaux 6.3 and 6.4.

Tableau 6.5: Preverbal negation (Italian, Spanish, formal Welsh ...) (final version)

¬p	FNEG	NEGFIRST	*NEG	FOCUSLAST
(S) V (O)	*!			
☞ (S) SN V (O)			*	*
(S) V SN (O)		*(!)	*(!)	
(S) SN V SN (O)			**!	

Tableau 6.6: Post-verbal negation (Piedmontese, German, Dutch, ...) (final version)

¬p	FNEG	FOCUSLAST	*NEG	NEGFIRST
(S) V (O)	*!			
(S) SN V (O)		*(!)	*(!)	
☞ (S) V SN (O)			*	*
(S) SN V SN (O)			**!	

Tableau 6.7: Discontinuous negation (Old English, written French, colloquial Welsh, Kanakuru, ...) (production)

¬p	FNEG	NEGFIRST	FOCUSLAST	*NEG
(S) V (O)	*!			
(S) SN V (O)			*!	*
(S) V SN (O)		*!		*
☞ (S) SN V SN (O)				**

Tableaus 6.5, 6.6 and 6.7 indicate that FNEG is always the highest ranked constraint. *NEG is a gradable constraint that incurs one violation for every instance of a negative form. In Tableau 6.5, the ranking of FOCUSLAST below both *NEG and NEGFIRST leads to preverbal negation as the optimal candidate. The ranking of *NEG with respect to NEGFIRST is irrelevant, so we represent them as tied constraints, which are ranked equally high (cf. Chapter 3 for tied constraints). In Tableau 6.6, we obtain post-verbal negation, because NEGFIRST is ranked below both *NEG and FOCUSLAST. In the case of discontinuous negation (Tableau 6.7), *NEG is violated twice, because there are two 'bits' of negative form present in the sentence. Economy reasons would avoid an extra violation of the markedness constraint, but the high ranking of both NEGFIRST and FOCUSLAST above *NEG overrules economy. The ranking of NEGFIRST and FOCUSLAST does not influence the outcome, so they are represented as tied constraints in Tableau 6.7.

6.2.3 The semantics of discontinuous negation

Discontinuous negation raises new problems for the semantics of negation. Tableau 6.7 is an OT syntactic evaluation, i.e., it determines the best form for a given meaningful input. If the optimal form for the expression of a single negation is a discontinuous negation, the question arises whether the input meaning is recoverable. In order to address this issue, we need to take a closer look at the OT semantics. If we have two negative forms in the sentence, we need to specify whether the sentences conveys a single negation as in (13), or a double negation as in the English example (14a) or the Dutch example (14b).

(14) (a) Common people are *not nothing.*

     (b) In tegenstelling tot het lege gebaar van Sun is dit *niet niets.*   [Dutch]
       'In contrast to the empty gesture by Sun, this is not nothing.'

Sentences conveying double negation typically require a special intonation (cf. Postal, 2004). Note that not all varieties of English give rise to double negation readings with multiple negative expressions; compare de Swart (2009: Chapter 5) for discussion of negative concord varieties of English.

The constraint FNeg is at the top of the ranking for all languages under consideration. In the OT semantics, FNeg determines that negation in the input cannot be ignored, but it does not determine whether each and every negative expression in the sentence contributes its own negation (as in 14), or not (as in 13). So this constraint cannot be responsible for the interpretive difference between discontinuous negation (13) and double negation (14). De Swart (2006) focuses on negative indefinites like *nothing, nada, rien,* and proposes the constraint IntNeg for the interpretation of negative expressions in OT semantics:

(15) IntNeg: Force Iteration (i.e., interpret every Neg-expression in the input form as contributing a semantic negation in the output.)

IntNeg is crucial to establish the distinction between so-called double negation languages (English, Dutch) and negative concord languages (Romance, Slavic, Hungarian, etc.) in the semantics. If the grammar adopts the ranking *Neg >> IntNeg, multiple instances of negation will be absorbed into a resumptive negative quantifier that binds all the variables in its scope (de Swart and Sag,

2002). The optimal interpretation of a sentence containing multiple negative expressions is a single negation reading (negative concord) (de Swart, 2006, 2009). If the OT grammar adopts the ranking IntNeg >> *Neg, every negative expression contributes its own negation to the interpretation by interpreting the sequence in terms of iteration (function application). As a result, the combination of two negative expressions leads to a double negation reading (de Swart, 2006, 2009). Languages like English and Dutch exemplify this ranking, as illustrated in (14). The insight about negative indefinites extends to expressions of propositional negation. If a single marker of negation shows up in a sentence, we cannot determine whether the language is a double negation language (7a; 9e; 10b, c) or a negative concord language (7c, d, e; 8a; 9a, b; 10a). Indeed, we are unable to classify the languages exemplified in (8b), (9c), (9d) or (10d), because the literature we are familiar with does not provide the relevant data with negative indefinites to decide the issue. However, the presence of discontinuous negation in (13) is a clear signal of a negative concord language, with a ranking *Neg >> IntNeg in the grammar. Only this ranking allows us to recover the single negation reading of a discontinuous negation, as illustrated in Tableau 6.8.

Tableau 6.8: Discontinuous negation (Old English, written French, colloquial Welsh, Kanakuru, …) (interpretation)

(S) SN V SN (O)	FNEG	NEGFIRST	FOCLAST	*NEG	INTNEG
p	*!				**
☞ ¬ p				*	*
¬ ¬ p				**!	

The input is a sentence with discontinuous negation, so there are two overt expressions of negation in the sentence. Their position with respect to the verb is irrelevant to the interpretation of the sentence, for NegFirst and FocusLast are syntactic constraints that do not play a role in the OT semantics. FNeg is relevant. It requires the sentence to have a non-assertive interpretation, because the sentence is formally marked as negative. The high ranking of FNeg in all natural languages immediately wipes out the affirmative meaning p as the optimal interpretation of the sentence. The real competition is between the single and the double negation interpretations $\neg p$ and $\neg \neg p$. The single negation reading incurs one violation of *Neg, and one violation of the interpretative constraint IntNeg, whereas the double negation reading incurs two violations of *Neg, but satisfies IntNeg. This means that the order of the two constraints is crucial. Given the ranking *Neg >> IntNeg in Tableau 6.8, the single negation reading is the preferred interpretation of the discontinuous negation in sentences like (13). This corresponds with the semantic input in the OT syntax Tableau 6.7, so the original meaning has been recovered under this ranking. According to this analysis, the study of the syntactic position of the expression of sentential negation in the sentence has important semantic implications.

6.2.4 A typology of negation in natural language

As far as the syntax is concerned, a full factorial typology would lead to six possible constraint rankings for the three constraints *Neg, NegFirst and FocusLast, which together determine the position of negation in the sentence. However, we find only three main patterns in natural language, namely preverbal negation, post-verbal negation, and discontinuous negation. How do these three patterns relate to the six possible constraint rankings? If we look more closely at the possible rankings, we observe that each pattern involves the joint ranking of two constraints as higher than the third one. Note that the two highest constraints in Tableaus 6.5, 6.6 and 6.7 are connected by a dotted line rather than a hard line. This indicates that we cannot decide on their ranking on the basis of the candidates displayed here. The constraints can be tied (cf. Chapter 3), or can remain unranked with respect to each other, so that each ranking of adjacent constraints leads to the same result.[11] If the relative order of the two highest constraints of each ranking is in fact irrelevant, the three grammars can be summarized as follows.

(16) Typology of placement of negation:
    preverbal negation: {NegFirst, *Neg} >> FocusLast
    discontinuous negation: {NegFirst, FocusLast} >> *Neg
    post-verbal negation: {FocusLast, *Neg} >> NegFirst

Two different constraints are paired up in each case, so no reduction in the number of constraints is possible. However, the result of the pairing up of constraints is that we obtain three main rankings, rather than the six that a full factorial typology would predict. The idea behind the three-way partition in the placement of negation is that all three constraints capture a fundamental and highly valued aspect of the expression of negation, namely the markedness of negation, and its preference for either a preverbal position or a focus position late in the sentence. It is impossible to satisfy all three constraints at the same time, because they are partially conflicting. However, it is possible to maximize the satisfaction of two constraints by accepting the violation of the third one. The joint maximization of two constraints as opposed to a third, weaker constraint leads to three possible rankings, instead of a full factorial typology. The three way partition then reflects an optimization strategy under which we find the least number of violations, with the largest degree of cross-linguistic variation. The three rankings account for the three main patterns of negation found in natural language that were described as early as Jespersen (1917).

6.3 Diachronic perspective

(Synchronic) typological variation and (diachronic) language change are two instances of the same phenomenon of cross-linguistic variation. In this section, we relate the main typological patterns of negation in natural language to the diachronic development of negation commonly referred to as the 'Jespersen cycle'.

6.3.1 The Jespersen cycle

Jespersen formulates the diachronic development of negation in the following terms: 'The history of negative expressions in various languages makes us witness the following curious fluctuation: the original negative adverb is first weakened, then found insufficient and therefore strengthened, generally through some additional word, and this in turn may be felt as the negative proper and may then in course of time be subject to the same development as the original word' (Jespersen, 1917:4, quoted by Horn, 1989:452). A few pages later, Jespersen adds: 'Now, when the negative begins a sentence, it is on account of that very position more liable than elsewhere to fall out, by the phenomenon for which we venture to coin the term of prosiopesis (the opposite of what has been termed of old aposiopesis): the speaker begins to articulate, or thinks he begins to articulate, but produces no audible sound (either for want of expiration, or because he does not put his vocal chords in the proper position) till one or two syllables after the beginning of what he intended to say. (…) The interplay of these tendencies – weakening and strengthening and protraction – will be seen to lead to curiously similar, though in some respects different developments in Latin with its continuation in French, in Scandinavian and in English.' (Jespersen, 1917:6).

The trajectory of the Jespersen cycle is well documented for English (Horn, 1989; Mazzon, 2004, and references therein), French (Bréal, 1900; Horn, 1989; Godard, 2004), German (A. Jäger, 2008, and references therein), and Dutch (Hoeksema, 1997; Zeijlstra, 2004). Although Borsley and Jones don't describe it in these terms, it is traceable for Welsh in their (2005) book. Horn (1989:455) summarizes the English and French development as follows:

Table 6.1: Summary of English and French development

Old French	Jeo *ne* dis I SN say	Old English	Ic *ne* secge I SN say
Modern French (written/standard)	Je *ne* dis *pas* I SN say SN	Middle English	Ic *ne* seye *not* I SN say SN
Modern French (colloquial)	Je dis *pas* I say SN	Early Modern English	I say *not* I say SN
		Modern English	I don't say I do SN say

The preverbal negation *ne* in Old French is reinforced by the post-verbal marker *pas*, which leads to the discontinuous negation *ne...pas* in modern written French. The discontinuous negation is currently giving away to a single post-verbal negation in spoken French (Ashby, 1981, 2001). In English, we find a similar development from the Old English preverbal negation *ne* via the discontinuous pattern in Middle English to the post-verbal negation *not* in Early Modern English. *Not,* which originates from *nawiht/nogh/nahtet* 'nothing', has taken over the negative force in this phase. The Jespersen cycle is iterative: over time, languages can move back from post-verbal negation to preverbal negation. In certain French creoles, spoken in Haiti, Guadeloupe, the Seychelles, the post-verbal marker *pas* from standard French has been reanalyzed as a preverbal negation. The Haitian Creole example in (17a) illustrates (from Posner, 1985).

(17) (a) li   past   a   ap   vi_ni_. [Haitian Creole]
       him SN   PAST   FUT   PROG   come
       'He wouldn't be coming.'

   (b) Nobody no   go   kam.   [Broken]
       nobody SN   will   come
       'Nobody will come.'

In (17b), we see that a similar development has taken place in the English-based Torres Strait Creole Broken (Haspelmath, 1997:205). Of course, Creole languages are not a straightforward historical development of the standard language, but the examples in (17) illustrate that it is possible in principle to shift back from a post-verbal to a preverbal negator.

Zeijlstra (2004: Chapter 4) reviews the diachronic development of negation in Dutch, and describes similar patterns.

Table 6.2: Summary of Dutch development

Old Dutch	Inde in uuege sundigero *ne* stûnt And in way sinners.ɢᴇɴ sɴ stood.3sɢ 'And didn't stand in the way of sinners'
Early Middle Dutch (13ᵗʰ century)	*En* laettine mi spreke *niet* sɴ let.he me speak sɴ 'If he doesn't let me speak'
Late Middle Dutch(16ᵗʰ century, Holland)	Mine herberge ontseggic u *niet* My tavern take.away.I you sɴ 'My tavern I won't take away from you'
Modern Dutch (Netherlands)	Jan loopt *niet* Jan walks sɴ 'Jan doesn't walk'

In certain Dutch dialects (mostly spoken in the south of the Netherlands and in Flanders, Belgium), discontinuous negation is still extensively used (cf. example (23) in Section 6.3.3 below), but the preverbal marker is optional.

In the OT system developed so far, we can informally describe the diachronic patterns as follows. NᴇɢFɪʀꜱᴛ is the driving force behind the expression of negation 'early' in the sentence. Negation is a focus operator, just like *only* (cf. Chapter 5), and as such it tends to directly precede its domain of application, i.e., the verb (de Swart, 2009). At the same time, this preverbal position is subject to erosion, which leads to a reinforcement of negation. Because the reinforcement of negation is emphatic, and bears focus, it occurs later in the sentence under the influence of FᴏᴄᴜꜱLᴀꜱᴛ. This leads to the strengthening of negation occurring in post-verbal position. Under the influence of NᴇɢFɪʀꜱᴛ, it is possible to reanalyze the post-verbal marker as a preverbal one. This development completes the cycle.

6.3.2 An OT implementation of the Jespersen cycle

In his sketch of two opposing tendencies, Jespersen describes the two roles of negation as a focus operator, and as carrying new (i.e., focused) information. By relating these opposing tendencies to the dynamics of language change, Jespersen sketches a pattern of diachronic change in which preverbal negation is first doubled with a post-verbal emphatic expression that reinforces negation. The post-verbal marker gradually takes over the negative force of the preverbal one, eventually leading to the disappearance of the preverbal marker of sentential negation. Furthermore, this process is subject to iteration.

We link the three main positions of the marker of sentential negation and their OT analysis in (16) to the three main stages of the Jespersen cycle. We propose a step-wise change in the grammar, whereby one constraint changes position in the ranking at every stage. This leads to the following modeling of the Jespersen cycle in OT:

(18) Jespersen cycle in OT (diachronic development of negation):

Stage 1 (preverbal negation)
    1.1 *NEG >> NEGFIRST >> FOCUSLAST
    1.2 NEGFIRST >> *NEG >> FOCUSLAST

Stage 2 (discontinuous negation)
    2.1 NEGFIRST >> FOCUSLAST >> *NEG
    2.2 FOCUSLAST >> NEGFIRST >> *NEG

Stage 3 (post-verbal negation)
    3.1 FOCUSLAST >> *NEG >> NEGFIRST
    3.2 *NEG >> FOCUSLAST >> NEGFIRST

In accordance with the results from Section 6.2.4, the joint ranking of two constraints as opposed to the weaker position of the third constraints captures each of the three stages in (16). In this way, a complete ranking for each stage always involves two possible ordinal rankings. The distinction between the two rankings posited for each stage is invisible in the language production. For example, the rankings in 1.1 and 1.2 both lead to the expression of negation in a preverbal position. However, under a gradual perspective on language change, the ranking has to have shifted to the second possible ranking of a stage before the transition to the next stage can take place. For example, the ranking in 1.2 allows the transition to the ranking in 2.1 by means of the raising of FOCUSLAST above *NEG. This transition in the grammar indicates the weakening of the preverbal negation and the reinforcement by a post-verbal negation. Note that a single change in the ranking of FOCUSLAST and NEGFIRST leads back from stage 3.2 to stage 1.1. This completes the cycle, and allows the diachronic process to repeat itself, as Jespersen suggested. In general, a change in stage occurs when re-ranking affects the lowest two constraints in the ranking. Re-ranking of the highest two constraints in the ranking does not affect the stage the grammar is in (cf. Section 6.2.4).

6.3.3 Intermediate stages: stochastic OT

The three typologically established cases of preverbal, discontinuous and post-verbal negation defined in Section 6.2 represent stages in a diachronic development. A diachronic development is typically not instantaneous, so we find intermediate stages in which the language wavers between stage 1 and stage 2, or between stage 2 and stage 3. We can model such intermediate stages by adopting a formulation of the rankings in terms of stochastic OT.

Standard Optimality Theory has an ordinal ranking. That is, in a ranking $C_1 \gg C_2$, constraint C_1 is always stronger, and the violation of constraint C_2 is always allowed in order to satisfy C_1. The ordinal ranking of standard OT is abandoned in stochastic OT, and replaced by a continuous ranking of constraints (Boersma, 1998; Boersma and Hayes, 2001; Jäger, 2004). The result is that constraints have overlapping ranges. This is illustrated in Figure 6.2.

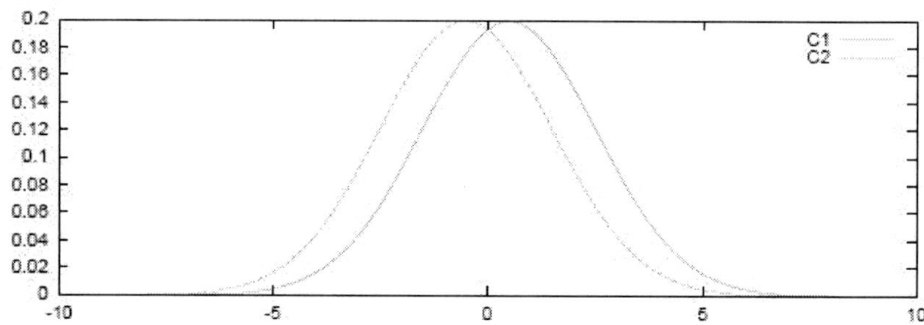

Figure 6.2: Overlapping constraints (from Jäger, 2004)

If two constraints C_1 and C_2 have overlapping ranges and chance determines the exact ranking at every evaluation of an input, we mostly find the order $C_1 \gg C_2$, but the order $C_2 \gg C_1$ in some cases. Jäger and Rosenbach (2006) use stochastic OT to model diachronic change and grammaticalization of possession relations. The use of stochastic OT to model intermediate stages of the Jespersen cycle is a direct extension of their approach.

Several languages have been argued to exemplify negation systems in between stages 1 and 2, or in between stages 2 and 3. A language that is between stage 1 and stage 2 has an obligatory preverbal marker of negation that is optionally reinforced by post-verbal emphatic negation. Such a language is moving away from a preverbal negation towards a system with a discontinuous negation. We find this in Welsh, as illustrated in (19) (data from Borsley and Jones, 2005):

(19) (a) *Nid*   oedd   Sioned   yn   gweithio.   [formal Welsh]
        SN   be.IMPF.3SG   Sioned   PROG   work
        'Sioned was not working.'

     (b) *Ni* soniodd   Sioned *ddim* am   y   digwyddiad. [formal Welsh]
        NEG mention.PAST.3SG   Sioned NEG   about the event
        'Sioned did not talk about the event.'

     (c) *Doedd*   Gwyn *ddim* yn   cysgu.   [informal Welsh]
        NEG.be.IMPF.3SG Gwyn NEG   PROG   sleep
        'Gwyn was not sleeping.'

     (d) Na'th   Emrys   *ddim* gweld dim byd.   [informal Welsh]
        do.PAST.3SG   Emrys   NEG   see   NEG world
        'Emrys didn't see anything.'

In (19a), the preverbal particle *nid* alone carries the negative force of the sentence. In (19b), *ni* is reinforced by the post-verbal adverb *ddim*. The data indicate that formal Welsh is moving from a preverbal negation to a discontinuous negation pattern. Discontinuous negation is well established in colloquial Welsh, with verbs that have a distinctive negative form as in (19c). In Welsh, sentences that involve verbs which do not have a distinctive negative form, such as *na'th* in (19d), the presence of *ddim* is the only indication of the negative force. The situation in (19d) reflects a stage 3 grammar. In formal Welsh, the post-verbal marker is optional, and both (19a) and (19b) are grammatical. However, in the informal Welsh examples (19c) and (19d), the presence of *ddim* is mandatory. Without *ddim* (18c) is ill formed, and the version of (19d) without *ddim* expresses an affirmative sentence. If we follow Borsley and Jones in their assumption that formal Welsh reflects an earlier stage of the language, we can see the Jespersen cycle at work in the data in (19).

We can model such an intermediate situation in terms of an overlapping range (0) of *NEG and FocusLast in the ranking NegFirst >> *NEG 0 FocusLast. The high ranking of NegFirst guarantees an obligatory preverbal marker of negation. The overlap between *NEG and FocusLast means that in some cases, *NEG wins (and we only have a preverbal marker of negation), whereas in other cases FocusLast wins (and the preverbal marker is reinforced by post-verbal emphatic negation). During the phase of language change, the overlap between the constraints shifts, so that we end up with a new ordinal balance in which FocusLast outranked *NEG.[12]

Stochastic OT can also describe transitions between stage 2 and stage 3. If we allow NegFirst and *NEG to have an overlapping range in the ranking FocusLast >> NegFirst 0 *NEG, we account for the co-existence of verbs that have a special negative form (*doedd* in 19c) and verbs that do not (*na'th* in

19d). In informal Welsh, it depends on the verb whether we find a discontinuous pattern (19c) or a single post-verbal marker (19d). In other languages, other syntactic properties may come into play. The overlapping range of constraints allows for an intermediate stage in the Jespersen cycle in which the preverbal marker of negation becomes optional, but the post-verbal marker is obligatory. This also is the case in modern French, where the formal version of the language requires the presence of preverbal *ne* as illustrated in (20a). In colloquial French, it is quite common to find sentences like (20b), in which negation is exclusively expressed by means of the post-verbal adverb *pas*:

(20) (a) Je *n'* ai *pas* vu Sophie. [formal/written French]
        I SN have SN seen Sophie.
        'I have not seen Sophie.'

    (b) J' ai *pas* vu Sophie. [colloquial French]
        I have SN seen Sophie

Even in the higher registers of spoken French, *ne* is frequently dropped (Ashby, 1981, 2001), so in diachronic terms, discontinuous negation is losing against the post-verbal marker of negation. Written French is a stage 2 language with discontinuous negation. Colloquial French is a stage 3 language, with a single, post-verbal marker of negation. Spoken French in the higher registers is in between a stage 2 and a stage 3 language: the use of *ne* is recommended by prescriptive grammars, but is not always realized.

In his description of the diachronic patterns of Dutch negation, Zeijlstra (2004) refers to Van der Horst and van der Wal's (1979) study of text frequencies of *en*-deletion in different constructions. Their results indicate that the use of preverbal *en* in the Dutch spoken in Holland gradually decreased between 1300 and 1600. By the end of the 17th century, the transition from a stage 2 to a stage 3 language was complete and the preverbal marker of negation had disappeared from the language. In other dialects of Dutch, this process took place later, and certain Flemish dialects are still in an intermediate stage, as witnessed by the West Flemish example (21) from Haegeman and Zanuttini (1996).

(21) Valère (*en-*)eet dienen boek *nie*. [West Flemish]
     Valère (SN.)has that book SN
     'Valère doesn't have that book.'

The preverbal marker *en* is optional, but the post-verbal marker *nie* is obligatory in (21).[13]

6.4 Double negation in negative concord languages

De Swart (2009) emphasizes that the analysis developed in Sections 6.2 and 6.3 is not the full story of the marker of negation in natural language. The interaction of the marker of sentential negation with negative indefinites brings new constraints into play. A full analysis of that interaction is outside the scope of this chapter, but a few remarks on the possibility of expressing double negation in negative concord languages are in order.

Recall from Section 6.2.3 that negative concord languages are languages in which multiple expressions of negation give rise to a single negation reading for the sentence as a whole. The ranking FNEG >> *NEG >> INTNEG in the OT semantics leads to a resumptive negative quantifier that binds all the variables in its scope (de Swart and Sag, 2002). On the basis of this ranking, and a strong bidirectional OT analysis, we expect double negation to be ineffable in negative concord languages (at least within the clause boundary, for resumption is clause-bound). Indeed, Giannakidou (2006) explicitly states that double negation readings do not arise in Greek, Hungarian and other so-called 'strict' negative concord languages, in which a marker of sentential negation always co-occurs with a negative indefinite. (22) illustrates.

(22) Sehol   *(nem) lát-t-am   senki-t.   [Hungarian]
      nowhere *(SN)   see.PAST.1SG nobody.ACC
      'I did not see anybody anywhere.'

There is no reason to doubt Giannakidou's insight for Greek, Hungarian, etcetera, but we need to enrich our analysis in order to account for double negation readings in the combination of negation with a negative indefinite in other negative concord languages, such as French, Afrikaans (from van Gass, p.c.) and Welsh (from Borsley and Jones, 2005:133), as illustrated in (23).

(23) (a) Il   n'est pas venu   pour   rien.   [French, DN]
           he   SN is   SN   come   for   nothing
           'He did not come for nothing.'

      (b) Hy kon   *nie niemand* gesien het *nie*.   [Afrikaans, DN]
           he could SN   nobody   saw   has SN
           'He could not have seen nobody.'

      (c) Dydy   hi *erioed ddim* wedi helpu.   [Informal Welsh, DN]
           NEG.be.3SG   she never SN   PERF help
           'She has never not helped.'

The double negation reading is the only possible interpretation of the sentences in (23). But how does the double negation reading come about under the constraint ranking *NEG >> INTNEG in the semantics? A closer investigation reveals that *ne...pas* (in 23a), sentence-medial *nie* (in 23b), and *ddim* (in 23c) do not occur when we construe these sentences with a single-negation reading as in (23'):

(23') (a) Il   est venu pour rien.   [French]
          he   is   come for   nothing
          'He came for nothing.'

     (b) Hy kon   *niemand*   gesien   het *nie*.   [Afrikaans]
         he could nobody   saw   has SN
         'He could have seen nobody.'

     (c) Dydy   hi *erioed* wedi helpu.   [Informal Welsh]
         NEG.be.3SG   she   never   PERF help
         'She has never not helped.'

The contrast between (23) and (23') indicates that negative concord languages pile up negative indefinites, but do not always pile up markers of sentential negation. And when the marker of sentential negation is not needed to convey single negation (as in 23'), its insertion gives to a double negation reading (as in 23). In the strong version of bidirectional OT that we have used so far, we cannot account for the double negation readings of *pas*, *nie* or *ddim* in combination with negative indefinites, for the combination of this form with this meaning is suboptimal under either direction of optimization. However, weaker versions of bidirectional OT have been studied in the literature (Blutner, 1998, 2000, 2004; Beaver, 2004; Beaver and Lee, 2004). The problem with double negation readings in negative concord languages seems to be best approached in the framework of weak bidirectional OT developed by Blutner (1998, 2000).

Blutner's (1998, 2000) weak bidirectional OT analysis was outlined in Chapter 1. In this framework, optimal forms and meanings are not calculated independently, but optimization proceeds over form-meaning pairs. A pair <f,m> is strongly optimal if there is no pair <f,m'> that is more harmonic than <f,m>, and there is no pair <f',m> that is more harmonic than <f,m>. A form-meaning pair <f,m> is a weakly optimal pair (also called 'super-optimal' pair) if there is no other super-optimal pair <f',m> such that <f',m> is more harmonic, and there is no other super-optimal pair <f,m'> such that <f,m'> is more harmonic than <f,m>. Weakly optimal pairs involve pairs of a marked form and a marked meaning that couldn't be paired up otherwise. If we calculate not only strongly optimal, but also weakly optimal ('super-optimal') pairs for the French and Afrikaans sentences with a marker of sentential negation and a neg-expression in (23a) and (23b), we can derive the double negation readings as an instance of weak bidirectional optimality. For French, this is illustrated in Tableau 6.9.[14]

Tableau 6.9: French double negation in weak bidirectional OT

f_1: neg; f_2: *pas*+neg m_1: $\neg\exists$xp; m_2: $\neg\,\neg\exists$xp	*NEG	INTNEG
☞ <neg, $\neg\exists$xp>	**	
<neg, $\neg\,\neg\exists$xp>	***	
<*pas*+neg, $\neg\exists$xp>	**	*
☞ <*pas*+neg, $\neg\,\neg\exists$xp>	****	

We take the negative indefinite (neg) to be the unmarked form compared to the combination of *pas* with a negative indefinite, because it is formally simpler and shorter. Of course, Section 6.1 argued that negation is semantically marked compared to affirmation, but everything is relative, and in the comparison with double negation, the single negation meaning is unmarked. The pair <neg, $\neg\exists$xp> is strongly optimal, because there is no better interpretation for this form, and no better form to express this meaning. No other form-meaning pair is strongly optimal according to Tableau 6.9. <neg, $\neg\,\neg\exists$xp> is not a strongly optimal pair, because single negation is a better (less complex) interpretation for this form. <*pas*+neg, $\neg\exists$xp> is not a strongly optimal pair, because neg is a better (more economical) form to express this meaning. <*pas*+neg, $\neg\,\neg\exists$xp> is not a strongly optimal pair, because there are both simpler forms to express this meaning, and simpler meanings for this form under the ranking given in Tableau 6.9. However, in a secondary (not optimal but 'super-optimal') round of evaluation, the restriction of the comparison to super-optimal pairs eliminates both <neg, $\neg\,\neg\exists$xp> and <*pas*+neg, $\neg\exists$xp> from the set of competing form-meaning pairs, because both lose against the strongly optimal pair <neg, $\neg\exists$xp>. Of course, <neg, $\neg\exists$xp> does not offer a better form for the double negation meaning, or a better meaning for the combination of pas+neg, so this strongly optimal pair does not directly compete with <*pas*+neg, $\neg\,\neg\exists$xp>. Given that there is no better super-optimal alternative, <*pas*+neg, $\neg\,\neg\exists$xp> itself becomes weakly optimal, or super-optimal. Note that we would never be able to obtain this in a unidirectional system, because pas+neg is a suboptimal form, and $\neg\,\neg\exists$xp is a suboptimal meaning. So we crucially need the notion of weak optimality, and optimize in both directions at the same time in order to derive this result. We conclude that weak bidirectional optimality allows the expression of double negation in negative concord languages, whereas this is impossible under strong bidirectional optimality.

The double negation readings of the Afrikaans and Welsh examples (23b) and (23c) are obtained in a similar way. If medial *nie* is not required to convey negation in the presence of the negative indefinite *niemand*, *ddim* is not required to convey negation in the presence of the negative indefinite *erioed*, the candidates in (23b) and (23c) incur an extra violation of *NEG. Economy blocks this as the optimal candidate for the single negation reading, but the double negation reading of the sentences arises as the result of a weak bidirectional optimization process. The fact that French, Afrikaans and Welsh pattern alike in allowing double negation readings for sentences that insert a negation marker in constructions that do not require this negation marker to convey a single negation reading shows that natural languages systematically exploit the economy constraint *NEG in the syntax as well as the semantics. Weak bidirectional OT provides us with a mechanism to account for these readings in a systematic and insightful way. Not all languages exemplifying negative concord allow the expression of double negation under weak bidirectional optimality. De Swart (2009: Chapter 6) discusses relevant linguistic constraints on this mechanism, as a result of which no double negation readings are predicted for strict negative concord languages such as Greek and Hungarian, cf. (22).

One objection that has been raised against weak bidirectional OT is that its recursive optimization process generates too many weakly optimal pairs. Blutner, de Hoop and Hendriks (2006) suggest a cognitive restriction that would lead to a single repetition of the optimization procedure, see also Chapter 1 and Chapter 5 (Section 5.6.1) for discussion. This restriction fits in with the data on double negation we observe in French, Afrikaans and Welsh.

6.5 Conclusion

In this chapter, we investigated patterns of negation in natural language. Negation is semantically marked with respect to affirmation, because it is expressed less frequently than affirmation. Evolutionary pressure as modelled by Horn's division of pragmatic labor leads to a situation where negative sentences have a special formal reflection, whereas affirmative sentences need not be marked in any way. If we furthermore assume that human cognition requires the expression of negative meanings in natural language, negation emerges as a universal category of all natural language communication systems. The faithfulness constraint FNEG and the markedness constraint *NEG provide the core constraints governing the expression of negation. The universal ranking FNᴇɢ >> *Nᴇɢ is found in all natural languages. The position of the negation marker with respect to the verb is subject to typological and diachronic variation. NᴇɢFɪʀsᴛ, FᴏᴄᴜsLᴀsᴛ and *Nᴇɢ come into play to derive preverbal, post-verbal and discontinuous negation. Unexpected patterns of double negation in negative concord languages are explained in terms of weak bidirectional Optimality Theory. The study of the expression and interpretation of negation carried out in this chapter shows that a universal set of violable constraints, combined with the possibility of a language specific ranking provides new insights into semantic variation. In the next chapter, we will use a very similar approach to account for patterns of referentiality in natural language. It is part of human cognition that we use nominals to create anchors for referents set up in conversational space. The linguistic machinery languages use to reflect this referential force in the form of the nominal depends on their ranking various faithfulness constraints with respect to a general markedness constraint blocking functional structure in the nominal domain.

Notes

1   Van Rooy (2004) develops this idea in terms of game theory. We will not discuss his approach here, but the insight is the same. See de Swart (2009) for more elaborate discussion.

2   An anonymous reviewer suggests a reformulation of FNᴇɢ and FAғғ exploiting the OT distinction between Mᴀx and Dᴇᴘ constraints. We do not use the labels of Mᴀx and Dᴇᴘ constraints here to avoid any possible confusion with the constraint MᴀxNᴇɢ that governs the use of negative indefinites in de Swart (2009).

3   Examples from Payne (1985)(3c), Borsley and Jones (2005)(3d) and de Groot (1993)(3e).

4   As de Swart (2009: Chapter 3) shows, we actually do find instances of the ranking *Nᴇɢ >> FNᴇɢ in pathological communication systems, such as the linguistic system of British Sign Language users suffering from brain damage, who neither produce nor understand negative utterances (Atkinson, Campbell, Marshall, Thacker and Woll, 2004). These findings provide indirect support for the inclusion of FNᴇɢ in a system based on soft constraints.

5   Evenki is a member of the Siberian subgroup of the Tungus family.

6   The Italian example is from Zanuttini (1991, 1996). The Baghdad Arabic example is from Payne (1985). The Welsh example is from Borsley and Jones (2005). The Koromfe example and the Gbaya Kaka example are from Dryer (2008). Koromfe is a Niger-Congo language spoken in Burkina-Fasso and Mali; Gbaya Kaka is a Niger-Congo language spoken in Cameroon.

7   The formulation of FocusLast we provide here is very general, for we take this to be a pragmatic principle that can affect many different relations between old and new information. This is not to say that we cannot find differences within a language as to the kind of construction FocusLast applies to. Aissen (1999, 2003) uses a general markedness constraint *Case, which can be split up into different sub-constraints. In a similar way, FocusLast can work out in different ways for negation and other constructions sensitive to focus within a language. We will ignore these complexities here, and only use FocusLast for negation in this chapter.

8   FNeg is always the highest ranked constraint (cf. Section 6.1). In order to avoid the discussion about word order, we give the tableaux in SVO form, but with S and O between brackets, to indicate that these could also get a different position. we am only concerned with the position of negation with respect to the verb. The reader is referred to Dryer (1988, 2008) for discussion of the relation between the position of negation, the subject, and the object.

9   The Romance examples in (13b,c) are from Zanuttini (1991, 1994). The Welsh examples (13e,f) are from Borsley and Jones (2005). The examples from Kanakura (13g) and Ewe (13h) are from Dryer (2008). Kanakura is a West Chadic language spoken in Nigeria. Ewe is a Kwa language spoken in Ghana.

10   Recently, this view has been criticized, for it cannot deal with the fairly stable situation of discontinuous negation we find in languages such as Afrikaans (Biberauer, 2007) and certain Flemish dialects (Breitbarth and Haegeman, 2008). These authors claim that emphasis comes into play to motivate the extra marker of sentential negation. In the picture we develop here, emphasis would require a more complex semantic representation, and additional constraints. Given that the discussion of emphatic negation has only just started (see also Zeijlstra, 2007), and has not been studied for a wide range of languages, we will not address these potential complications here, but leave them for further research.

11   Thanks to an anonymous reviewer for the second suggestion.

12   Other examples of languages that are in a transitional phase between a stage 1 and a stage 2 language are Tamazight Berber (Ouali, 2003, 2005), Catalan (Zeijlstra 2004:132) and Hausa (Dryer, 2008).

13   Dryer (2008) cites Mupun (a West Chadic language spoken in Nigeria) and Bongo (a Bonggo-Bagirmi language spoken in Sudan) as languages in which the preverbal marker of negation is optional, and the post-verbal marker is obligatory. The diachronic patterns of languages spoken in Africa are generally not well documented, but the synchronic data suggest that these languages are in a transitional phase between stage 2 and stage 3 languages.

14   Tableau 6.9 ignores the role of *ne*, which does not interact with the double negation reading. See de Swart (2006, 2009) for an account of French *ne* as a co-negative.

7 Nominals with and without an article: distribution, interpretation and variation

7.1 Articles and reference in conversational space

7.1.1 Observations about articles and plurality

In languages like English, we use articles to set up referents in a conversational space, and to refer back to them. Consider the following examples:

(1) (a) A student came to my office. He had a question about the exam.

(b) A child was playing in the park. The funny little creature wore a green hat, and purple socks.

Imagine that I am coming home from work, and that I am describing my day to my partner. I could utter the sequence (1a), and effectively share information with my interlocutor. The indefinite noun phrase *a student* in (1a) sets up a referent in the conversational space, which has the properties of being a student and of having called on me in my office. Of course there are many students in the world, and many may have come into my office (even today), but the indefinite article is simply setting up one such referent, without excluding that there are others. Once a referent with certain properties has been introduced, we can use a pronoun to refer back to it. Thus *he* in the subsequent sentence of (1a) functions as an anaphoric pronoun that refers back to the student who came into my office. The discourse in (1a) illustrates that the main contribution of pronouns like *he* is to establish coreference with an individual that has already been introduced in the context so far, and allow for further predication of properties of that discourse referent. An indefinite nominal like *a student* is not dependent on the discourse for its interpretation. It sets up a new referent in the joint conversational space, which is then available for further cognitive operations (additional specifications, coreference, etc.) by both conversational partners.

Instead of a pronoun, we can also use a definite description to refer back to an individual that has already been introduced in the conversational space.

The anaphoric use of the definite article is illustrated in (1b). The indefinite nominal *a child* sets up a referent in the conversational space. The definite nominal *the funny little creature* in the subsequent sentence of (1b) refers to the child that was playing in the park. Although the description *funny little creature* hasn't been used in the previous discourse, the referent of the definite nominal is construed as familiar and unique. In (1b), uniqueness is relativized to the context by the anaphoric interpretation of the definite nominal as pointing to a referent familiar from previous discourse.

These informal descriptions of the sequences (1a) and (1b) suggest that definite and indefinite articles play very specific roles in conversation, which are best evaluated at the discourse level. Rijkhoff (2002:185) states that definite articles are localizing elements that express 'weak deixis' in the sense of Anderson and Keenan (1985:261–2). Indefinite articles lack these features, but simply introduce a discourse referent in the terms of Discourse Representation theory (Kamp and Reyle, 1993).

The observations made so far extend to plural definites, as illustrated in (2a).

(2)   (a)   I saw some children playing in the park. The sweet little creatures were
              having lots of fun.

      (b)   I love you more than the sun and the stars.

Of course, plurals do not refer to a single individual, so plural definites cannot be construed as having unique reference, but are said to have maximal reference. Thus the indefinite *some children* sets up a plural discourse referent, which the definite *the sweet little kids* refers back to. The definite has maximal reference in the sense that it refers to the entire group of children introduced in the first sentence. (2b) illustrates that unique and maximal reference is not always context-dependent. *The sun* and *the stars* have unique and maximal reference with respect to the entire universe of discourse in this sentence. Farkas (2002) uses the term *determined reference* to describe the contribution of the definite article. This term generalizes over familiarity (anaphoric interpretations) and uniqueness/maximality.

7.1.2 The interpretation of functional structure

The examples discussed so far indicate that languages like English establish a clear contrast between singular and plural nominals, and use definite and indefinite articles to set up referents and refer back to them in conversational space. Plural morphology and articles are functional elements, as opposed to the lexical contribution made by nouns and verbs. Lexical elements are often viewed as the building blocks of language, and functional elements as the cement that keeps them together. Linguists have formulated correspondence rules that fix the contribution of functional elements to the interpretation of the sentence and the discourse. In this chapter, we limit ourselves to functional structure in the nominal domain, and focus on plural morphology and definite/indefinite articles. There is an extensive linguistic and philosophical literature on articles and plurality, that we cannot even begin to review here.[1] We rely on fairly widely accepted insights in the formulation of the following correspondence rules between functional structure and discourse meaning:

(3)   DR: A determiner (form) corresponds to the presence of a discourse referent (meaning).

(4)   DEF: A definite article (form) corresponds to a discourse referent with determined reference (meaning).

(5)   PL: Plural morphology on the noun (form) corresponds to a predication of plurality on a presupposed discourse referent (meaning).

The correspondence rule DR builds on much work in dynamic semantics in which the role determiners play in the introduction of discourse referents is investigated (Kamp and Reyle, 1993; Higginbotham, 1985; Kamp and van Eijck, 1997; etc.). It suggests that determiners are responsible for managing reference in a conversational space. The examples (1) and (2) illustrate the role of DR in English. The correspondence rule DEF describes the contribution made by a definite article in terms of a discourse referent that has determined reference (uniqueness/maximality and/or anaphoric reference, cf. 1b and 2). According to Farkas and de Swart (2003), plurality is a notion that only applies to discourse referents. In order to apply a predicate of plurality to a discourse referent (as in 2), we need to take the presence of an available discourse referent for granted. This is why the correspondence rule PL is phrased in terms of a presupposed referent.

7.1.3 Article use and language variation

The correspondence rules DR, DEF and PL are our starting point in the study of language variation. The examples in (1) and (2) illustrate the role of DR, DEF and PL in English. Cross-linguistic research indicates that articles and plural morphology in other languages make roughly the same contribution to the meaning of the sentence and the discourse.[2] However, we don't necessarily find articles and plural morphology in all languages. More precisely, although a plural form conveys a plural meaning, plural reference is not in all languages expressed by plural morphology. Although a definite article conveys determined reference of a discourse referent, familiar, unique or maximal reference is not always expressed by a definite article. Although a determiner sets up a discourse referent in the conversational space, not all languages use articles to express discourse reference. Many languages use *bare nominals*, i.e., noun phrases that lack an article or determiner in environments in which English would use a definite or indefinite noun phrase. Depending on the language, such a bare nominal may have a definite or an indefinite, a singular or a plural meaning. In (6), we see Chinese examples, in which the interpretation of the bare nominal is heavily context-dependent.[3]

(6)　(a)　Wǒ　　kànjiàn　xióng　　le.　　　　　[Mandarin Chinese]
　　　　　 I　　　see　　　 bear　　 ASP
　　　　　'I saw a bear/some bears.'

　　　(b)　Gou　 hen　　jiling.
　　　　　 dog　 very　 smart
　　　　　'The dog is intelligent/dogs are intelligent.'

The bare nominal in (6a) has an existential reading; in (6b), the bare nominal can have a definite or a generic interpretation. In this chapter, we focus on definite and indefinite interpretations of bare nominals. For an analysis of article selection in relation to genericity, we refer the reader to Farkas and de Swart (2007). Chinese does not have a formal singular/plural distinction, and no system of definite/indefinite articles either. As a result, we find bare nominals in a wide range of contexts, with a wide range of meanings.

In the face of such typological variation, linguists are faced with the question how articles are distributed over languages, and how nominals without an article are interpreted. In the broader perspective of cognitive science, we wonder how this typological variation arises from language as a single cognitive faculty. Language is one of the most important cognitive faculties of human beings, and constitutes one of the most striking differences between us and other animals. We assume that setting up referents in discourse space, and referring to them involves general cognitive operations, which are related to the way we organize our conversational space around the individuals that we talk about. Furthermore, we assume that people possess the same cognitive abilities, independently of their mother tongue. In the face of those assumptions about general cognitive abilities, we wonder why certain languages (such as English) encode these cognitive operations in the functional structure of nominals, whereas other languages (such as Chinese) don't.

Linguists generally maintain that there is a universal grammar that underlies all languages. This universal grammar is the direct reflection of the human language faculty. By necessity, the concept of universal grammar is as abstract as the notion of language as a cognitive faculty, and in the literature we find different ways of working out the relation between language variation, and language as a universal cognitive faculty. As far as the functional structure in the nominal domain is concerned, some linguists would maintain that languages like Chinese, which do not project overt number morphology and articles project them covertly (e.g., Borer, 2004). In such an approach, functional complexity is posited that is not 'visible', because there is no lexical material filling these positions. The advantage of such an approach is that we maintain that languages have the same functional structure in the nominal domain, which is always covertly present, if not necessarily overtly. However, it is difficult to answer the question why languages would project functional structure, if they don't fill it in with lexical material. Others defend the view that universal grammar leaves room for parametrization. Article use would be related to a particular parameter, which is turned on for English, and turned off for Chinese (cf. Chierchia, 1998a). Parametrization does not answer the question why languages would differ in this way, though. Furthermore, a strict parametrized approach would predict that we don't find any bare nominals in a language like English. However, this prediction is too strong. Although English does not allow bare singulars in the environments in (7a), and a definite or indefinite article is required (7b), bare singulars occur in a range of special constructions, as illustrated in (8).[4]

(7) (a) * I saw bear.
     (b)   I saw a/the bear.

(8) (a)   John is *in jail*.   (Bare location)
     (b)   the way to use *knife and fork*   (Bare coordination)
     (c)   Mary *is chair* of the department.   (Bare predication)
     (d)   He found *door after door* closed.   (Bare reduplication)
     (e)   She is *playing piano* for the choir. (Bare incorporation)

A parametrized approach might explain the contrast between (7a) and (7b), but does not account for the occurrence of bare nominals in the special constructions in (8). Moreover, it does not account for the richer, stereotypical interpretation of the bare nominals in (8). (8a) for instance means that John is in jail as a prisoner, not simply as a guest. And a person who plays piano as in (8e) plays the instrument in a proper way, rather than just producing noise. Such constructions are not only found in English, but also in other languages that usually require singular count nouns like *hospital, knife, fork, chair, door, sergeant* and *piano* to have a determiner (e.g., the Germanic and Romance languages). We infer from the data in (6)-(8) that differences in the syntax-semantics interface between English-type languages and Chinese-type languages are unlikely to reside in a single parameter.

In this chapter, we pursue a different approach to the tension between a single universal language faculty, and the language variation we find in the functional structure of nominals. We start from the claim that setting up referents in conversational space, and referring to them in subsequent discourse are indeed general cognitive operations that are available to speakers of all languages. This implies that we take the correspondence rules proposed in Section 7.1.2 above to be rules of universal grammar. Language variation in the expression of plurality, discourse reference, and determined reference arises from the interaction of these correspondence rules with a general economy constraint blocking functional structure in the nominal domain. This economy constraint is also a rule of universal grammar, but it obviously conflicts with the correspondence rules. The conflict is resolved by taking the rules to be soft, violable constraints, which can be ranked with respect to each other, in an Optimality Theoretic way. Although the cognitive operations are universal, the ranking is language-specific (cf. Chapter 6, for a similar approach to the expression and interpretation of negation in natural language). Note that the economy constraint is speaker oriented, so it operates on forms, not on meanings. Its ranking with respect to the correspondence rules governing functional structure explains the asymmetry between the expression and interpretation of functional structure observed in Section 7.1.3. The approach accounts for the contrast between (6) and (7) in terms of different constraint rankings of the two languages involved. We argue that the data in (8) are an instance of 'emergence of the unmarked': bare nominals can be used in English, because the correspondence rules do not block the preference for a minimal structure in these particular configurations. The general contrast as well as the exceptional cases then fall out of the same set of conflicting constraints.

The organization of the chapter is as follows. Section 7.2 develops a typology of bare nominals in Optimality Theoretic terms. The starting point of the typology is the intuition that bare nominals, lacking functional projections containing number and determiners constitute the unmarked case. Unmarked forms are economical from the point of view of the speaker, but they leave the interpretation of the bare nominal underdetermined for the hearer, so we have two opposing tendencies. The grammar of a language strikes a balance between the drive towards unmarked forms, and the desire to reflect semantic distinctions in the form of the nominal. Faithfulness constraints driving towards the expression of information concerning number and the referential status of the nominal carry more weight than markedness constraints avoiding functional structure in some languages (e.g., English), but not in others (e.g., Chinese). The ranking of the constraints has consequences for the interpretations that are available for bare nominals in a language, as we argue in Section 7.3. Even in languages like English, we find constructions in which the faithfulness constraints promoting functional structure are not active. In Section 7.4, we argue that this is what happens in examples such as (8). A bidirectional analysis accounts for the relation between bare forms and strong, stereotypical meanings in these environments. Section 7.5 concludes.

7.2   A typology of bare nominals

We know that languages vary in the ease with which they use article-less nominals. Typological theory (e.g., Greenberg, Ferguson and Moravcsik, 1978) puts forward generalizations about article use and number systems. In the framework of Optimality Theory, typological variation is accounted for by positing a range of possible rankings of the same universal constraints. Every meaning can be expressed in every language, but when the distribution of bare nominals is governed by different constraint rankings, we find that these expressions do not have the same range of meanings across languages. Section 7.2.1 introduces the basic syntactic assumptions, and sets up the language classification we intend to account for. Sections 7.2.2 to 7.2.6 define the relevant markedness and faithfulness constraints that underlie the typology. Section 7.2.7 shows how these constraints account for the language classification set up in Section 7.2.1.

7.2.1 Projections and language classes

As far as the syntactic structure of nominals is concerned, we assume that full DPs have the layered structure $[_{DP} [_{NumP} [_{NP}]]]$. Both articles and quantifiers are assumed to reside in D. We will only be concerned with articles here, and we do not spell out the constraints pertaining to other determiners. We try to avoid null elements in the functional projections Num and D in the absence of evidence that they need to be projected. Whether nominals project at the functional levels of NumP and DP depends on the presence of number morphology on the noun and on the presence of articles or other determiners. We know that bare nominals do not have an overt D, so we assume that they are not DPs. Furthermore, we observe that bare nominals are number neutral. The paraphrases in (6) make this clear for the Mandarin examples under consideration. Bare nominals in the special constructions exemplified in (8) also display number neutrality, as illustrated by (9a, b).

(9) (a) Mari bélyeget   gyüjt.   [Hungarian]
         Marie stamp.ACC collect

     (b) Jan en Sofie zijn leraar.   [Dutch]
          Jan and Sofie are teacher
          'Jan and Sofie are teachers.'

Incorporated singulars as in (9a) can have singular or plural reference, so Farkas and de Swart (2003) claim that they lack a Num projection. According to de Swart, Winter and Zwarts (2005, 2007), bare predicate nominals do not have a Num projection either, which explains why they can be used with singular (8c) or plural subjects (9b). Generalizing over these observations, we assign the bare singulars in (6), (8) and (9) the structure of an NP.

The second assumption we make about the functional structure of nominal expressions is that higher levels of projection imply lower levels, so a full DP also has a NumP and an NP; a NumP also has an NP. But lower levels do not necessarily imply higher levels. All nominals project at least at the lexical level of NP. This means that nominals in a language can have the structure of an NP (bare singulars), of a NumP (bare plurals) or of a DP (nominals with an article or another determiner). Bare singulars have the minimal syntactic structure possible for a nominal expression. In that sense, bare singulars constitute the unmarked nominal form.

As the contrast between (6) and (7) in Section 7.1 showed, not all languages allow bare nominals in regular argument position. In order to get a better grip on the distribution of bare nominals, we distinguish the following six major classes of languages in our typology, and give an illustrative example of each class:

(i)   Languages that have functional structure in the nominal domain, but no morphological number, no articles (Chinese);

(ii) Languages that establish a singular/plural distinction, but do not use articles (Georgian);

(iii) Languages that use a definite article, but no indefinite one (Hebrew);

(iv) Languages that don't exemplify a definite/indefinite contrast, but that require a determiner on all nouns in argument position (St'át'imcets);

(v)   Languages that use both a definite and an indefinite article in the singular, but only a definite article in the plural; definite plurals contrast with bare plurals (English, Spanish);

(vi) Languages that use definite and indefinite articles in the singular as well as in the plural (French).

This classification does not cover all the languages in the world, but it seems to capture some major classes of languages as far as their use of number morphology and articles is concerned. As usual in OT, the typology is established by a weighting of faithfulness and markedness constraints. The same constraints are relevant to all the languages in the classification, so we take them to be universal. The ranking determines the language-specific grammar. Cross-linguistic variation is constrained by the possible rankings of the constraints in a factorial typology. Not all rankings necessarily lead to a different grammar. Some constraints do not directly interact, or only interact in certain rankings, so grammars may correspond to sets of rankings. In Sections 7.2.2 to 7.2.5, we will define five different grammars, based on a total of two markedness constraints and three faithfulness constraints.

7.2.2 Markedness constraints in the nominal domain

In Section 7.2.1, we claimed that bare nominals constitute the unmarked form, because they have the simplest possible nominal structure. In our typology, we value this insight by means of a core markedness constraint, *viz.* *FUNCTN, which avoids all functional structure in the nominal domain:

(10) *FUNCTN: Avoid functional structure in the nominal domain.

Each functional projection in a noun phrase presents a violation of the markedness constraint. If the constraint *FUNCTN is ranked higher than faithfulness constraints involving the expression of meanings that are characteristically expressed in the functional layer above NP (call them FNOM), we obtain the ranking *FunctN >> {FNOM$_1$, FNOM$_2$, ... FNOM$_N$}. The relevant faithfulness constraints will be introduced in Sections 7.2.3–7.2.5. As we will see there, the FNOM constraints concern the faithful expression in the form of plurality, determined reference, and discourse reference. Under the ranking *FUNCTN >> {FNOM$_1$, FNOM$_2$, ... FNOM$_N$}, we have no number distinctions, no articles, no indefinite determiners (like *some, several*), no numerals (like *four, at least three*), and no D-quantifiers (like *every, most*). The mutual ranking of the constraints FNOM$_1$, FNOM$_2$, ... FNOM$_N$ is irrelevant if all functional structure is blocked by the highly ranked markedness constraint *FUNCTN. Arguably, this ranking would give us the perfectly unmarked nominal system. It is likely that communicative systems in which *FUNCTN is ranked higher than any other constraints in the nominal domain exist in the domain of restricted linguistic systems (primitive pidgins, early L2 acquisition, etc.). However, it is unclear to us whether any full linguistic system adopts this ranking. Abstracting away from restricted linguistic systems, we hypothesize that most if not all full natural languages have at least some level of functional structure in the nominal domain. Even if they don't have morphological number and do not use articles, they may have case markers, numerals, classifiers and/or quantifiers. Given that this chapter focuses on number and article systems, and does not address the full range of functional projections in the nominal domain, we formulate the constraint *ART that can be viewed as a special instance of the general constraint *FUNCTN:

(11) *ART: Avoid article.

If *ART is ranked higher than faithfulness constraints governing article use, we may see functional structure like determiners, classifiers, case marking, etcetera, but we don't see a formal reflection of plurality or information concerning referential status conveyed by articles. Such languages as Japanese, Thai and Chinese are then class (i) languages. Bare forms are used for definite, indefinite and kind reference, and do not display a singular/plural distinction. The Chinese examples in (12) are repeated from (6).[5]

(12) (a) Wò kànjiàn xióng le.　　　　　　　　　　[Mandarin Chinese]
　　　　　　I   see   bear ASP
　　　　　　'I saw a bear/some bears.'

　　　(b) Gou   hen   jiling.
　　　　　　dog   very   smart
　　　　　　'The dog is intelligent/dogs are intelligent.'

Under the ranking *ART >> *FUNCTN >> { $FNOM_1$, $FNOM_2$, ... $FNOM_N$ }, bare nominals emerge as the optimal form for the expression of singular/plural, indefinite, definite, and generic meaning. Tableau 7.1 illustrates how (12a) emerges as a result of existential quantification and plural meaning in the input meaning.[6]

Tableau 7.1: Bare singular with existential, plural meaning in a class (i) language, illustrated with Mandarin Chinese (production)

$\exists x[\text{Bear}(x) \,\&\, \text{PL}(x) \,\&\, \text{See}(I,x)]$	*ART	*FUNCTN	{$FNOM_1$, ... $FNOM_N$}
☞ Wò kànjiàn [NPxióng] le. I see bear ASP			**
Wò kànjiàn [NumP PL [NPxióng] le. I see bear.PL ASP		*!	
Wò kànjiàn [DP INDEF [NumP PL [NPxióng] le. I see INDEF bear.PL ASP	*!	**	

The bare nominal with just an NP projection constitutes the optimal form in Tableau 7.1, even though it violates some of the faithfulness constraints that will be introduced in Sections 7.2.3 to 7.2.5 below. As far as class (i) languages are concerned, the markedness constraints *ART and *FUNCTN carry more weight than FNOM$_1$, FNOM$_2$, ... FNOM$_N$. Note that definite and singular meanings would also lead to a bare singular as the optimal form under this ranking. As a result, Chinese bare nominals can have different interpretations in context. The bare nominal in (12a) has an existential reading. In (12b), the bare nominal can have a definite or a generic interpretation. These observations suggest that there is no one-to-one relation between bare forms and semantic interpretation, but that the meaning of a bare nominal is strongly context-dependent. We will come back to the interpretation of bare nominals in Section 7.3 below.

The ranking of the markedness constraints *ART and *FUNCTN with respect to faithfulness constraints involving the distinction between singular and plural, and definite and indefinite interpretations provides the key to a typology that opposes bare nominals to non-bare ones, as we will show in the following section.

7.2.3 Faithfulness to plurality

As we saw in Section 7.2.2, Mandarin Chinese is a language without a formal reflection of the singular/plural distinction. But in many languages, number is marked in the morphology on the noun. As a default, plural will be marked first, if there is a number distinction at all (Greenberg, 1963; Corbett, 2000). In line with these observations from typological theory, we assume a faithfulness constraint FPL, which rephrases the correspondence rule PL in Section 7.1.2:[7]

(13) FPL: Plural predication on a (presupposed) discourse referent corresponds with an expression in Num.

Languages that rank FPL higher than *FUNCTN project at least a NumP for plural nouns. However, the expression of number in the morphology on the noun is not necessarily connected to article use. In languages that adopt the ranking FPL >> {*ART, *FUNCTN} >> { FNOM$_1$, FNOM$_2$, ... FNOM$_N$ }, definite and indefinite meanings as well as kind reference will be expressed by bare nominals (singulars and/or plurals). Relevant class (ii) languages are Hindi, Russian, Georgian (Rijkhoff, 2002).[8] (14) provides an example from Georgian (from Harris, 1981:21–22, quoted by Rijkhoff, 2002); Chierchia (1998b) and Dayal (2004) discuss similar examples from Russian and Hindi.

(14) burtebi   goravs.   [Georgian]
balls.PL.NOM roll.3SG
'Balls/The balls are rolling.'

(14) illustrates that bare count nouns can occur in argument position in Georgian and Russian, and have both indefinite and definite interpretations. Tableau 7.2 illustrates how a definite plural input leads to the bare plural form in (14) under the ranking FPL >> {*ART, *FUNCTN} >> { FNOM$_1$, FNOM$_2$, ... FNOM$_N$ }.

Tableau 7.2: Bare plurals with a definite interpretation in type (ii) languages, illustrated with Georgian (production)

$\exists!$x Ball(x) & PL(x) & Roll(x)	FPL	*ART	*FUNCTN	{FNOM$_1$, ... FNOM$_N$}
[$_{NP}$ burt] goravs.	*!			*
☞ [$_{NumP}$ burtebi] goravs. balls.PL.NOM roll.3SG			*	
[$_{DP}$ DEF [$_{NumP}$ burtebi]] goravs.		*!	**	

The definite input meaning is here represented by means of $\exists!$x, in order to distinguish it from the indefinite input meaning $\exists$x (cf. Tableau 7.1), but note that an indefinite meaning would have led to the same optimal candidate under this ranking. The bare plural emerges in Tableau 7.2 as the optimal form, because of the ranking FPL >> *FUNCTN. Thus a language chooses the least marked expression that obeys the faithfulness constraints activated in that language.

If we compare this result to the class (i) languages discussed in Section 7.2.2 above, we observe that, although the input involved plurality in Tableau 7.1 as well, this aspect of the meaning was not reflected in the form of the nominal, because of the ranking *FUNCTN >> FPL. The motivation for typological variation in the position of *ART and *FUNCTN with respect to faithfulness constraints governing number morphology in the system is clear from the comparison between Mandarin Chinese in Tableau 7.1, and Georgian in Tableau 7.2. Although Mandarin Chinese and Georgian differ in their expression of number, they behave alike in their preference for article-less nominals. Note that neither the indefinite meaning in Tableau 7.1, nor the definite meaning in Tableau 7.2 receives an overt reflection in the form. The optimal candidate is a bare, determiner-less nominal in both class (i) and class (ii) languages, because of the high ranking of *ART. If singular number receives no formal expression, singular nouns are number neutral (cf. Farkas and de Swart, 2003, and the examples in 9 above).[9]

Although the high ranking of *Art and *FunctN in class (i) and class (ii) languages is economical from the speaker's perspective (it reduces speaker effort), it is not attractive from the hearer's perspective (it induces massive ambiguities). In languages like Chinese, Japanese, Hindi and Slavic, bare nominals can get definite, existential, and generic interpretations, and it is up to the hearer to construct the optimal interpretation in the context. For the hearer, it would be easier to interpret the utterance if the form would reflect some of these meaning distinctions. This is the intuition underlying the faithfulness constraints FDef and FDr, that we will introduce in Sections 7.2.4 and 7.2.5 respectively.

7.2.4 Faithfulness to definiteness

The definite/indefinite contrast is not quantificational in nature, but involves the referential status of the individual variable in the discourse (Farkas, 2002, 2006; Farkas and de Swart, 2007, and references therein). Farkas (2002, 2006) interprets the definite/indefinite contrast in the following terms: definites convey determined reference, indefinites don't convey anything. Determined reference involves the possibility to pick out a unique individual in the model as the referent of the definite expression. As we saw in Section 7.1.1, determined reference is established by uniqueness or anaphoricity. In Farkas' view, indefinites simply lack the property of determined reference, but they are not necessarily incompatible with it. If faithfulness constraints come into play that relate the referential status of the discourse referent to the form of the nominal, the asymmetric treatment of definites and indefinites leads us to posit a faithfulness constraint FDef, that requires the expression of determined reference. FDef rephrases the correspondence rule formulated in Section 7.1.2 above.

(15) FDef: Determined reference of a discourse reference corresponds with a definite article in D.

The prototypical way to realize determined reference is by means of a definite article. [10] With the ranking FDef >> *Art, we obtain a system that exemplifies an alternation between definites and bare nominals. Such class (iii) languages are Hebrew and Bulgarian. The following Hebrew examples illustrate. (16a) is from de Swart, Winter and Zwarts (2007); (16b) is from Corbett (2000:95) and (16c) is from Doron (2004).

(16) (a) dan   ra'a   namer.   [Hebrew]
        Dan   saw   tiger
        'Dan saw a tiger.'

(b) ha-yam-im   'avru   maher.
    the day.PL   pass.PAST.3PL   quickly
    'The days passed quickly.'

(c) namer / ha-namer hu   xaya   torefet.
    tiger / the.tiger is   animal   carnivorous
    'The tiger is a carnivorous animal.'

The bare singular gets an existential (16a) or a generic interpretation (16c). The definite singular or plural gets a regular definite (16b) or a generic interpretation (16c). Tableau 7.3 derives the use of a marked, definite form for an input meaning where the discourse referent has determined reference.

Tableau 7.3: Definite nominal in type (iii) languages, illustrated with Hebrew (production)

$\exists!x$ Day(x) & PL(x) & Go-by(x)	FPL	FDEF	*ART	*FUNCTN
[NP yam] 'avru maher.	*(!)	*(!)		
[NumP yam-im] 'avru maher.		*!		*
☞ [DP ha [NumP yam-im]] 'avru maher. The day.PL pass.PAST.3PL quickly			*	**

If we compare Tableau 7.3 with Tableaux 7.1 and 7.2 above, we observe that the ranking FPL >> *FUNCTN gives rise to a preference of plural forms over unmarked nominals if the input predicates plurality of the discourse referent. The expression of determined reference was not visible in the bare form in Tableau 7.2, but the ranking FDEF >> *ART in Tableau 7.3 leads to the use of a definite article in Hebrew.

The asymmetric treatment of the definite/indefinite contrast that leads us to posit FDEF as a relevant faithfulness constraint makes a fairly straightforward prediction. It predicts that languages typically oppose bare and definite nominals, but not bare and indefinite ones. As such, this is in line with the typological literature (Greenberg, Ferguson and Moravcsik, 1978). From the semantic literature, it is also clear that bare nominals, in languages in which they occur, can always have an existential meaning (possibly besides definite and generic readings). The availability of an existential interpretation for bare nominals is common to class (i), (ii) and (iii) languages.[11]

7.2.5 Faithfulness to referential status

Class (iii) languages have a stable system that reflects the asymmetry between definite and indefinite (or rather: non-definite) nominals. The introduction of faithfulness constraints concerning the referential status of the discourse referent can also be viewed in the broader perspective of how discourse referents are introduced. Farkas and de Swart (2003) establish a relation between discourse referents and argument structure. As spelled out in Chapter 2 of their book, a verb comes with one or more thematic arguments, 'slots' that can be 'filled' by nominals fulfilling certain roles in the action. For instance, a transitive verb like *read* comes with two thematic arguments, one of which is related to the reader, and the other one to the object of the reading. The role of thematic arguments within the boundaries of lexical semantics is uncontroversial. But Farkas and de Swart argue that we need to make room for them in the discourse representational structure resulting from the combinational semantics as well. Given that nominal expressions, but not verbs, are responsible for the introduction of discourse referents into the discourse representation structure, the thematic argument of a verb needs to be instantiated by the discourse referent introduced by the nominal that combines with the verb. Following much work in DRT, Farkas and de Swart (2003) focus on the role of determiners as the linguistic expression that introduces a discourse referent. If we assume with Farkas and de Swart (2003) that nouns basically just come with thematic arguments, but verbs normally combine with arguments that have discourse referential status, we can posit a constraint that requires discourse referents to be introduced by a functional layer above the NP. We label this constraint FDR, and define it as a rephrasing of the correspondence rule introduced in Section 7.1.2 above.

(17) FDR: The presence of a discourse referent in the semantics corresponds with a
     strong functional layer above NP.

Languages that rank FDR below *FUNCTN don't require a functional layer above NP to parse discourse referents, so bare nominals are fully adequate in regular argument positions, as is commonly established for class (i) to (iii) languages. Class (iv) languages that adopt the ranking {FPL, FDR} >> {*ART, *FUNCTN} >> FDEF do not establish a definite/indefinite contrast, but use a determiner on all nominals in argument position. The Salish languages (a family of Amerindian languages spoken on Canada) exemplify this ranking. Matthewson (1998, 2005) provides examples from St'át'imcets, and points out that all argument nominals are introduced by an overt determiner (18).

(18) (a) tecwp-mín-lhkan   ti   púkw-a   lhkúnsa.   [St'át'imcets]
buy.APPL.1SG.SUB   DET book.DET   today
'I bought a/the book today.'

(b) túp-un'-as   [tiplísmen-a]   s-John.
punch.TR.3ERG   DET policeman.DET   NMLZR.John
'John hit a/the policeman today.'

As the translation of (18a) and (18b) indicates, the determiner is compatible with a definite or an indefinite interpretation. Matthewson (1998) extensively argues that the St'át'imcets determiners do not encode either definiteness or specificity. She defends the view that Salish determiners encode 'assertion of existence', and models this notion in Discourse Representation Theory (Kamp and Reyle, 1993). For our purposes, the notion of 'assertion of existence' can be identified with the introduction of a discourse referent. In St'át'imcets, number is incapable of licensing a discourse referent (18b), so the presence of an overt determiner is required, even in the plural (19a) (cf. below for a treatment of French as involving weak number in a similar way).

(19) (a) léxlex   I   smelhmúlhats-a.
intelligent DET.PL   woman(PL).DET
'Women/the women are intelligent.'

(b) *léxlex   smelhmúlhats
intelligent   woman(PL)

The ranking {FPL, FDR} >> {*ART, *FUNCTN} >> FDEF postulated for St'át'imcets derives full DPs as soon as the input contains a discourse referent. Tableau 7.4 illustrates.

Tableau 7.4: Definite nominal in type (iv) languages, illustrated with St'át'imcets (production)

∃!x Woman(x) & PL(x) & Intelligent(x)	FPL	FDR	*ART	*FUNCTN	FDEF
léxlex [NP smelhmúlhats].	*(!)	*(!)			*
Léxlex [NumP smelhmúlhats-a].		*!		*	*
☞ léxlex [DP I smelhmúlhats-a]. intelligent DET.PL woman(PL).DET			*	**	*

The optimal candidate *I smelhmúlhats-a* involves a full DP structure. Although the plural determiner *I* introduces a discourse referent, it does not convey determined reference, which explains the violation of FDEF for all candidates under consideration.

7.2.6 Combining FDEF and FDR

Languages that rank both FDEF and FDR above *ART exemplify a full contrast between definite and indefinite forms for all nominals. In line with Farkas and de Swart (2003), we assume that plural morphology on the noun may also be capable of licensing a discourse referent. For Farkas and de Swart this possibility is related to the fact that plural number morphology is interpreted in terms of a condition on the discourse referent. In order for this condition to be verified, a discourse referent needs to be posited. Singular nouns on the other hand, do not come with number morphology, project just a thematic argument, and are interpreted as number neutral. Assuming that singular nouns do not have a Num projection, but plural nouns do, we end up with an asymmetry between singular and plural nouns. If either Num or D is sufficient to introduce a discourse referent, class (v) languages end up with a system of definite and indefinite articles in the singular, and an opposition between definites and bare nominals in the plural. This is the system characterizing languages like English (but also Dutch, German, Norwegian, Swedish, Spanish, Italian, etc.).

(20) (a) I read *(a) book. [English]
   (b) I read books.
   (c) I read the book.
   (d) I read the books.

Tableaux 7.5 and 7.6 illustrate how the ranking {FPL, FDR, FDEF} >> {*ART, *FUNCTN} derives the possibility of bare plurals, but not of bare singulars.

Tableau 7.5: Blocking of bare singular in class (v) languages, illustrated with English (production)

$\exists x$ Book(x)	FPL	FDR	FDEF	*ART	*FUNCTN
[NP book]		*!			
[NumP SG [NP book]]		*!			*
☞ [DP a [NumP SG [NP book]]]				*	**

Tableau 7.6: Bare plurals in class (v) languages, illustrated with English (production)

$\exists x$ Book(x) & pl(x)	FPL	FDR	FDEF	*ART	*FUNCTN
[NP book]	*(!)	*(!)			
☞ [NumP PL [NP book]]					*
[DP INDEF [NumP PL [NP book]]]				*(!)	**(!)

In English-type languages, bare singulars are blocked, because of the ranking of FDr > {*Art, *FunctN}, as Tableau 7.5 illustrates. It does not help to project a NumP, because there is no singular morphology in English, capable of parsing the discourse referent. The only way to satisfy FDr with a singular, indefinite meaning in the input is to project an indefinite article *a* in D. As we see in Tableau 7.6, plural morphology satisfies FDr in English. The insertion of a plural indefinite article would constitute an unnecessary violation of *Art and *FunctN. The contrast between Tableaux 7.5 and 7.6 illustrates that the more economical bare form is preferred whenever it does not violate the higher ranked faithfulness constraints.

If Num is not strong enough to introduce a discourse referent, then we end up with a definite/indefinite contrast in the singular as well as the plural. An analysis in terms of weak number has been defended for French (Delfitto and Schroten, 1991; Le Bruyn, 2005). We label French as a class (vi) language.

(21) (a) J'ai   lu   *(un)   livre.   [French]
          I have read   *(SG-INDEF) book

     (b) J'ai   lu   *(des)   livres.
          I have read   *(PL-INDEF) book

     (c) J'ai   lu   le   livre.
          I have read   the book

     (d) J'ai lu   les livres.
          I have read the books

Interestingly, we do not need additional constraints to account for this case: FDr allows number to introduce a discourse referent, but only if this functional projection is strong. Tableau 7.7 illustrates how bare plurals are blocked in French under the ranking {FPL, FDr, FDef} >> {*Art, *FunctN}.

Tableau 7.7: Bare plurals are blocked in class (vi) languages, illustrated with French (production)

$\exists$x Book(x) & PL(x)	FPL	FDR	FDEF	*ART	*FUNCTN
[NP livre]	*(!)	*(!)			
[NumP PL_w [NP livre]]		*!			*
☞ [DP des [NumP PL_w [NP livre]]]				*	**

The singular form *livre* and the plural form *livres* are phonetically indistinguishable in French. As a consequence of the weak number morphology on the noun, the bare plural *livres* implies a violation of FDr, whereas its counterpart *books* in Tableau 7.6 does not. The fact that class (vi) languages have weak number leads to a striking contrast between French and English as far as the possibility of having bare plurals is concerned. French is treated along the same lines as St'át'imcets. As we saw in Tableau 7.4 above, bare plurals in this language are blocked, and full DPs are required, because plural morphology on the noun is unable to satisfy FDR.

7.2.7 Typology of bare nominals

The introduction of the constraint FDR completes the set of constraints we need to define our typology. We can sum up the results as follows:

Table 7.1: A typology of bare nominals

Class	*Ranking*	*Characteristics*	*Example*
(i)	{*ART, *FUNCTN} >>{FPL, FDEF, FDR}	no number, no articles	Chinese
(ii)	FPL >> {*ART, *FUNCTN} >> FDEF, FDR	sg/pl distinction, no articles	Georgian
(iii)	{FDEF, FPL} >> {*ART, *FUNCTN} >> FDR	definite/bare contrast	Hebrew
(iv)	{FDR, FPL} >> {*ART, *FUNCTN} >> FDEF	no def/indef contrast; no bare nominals (weak Num)	St'át'imcets
(v)	{FDR, FDEF, FPL} >> {*ART, *FUNCTN}	def/indef contrast, bare plurals OK	English, Dutch, Italian
(vi)	{FDR, FDEF, FPL} >> {*ART, *FUNCTN}	def/indef contrast, no bare nominals (weak Num)	French

- Class (i) languages have the ranking {*ART, *FUNCTN} >> {FPL, FDEF, FDR}, but probably allow other faithfulness constraints to intervene between *ART and *FUNCTN. Thus they effectively introduce functional structure (classifiers, case marking, quantification) in the nominal domain, without projecting number or using articles, though. Examples are Thai, Japanese and Chinese, as discussed in Section 7.2.2.

- Class (ii) languages have the ranking FPL >> {*ART, *FUNCTN} >> FDEF, FDR. The high ranking of *ART blocks the use of articles to express the definite/indefinite contrast. Bare nominals occur in regular argument positions and both singulars and plurals have a range of meanings, including definite, existential, and kind referring. Examples are Hindi, Russian and Georgian, as discussed in Section 7.2.3.

- Class (iii) languages exemplify the ranking {FDEF, FPL} >> {*ART, *FUNCTN} >> FDR. These languages establish a contrast between definites and bare nominals. Bare nominals occur in regular argument positions, but their interpretation is more restricted than in class (ii) languages. In particular, definite interpretations are blocked. Examples are Bulgarian, Brazilian Portuguese and Hebrew, as discussed in Section 7.2.4.

- Class (iv) languages exemplify the ranking {FDʀ, FPʟ} >> {*Aʀᴛ, *FᴜɴᴄᴛN} >> FDᴇꜰ. In combination with weak number, these languages mark every nominal in argument position with a determiner. Bare nominals are restricted to non-referential positions. A definite/indefinite contrast is absent. An example is St'át'imcets, as discussed in Section 7.2.5.

- Class (v) and (vi) languages have the ranking {FDʀ, FDᴇꜰ, FPʟ} >> {*Aʀᴛ, *FᴜɴᴄᴛN}. They require the introduction of discourse referents to be regulated by a functional layer above NP. If either Num or D can take up this role, *Aʀᴛ will make sure we do not use an indefinite article if we can avoid it. As a result, class (v) languages typically exemplify an asymmetry between singulars and plurals: indefinite plurals can be bare, indefinite singulars need an article. Examples are English, Germanic, Italian, and Spanish, as discussed in Section 7.2.6. If Num is weak, D is always required, and we have a definite/indefinite contrast in both the singular and the plural. An example of a class (vi) language is French, as discussed in Section 7.2.6.

The typology indicates that several distinctions are relevant in natural language. As a result, a bare nominal in one language (belonging to one class) need not have the same range of meanings or the same distribution as a bare nominal in some other language (belonging to some other class). In Section 7.3, we work out the implications of the typology for the semantics of bare nominals.

7.3   Bare nominal interpretations across languages

7.3.1 Interpretation of functional structure

The language typology developed in Section 7.2 allows us to recover the range of interpretations of a bare nominal in a language. The faithfulness constraints FPʟ, FDᴇꜰ and FDʀ rephrase the correspondence rules developed in Section 7.1.2. We assume that the ranking of the constraints in the syntax mirrors the ranking of the constraints in the semantics. The main difference between the two directions of optimization is that *FᴜɴᴄᴛN and *Aʀᴛ are operative in the syntax, but not in the semantics.

Under these assumptions, the syntax-semantics interface of class (iv) languages like St'át'imcets and class (vi) languages such as French follows immediately. Syntactic projections and semantic interpretations are in full correspondence. No bare nominals are generated in regular argument position in class (iv) and class (vi) languages (cf. 11 and 13).

The main difference between class (v) (English, Germanic) and class (vi) languages (French) resides in the strength of number morphology. According to FDR, either Num or D can express discourse referential status. This means that bare singulars are blocked in class (v) languages, but bare plurals are allowed, as we see in (20) and Tableaux 7.5 and 7.6. Following Farkas and de Swart (2003), a bare plural, which projects a NumP, rather than a DP, relies on presupposition accommodation to guarantee discourse referential status. Bare plurals have a non-definite, plural meaning. The plural meaning of a bare plural is directly derived from the plural morphology, under the assumption, defended here, that functional structure is interpreted in terms of the correspondence rules. The non-definite meaning arises, because the definite meaning is blocked by the definite DP under the high ranking of the constraint FDEF in English-type languages, and the rules for the interpretation of functional structure that we adopt. A strong bidirectional analysis immediately accounts for this situation, as illustrated in Diagram 7.1.

Diagram 7.1: Strong bidirectional optimization (English bare plurals)

	non-definite	definite
	non-definite	definite
bare plural	○ ✌	○
	↑	↓
definite plural	○ →	○ ✌

According to the strong bidirectional analysis in Diagram 7.1, the only bare nominals we find in English-type (class v) languages are bare plurals, and bare plurals always get a non-definite, plural interpretation.

This completes the syntax-semantics interface for class (iv) to (vi) languages. The main difference between classes (i) to (iii) on the one hand, and class (iv) to (vi) on the other hand concerns the referential status of bare singulars. In English, French and St'át'imcets, bare singulars do not appear in regular argument position, because of the high ranking of the constraint FDR. In Chinese, Georgian and Hebrew, bare nominals freely occur in a wide range of positions. The typology developed in Section 7.2 reflects this situation. However, we need to make an extra assumption in order to account for the range of interpretations of bare singulars in these languages.

7.3.2 Bare singulars in argument position

The OT typology developed in Section 7.2 splits the classes of languages into two groups. Languages falling into class (i) through (iii) allow bare singulars to appear in regular argument position, languages in classes (iv) to (vi) do not. The question we want to address in this section is how the constraint rankings summarized in Section 7.2.6 relate to this distribution. In order to achieve this, we need to connect the syntactic constraints introduced so far to an interpretational rule governing argument structure and discourse referents.

Most of the work in dynamic semantics focuses on the role of determiners as the linguistic expression that introduces a discourse referent (cf. Section 7.1.2). The inclusion of bare plurals into the discussion widened the perspective (Farkas and de Swart, 2003). However, we need to go further, for discussions in Dayal (1999, 2003, 2004) indicate that bare nominals in class (i) to (iii) languages can have full discourse referential power (cf. examples 6, 12, 14 and 16), even though there is nothing in the functional structure of the nominal that licenses a discourse referent. We assume the general interpretation rule ARG as a way to connect verbs and different nominal projections in regular argument position.

(22) ARG: Parse an XP in argument position as a discourse referent.
(where X = N, Num or D)

ARG relates the presence of some nominal projection (an NP, NumP or DP) in regular argument position to a semantic representation involving a discourse referent. A nominal occurs in a regular argument position if it instantiates a thematic argument of the predicate (Farkas and de Swart 2003). At a more general level, ARG is an instance of a condition of normality: standard syntax leads to a standard (compositional) interpretation. We could also call this semantic *closure*: the interpretation of the constituent needs to be semantically closed at the level required by the construction. Semantic closure or a condition of normality could be viewed as a very general faithfulness constraint operating on the semantics of sentences. We will not try to formulate the principles at this abstract level, but ARG is clearly a particular spell out of a much more general notion: we take it to be a standard feature of the normal syntax-semantics interface that a nominal in regular argument position introduces a discourse referent.

The appeal to ARG is sufficient to interpret bare singulars in regular argument position in class (i) to (iii) languages as introducing a discourse referent. In the absence of a marked form expressing determined reference, bare nominals in class (i) and (ii) languages can have both definite and indefinite meanings, as illustrated in (6) and (14). Class (iii) languages such as Hebrew have a definite/bare contrast, as illustrated in (16). Under the bidirectional analysis, the bare singular in Hebrew is restricted to non-definite meanings, along similar lines as the restriction of English bare plurals to non-definite meanings (cf. Diagram 7.1).

The range of interpretations of a bare nominal in a language is thus immediately recoverable from the grammar. The most striking result is that the analysis accounts for the observation that bare nominals in class (i) to (iii) languages have full discourse referential status, in line with the claims made by Dayal (1999, 2003, 2004), and others. All nominals in regular argument position introduce discourse referents according to Arg. Class (i) to (iii) languages just don't reflect the discourse referential status of the nominal argument in the functional projection of the nominal, but use an unmarked (bare) form.

7.3.3 Non-referential bare singulars

The interpretive rule ARG, introduced in Section 7.3.2 plays a central role in the syntax-semantics interface of bare nominals in all languages under consideration. Bidirectionality requires that the produced form PROD(M) for the meaning M that the speaker wants to convey is optimal if and only if the interpretation INT(PROD(M)) of the form PROD(M) by the hearer is identical to M, that is, INT(PROD(M)) = M. If ARG must be satisfied in the semantics, the speaker cannot express argument structure without a discourse referent, because the interpretation of the argument structure always involves a discourse referent. A speaker who decides on the optimal form of a nominal in argument position thus starts from a semantic representation involving a discourse referent. So far, we have taken it for granted that the input meaning in the tableaux given in Section 7.2 contains a discourse referent, but ARG makes the semantics of argument structure explicit.

Under the bidirectional analysis, ARG and FDR work together in class (iv) to (vi) languages to block bare singulars in argument position. ARG parses the nominal as introducing a discourse referent, because of its occurrence in a regular argument position. FDR requires this discourse referent to be parsed by a functional level above NP. This pairing up of syntax and semantics effectively requires a marked nominal (with an article or a plural) in regular argument position, and only allows non-referential interpretations of bare singulars under a strong bidirectional OT analysis, as illustrated in Diagram 7.2.

Diagram 7.2: Strong bidirectional optimization (bare singulars in English)

	non-referential	referential
bare singular	○ ✌	○
	↑	↓
marked nominal	○ →	○ ✌

In Diagram 7.2, the bare singular form is in competition with a marked nominal (i.e., a nominal with some level of functional structure). Any functional projection (either Num or D) satisfies FDr, and is interpreted in terms of information about a discourse referent. Because of the way the syntax-semantics interface works, bare singulars in Germanic/Romance languages are pushed back into the parts of the grammar where no discourse referent is introduced, and we obtain a non-referential interpretation. Because of the way ARG works, this must be a position that doesn't qualify as an argument position, because argument positions correlate with discourse referents. What emerges from the way ARG and FDR determine the syntax-semantics interface in class (iv) to (vi) languages is that bare singulars can only appear in constructions that are semantically characterized as non-referential, and that are syntactically characterized as not involving a regular argument position. We argue that this includes the constructions of location, bare incorporation, bare predication, bare coordination, etcetera, illustrated in (8) above.

Strong support for the view that bare singulars in the examples in (8) should be characterized as non-referential comes from the literature bearing on these constructions. Bare singulars appearing in prepositional phrases typically cannot function as the antecedent of a pronoun in later discourse. Stvan (1998:224) gives the following contrast for bare location:

(23) (a) Pat is in prison. ?It is a 3-story concrete building.
     (b) Pat is in a/the prison. It is a 3-story concrete building.

Similar observations have been made by Baldwin, Beavers, van der Beek, Bond, Flickinger and Sag (2006):

(24) I traveled to San Francisco by car. They're/It's a great way to travel/#It rattled a lot.

The non-referentiality of bare reduplication constructions has been discussed by Roodenburg (2004: Chapter 2). Notice also the contrast between bare and full predication in the Dutch examples (25).

(25) (a) Jan is *(een) leraar   en Piet is *er*   ook één.   [Dutch]
          Jan is a   teacher and Piet is there   also one
          'Jan is a teacher and Piet is one too.'

     (b) Jan is (een) leraar   en Piet is *dat* ook.
          Jan is a   teacher and Piet is that also
          'Jan is a teacher and Piet is that too.'

Bare predication allows anaphoric reference to the property (through the demonstrative pronoun *dat* in 25b), but we can only pick out individuals from the set of teachers (through the indefinite *er* in 25a) with a full nominal.

Incorporated nominals in Dutch (26a), Hungarian (26b) (Farkas and de Swart, 2003), and Hindi (26c) (Dayal, 1999, 2003) are discourse opaque, that is, anaphoric pronouns in discourse cannot refer back to the incorporated (singular) nominal.

(26) (a) Ik   weet   dat Peter   viool$_i$ speelt. #Kan hij   'm$_i$ meenemen?
        I   know   that Peter   violin$_i$ plays. #Can he   it$_i$ take along?

   (b) Janós$_i$ beteget$_j$ vizsgált   a   rendelöben.
        Janós$_i$ patient.ACC$_j$ examine.PAST   the   office.in
        'Janos patient-examined in the office.'

        ??pro$_i$ Túl sulyosnak   találta   öt$_j$ és
         pro$_i$ too severe.DAT   find.PAST   he.ACC$_j$ and

        beutaltatta   pro$_j$ a   korházba.
        intern.CAUSE.PAST   pro$_j$ the hospital.in
        'Janós patient-examined in the office. #He found him too ill, and sent him to
           hospital.'

   (c) anu-ne   kitaab paRhii. #Vo/kitaab/Ø   bahut acchii thii.
        Anu   book   read.   It/book/e   very good was.
        'Anu read a book. #It/the book/[pro] was very good.'

We generalize these observations to the claim that bare singulars in class (iv) to (vi) languages only appear in non-argument position with a non-referential meaning. The syntax-semantics interface developed here accounts for this observation in a straightforward way. Tableau 7.8 illustrates this for predicative constructions in Dutch.

Tableau 7.8: Bare singular in non-argument position in class (v) languages, illustrated with Dutch predicative constructions (production)

Teacher (j)	FPL	FDR	FDEF	*ART	*FUNCTN
☞ Jan is [NP leraar].					
Jan is [NumP SG [NP leraar]].					*!
Jan is [DP een [NumP SG [NP leraar]]]. Jan is a teacher				*!	*(!)*

FDR is vacuously satisfied in the OT syntax, because no discourse referent is involved in the semantic input. If FDR is vacuously satisfied, the lower ranked constraints *ART and *FUNCTN determine that a bare nominal is preferred over a nominal marked with an article, and a bare singular is preferred over a bare plural. Although these constraints are ranked so low that they become 'invisible' in major parts of the syntax, they emerge as decisive when higher ranked constraints are vacuously satisfied in predication, location, coordination and incorporation constructions. The use of bare singulars in such environments can thus be properly viewed as a case of emergence of the unmarked in OT terms.

The analysis works well in the sense that we have derived the use of bare singulars in non-argument position from the interaction of the constraints. However, the analysis seems to be overly strong. Tableau 7.8 gives us only one optimal candidate, namely the bare singular. But it is well known that we also find full DPs in predicative position in Dutch (27).

(27) (a) Meneer Schouten is   slager.
          Mister Schouten is   butcher

     (b) Meneer Schouten is een slager.
          Mister Schouten is a   butcher

When we compare the bare with the non-bare case, we see that the bare case only has a literal, professional interpretation (the subject is working or trained as a butcher), while the non-bare case does not necessarily have that interpretation; it can also be metaphorically applied to a surgeon (working like a butcher). The special interpretation of bare predicates has been documented in recent work of de Swart, Winter and Zwarts (2005, 2007), Matushansky and Spector (2005), Munn and Schmitt (2005) and Zamparelli (2005). The bare predicates carry the effect that the subject is part of the predicate in a professional, permanent way.

The alternation between bare and non-bare nominal predicates in (27) implies that bare forms do not block non-bare forms in the special constructions in which bare nominals in non-argument positions have non-referential interpretations. A strong bidirectional OT analysis does not account for cases of partial blocking, because it would only generate the form-meaning combination in (27a). In Section 7.4, we develop an analysis in terms of weak bidirectional OT, which explains the contrast in (27) as an instance of Horn's division of pragmatic labor, according to which unmarked forms go with unmarked meanings, and marked forms go with marked meanings.

7.4   Bare singulars in weak bidirectional OT

So far, we have established not only the syntactic unmarkedness of bare singulars in the typology of natural languages, but we have also restricted the use of bare singulars in languages like English, Dutch, and French to non-argument positions, in which these nominals get a non-referential interpretation. In this section, we explain the alternation between bare singulars and marked nominals in a range of 'special' constructions in terms of weak bidirectional OT.

7.4.1 Stereotypical interpretations

In Section 7.3.4 we already pointed out that bare predicate nominals in Dutch have a 'special' interpretation that we do not find with their non-bare counterparts. The effects are not limited to Dutch. We find similar contrasts in other Germanic and Romance languages. De Swart, Winter and Zwarts (2007) discuss the following examples from Spanish and Danish, and observe that the bare nominal predicates in (28a) and (29a) have a literal, professional meaning, whereas their non-bare counterparts in (28b) and (29b) have a more general, most likely metaphorical interpretation.

(28) (a) Es negrero.   [Spanish]
         'He is a trader in black slaves.'

     (b) Es un negrero.
         'He is a slave driver.' (i.e., makes you work too hard)

(29) (a) Olivier var skuespiller.   [Danish]
         Olivier was actor
         'Olivier was an actor.'

     (b) Din   lille   pige   er   en   skuespiller.
         your   little   girl   is   an   actress
         'Your little girl is an actress.'

We use stereotyping as a general term for the special meaning effects that arise with bare nominals. The interpretation gets enriched in a way that goes beyond what the construction compositionally gives us. This leads to clear interpretive differences between the parallel bare and full constructions. Most of these effects have been documented in the literature.

Stereotypical interpretations of bare location are extensively described in Stvan (1998) and Pérez-Leroux and Roeper (1999). With social spaces, bare location usually has, what Stvan (1998) calls, an activity sense:

(30) (a) to be in prison   'to be a prisoner'
     (b) to be in the prison   'to be in the location designated by 'prison''

To be in prison (hospital, school, church) does not just refer to a physical location in a building, but to the most typical way to participate in the social institution that corresponds to that location, e.g., be a prisoner (patient, student, church-goer). Another effect is that the bare construction has a possessive interpretation that is lacking in the normal construction:[12]

(31) (a)   John is at school.   'at *his* school'
     (b)   John is at a/the school.

We can say in general that the subject of the PP is a typical participant in the defining activities/states of the institution that corresponds to N: the religious service with *in church*, education with *to school*, medical care with *in hospital* and detention with *in prison*. This is not necessary with full PPs like *in the church, to a school, in the hospital* and *in a prison*.

The stereotypical interpretation of bare coordination is noted in Lambrecht (1984). The semantic effect carried by a bare coordination is that these two objects corresponding to N_1 and N_2 occur together *naturally*. The full construction has to be used when the two objects come together accidentally. They fit together in one *frame*, as Lambrecht calls it. In other words, the referents of 'N_1 and N_2' go together naturally as part of some physical or social configuration, as we can see in *sun and moon, mother and child, knife and fork*. Many languages distinguish between natural and accidental coordination, as shown in Dalrymple and Nikolaeva (2006) and Haspelmath (2007). Bare coordination instantiates natural coordination in this sense.

Bare reduplication constructions have quantificational force: *N after N* necessarily implies that most or a great number of the referents of N are involved in the activity of the sentence. Strictly speaking, this is not a stereotypical interpretation, but it is clearly an enrichment of the bare construction vis-à-vis the full construction:

(32) (a)   He found door after door closed.
     (b)   He found one door after another door closed.

Most of the bare constructions that we have discussed are on the borderline of regular and idiomatic expressions. Lambrecht (1984) points out that bare coordination is often 'formulaic' (*bow and arrow, hearth and home, rank and file*). Jackendoff (2008) is also concerned with this 'complex mixture of idiomaticity and productivity' with respect to bare reduplications. Stvan (1998) and Baldwin et al. (2006) discuss the same mixture for bare location. Stvan (1998) provides an extensive overview of the classes of nouns that occur in bare location, and identifies very specific clusters of nouns, like religious settings (chapel, church, seminary, synagogue, temple) or visual frames (camera, frame, range, screen, shot, sight, stage, view). The bare predication construction is limited to nouns that refer to professions, nationalities and religions (de Swart, Winter and Zwarts, 2005, 2007). The Dutch incorporation construction has but one productive subsystem: it is restricted to the verb *spelen* 'play' with nouns for musical instruments. As pointed out by Dayal (1999, 2003), the Hindi verb *dekhnaa* 'see' can incorporate *laRkii* 'girl' but not *aurat* 'woman'. The incorporated structure *laRkii-dekhnaa* 'girl see' cannot be used to describe a situation in which someone just happens to see some girl while looking out of the window: it refers to the viewing of girls as prospective brides.

Some of the bare nominal constructions could be regarded as fixed constructions. If this were true for all cases, an approach in terms of listing would be possible. Although we do not deny the fixed nature of some bare constructions, we agree with Baldwin et al. (2006) that listing may work for certain examples (*at large, on track*), but this cannot be the whole story. Even high frequency classes (*by train, by tax*) are productive (*by carpet* in the context of a flying carpet), which makes a simple listing in the lexicon impossible. Creative use of bare nominals is not only found with bare location, but also with bare reduplication, as illustrated by (33):

(33)   Then the humpback whale
         Held out his tail
         And on crawled snail after snail after snail.
         [Julia Donaldson, *The snail and the whale*]

For low frequency examples such as (33), an approach in terms of listing is impossible, because no list would ever be complete.

7.4.2 Horn's division of pragmatic labor

The analysis we will defend is that bare nominals with stereotypical interpretations, and full nominals with non-stereotypical interpretations exemplify Horn's division of pragmatic labor, which says that unmarked forms go with unmarked meanings, and marked forms go with marked meanings, along the lines of Horn (1984), Levinson (2000a) and Stvan (1998). Horn's division of pragmatic labor has been implemented in weak bidirectional OT, as we saw in Chapter 1. There are many examples that exemplify this kind of non-arbitrary correlation between form and meaning, in morphology, historical development, grammaticalization, binding theory, etcetera, as discussed throughout this book.

If we compare the two forms *in the jail* and *in jail*, we can maintain that *in the jail* is marked vis-à-vis *in jail* (which is shorter, less complex). As far as the two meanings 'incarcerated in the institution' and 'located in the building' are concerned, we observe that the first is the more stereotypical, the expected way of being located in a jail, namely as a prisoner, and therefore less marked. This gives the iconic Horn effect, which Diagram 7.3 derives in a bidirectional fashion.

Diagram 7.3: Weak bidirectional optimization (bare location)

	'incarcerated'		'just visiting'
in jail	○ ☝	←	○
	↑		↑
in the jail	○	←	○ ☝

The arrows point from the more marked to the less marked elements. The pair in the upper left corner is strongly optimal because there are simply no better alternatives. The pair in the lower right corner is weakly optimal or 'super-optimal' in terms of Blutner (2000), because there are alternatives, but these alternatives are not optimal themselves.

We can work out the bare/non-bare predication examples in a similar way. The bare form *slager zijn* ('be butcher') is shorter, less complex than the full form *een slager zijn* ('be a butcher'), and therefore constitutes the unmarked form. The property of being a professional butcher is the stronger, more stereotypical interpretation reserved for the unmarked form *slager zijn*. The full, marked form gets a non-stereotypical, possibly metaphorical interpretation. The weak bidirectional analysis in Diagram 7.4 runs parallel to the one in Diagram 7.3.

Diagram 7.4: Weak bidirectional optimization (bare predication)

	professional		metaphorical
slager zijn	○ ☝	←	○
	↑		↑
een slager zijn	○	←	○ ☝

Diagrams 7.3 and 7.4 both oppose bare and non-bare forms as unmarked and marked forms respectively. They also oppose stereotypical and non-stereotypical meanings, but the diagrams show that the way stereotypical meanings are defined is construction specific.

The bidirectional analysis relies on the notion of markedness, in the syntax as well as in the semantics. As far as the syntax is concerned, the unmarked status of bare singulars is well established in the typology developed in Section 7.2, through *FunctN and *Art. On the meaning side, we need to determine on what basis we can say that 'incarcerated' is semantically less marked than 'just visiting', and being a professional butcher is less marked than being a metaphorical one. It is not immediately clear that the former (stereotypical) meaning is less complex than the latter (non-stereotypical) meaning. Actually, it seems that we could formulate it either way, just the way we want, because we have no clear idea how stereotypicality relates to markedness. We need an independent way to order the two meanings, not just for these two examples, but in a more general way, in order to account for the range of stereotypicality effects that we observe in bare constructions.

7.4.3 Stereotypical interpretations as the unmarked meaning

Stereotyping is used in the pragmatic literature as a cover term for the addition of a special meaning effect on top of a normal interpretation. The existing practice has shown that we don't always need detailed formalized semantic analyses to understand what is going on. The minimum requirement for a bidirectional analysis are two meanings m and m´ that can be ordered, say m < m´, such that m is 'more harmonic' or 'less marked' than m´. But here we want to go a step further in understanding the stereotypical enrichments of bare constructions, and claim that these interpretations are semantically unmarked.

As a first step to determine the harmony relation, we use entailment between interpretations: the stereotypical meaning implies the general meaning. This is another way of saying that the stereotypical meaning is more informative, stronger, and richer. De Swart, Winter and Zwarts (2005) have made this clear for bare predication. A sentence with a bare predicate typically entails the sentence with the corresponding full predicate, but the reverse is not true:

(34) (a)   Jan is leraar   ⇒ Jan is een leraar
           Jan is teacher   ⇒ Jan is a teacher

    (b)   Meneer Schouten is een slager   *⇒ Meneer Schouten is slager
          Mister Schouten is a butcher   *⇒ Mister Schouten is butcher

The reason that (34b) is not valid is that a surgeon can be a (metaphorical) butcher, without being a butcher by profession. In other words, the stereotypical meaning is a proper subset of a wider meaning that includes both stereotypical and non-stereotypical situations:

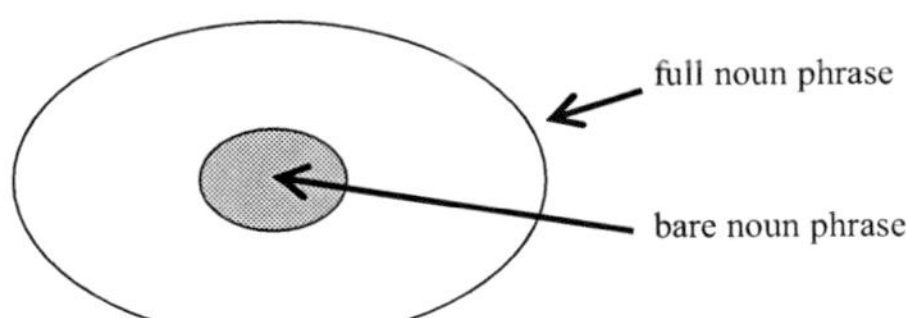

Figure 7.1: Stereotypical meaning as a proper subset

But what kind of information is added to distinguish this subset from the rest? We want to take an example to make this concrete with some formal representations.

De Swart, Winter and Zwarts (2007) defend the view that bare predication involves reference to capacities. Capacities are special ontological entities of the same type as kinds, but sortally distinct from them. Along the lines of Carlson (1980), kinds are related to entities via a realization relation REL. Similarly, capacities are related to entities via the capacity relation CAP. Whereas REL provides the set of entities that instantiate the kind, CAP is more specific, and provides the set of entities that realize the capacity in the proper way. The contrast between the bare and non-bare predication constructions in (34) then corresponds with the two semantic representations in (35).

(35) (a)   Meneer Schouten is slager.

   $s \in$ CAP(**butcher'**)

   (b)   Meneer Schouten is een slager.

   $s \in$ REL(*kind*(**butcher'**))

With the bare nominal, the predication is $s \in$ CAP(**butcher'**), which means that Mr. Schouten is in the set of individuals who are butchers by profession. The predication with full indefinite nominals is $s \in$ REL(*kind*(**butcher'**)), where *kind* is the operator coercing the capacity into a kind. Hence, the predication now means that Mr. Schouten is a member of the set that realizes the kind butcher. Metaphorical interpretations are incompatible with the CAP operator, but not with the REL operator. What we see in (35) is that the interpretation of the bare construction is narrowed down, so that the stereotypical meaning will always be a proper subset of the other meaning.

However, in the bidirectional optimization of labor between marked and unmarked forms, we often need a picture that is slightly different from Figure 7.1. Ultimately, as a result of bidirectional optimization, the meaning that is assigned to full noun phrases, as opposed to bare noun phrases, is not the general meaning in Figure 7.1, but the *complement* of the stereotypical meaning with respect to the general meaning.

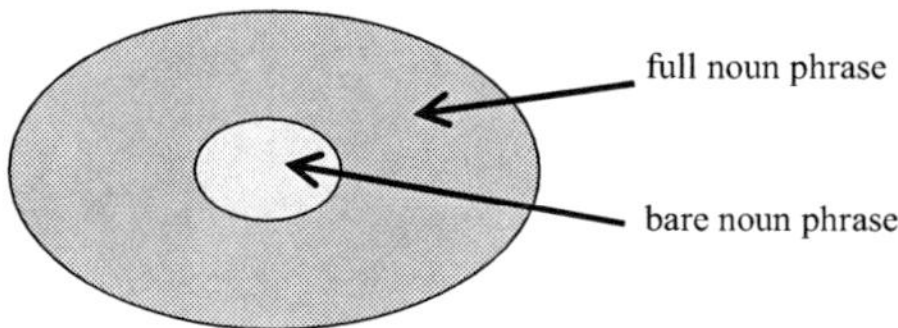

Figure 7.2: Non-stereotypical meaning as the complement

In other words, the semantics in (35b) is frequently strengthened with an implicature that excludes the meaning in (35a). In this case, the meaning can be described as: being a butcher, but not in a professional sense:

(36) Mr. Schouten is (een) slager.

   (a) $s \in$ CAP(**butcher'**)

   (b) $s \in$ REL(*kind*(**butcher'**)) − CAP(**butcher'**)

In the bidirectional approach the stereotypical meaning (36a) does not compete with the *general* meaning of (35b), but with the *non-stereotypical* meaning of (36b). This fits in with the observation that full indefinite nominals are not used in predication relation unless the intended meaning is different from the capacity reading.

Still, the ordering between the two meanings in (36) has to be derived from the implicational relation in (34). Cohen (2006) suggests that stereotypical interpretations are preferred because of their stronger potential to support inferences. We assume that the stereotypical and the non-stereotypical meaning can be ordered through a constraint STRENGTH that favors informationally stronger, richer meanings (Zwarts, 2004, and references cited there):

Tableau 7.9: Selection of the stereotypically restricted meaning

Meneer Schouten is (een) slager	STRENGTH
s ∈ REL(*kind*(**butcher'**)) - CAP(**butcher'**)	*!
☞ s ∈ CAP(**butcher'**)	

In this way we actually hide all the enrichment complexities in the generator GEN of the system. We do not specify here how GEN manages to yield enriched meanings from the compositional, lexically based meanings, and how this enrichment is driven or constrained by convention, encyclopedic knowledge, cultural models, qualia, frames, scripts and scenarios, etcetera. We just claim that it is these factors that determine what is normal, natural, typical, customary, conventional, and institutionalized for the different constructions. What bidirectional optimization now does for us is lining up the forms and the meanings in an iconic way, through the constraints *ART and STRENGTH:

Tableau 7.10: Selection of two optimally aligned form-meaning pairs

		*ART	STRENGTH
☞	*<slager zijn*, CAP(**butcher'**)>		
	<een slager zijn, CAP(**butcher'**)>	*	
	<slager zijn, REL(*kind*(**butcher'**)) - CAP(**butcher'**)>		*
☞	*<een slager zijn*, REL(*kind*(**butcher'**)) - CAP(**butcher'**)>	*	*

With Tableau 7.10, we have recovered the bidirectional analysis proposed in Diagram 7.4 in Section 7.4.2 above. The main gain of the markedness constraint *ART and the appeal to the strongest meaning constraint is that they allowed us to define the syntactic and semantic markedness dimensions that we needed to ground the bidirectional analysis in the grammar.

7.5 Conclusion

In this chapter, we studied the distribution and interpretation of bare nominals in a range of languages. We argued that an OT typology is responsible for the differences in distribution. The semantics is directly recoverable from the syntax, under the assumption of a small set of correspondence rules between form and meaning. Thus, we maintain the view that setting up referents in conversational space and referring to them are universally available cognitive operations. However, language variation arises from the resolution of the conflict between these universal correspondence rules, and a general drive towards speaker economy. This approach embeds language variation in a more principled view on the universal nature of language as a human faculty, along similar lines as the analysis proposed for negation in Chapter 6. Independent support in favor of the OT approach comes from a number of constructions in which languages like English allow nominals to appear without an article. These include bare location, bare coordination, bare predication, bare reduplication, and bare incorporation. We applied weak bidirectional Optimality Theory to these constructions, and argued that the special meaning of these constructions is the result of the pairing up of unmarked forms with unmarked meanings, and marked forms with marked meanings. Although the use of bare singulars in languages like English is extremely restricted, their occurrence does tell us something about the special nature of these nominals.

Notes

1 Some relevant references: Chierchia (1998b), Corbett (2000), Heim (1982), Kamp and Reyle (1993), Lyons (1999), Link (1983).

2 Compare Rijkhoff (2002), Heine and Kuteva (2002), Farkas and de Swart (2003), etc.

3 The examples in (6a) and (6b) are from Krifka (1995) and Dayal (2004) respectively.

4 A selection of relevant recent studies of bare singulars in English: Stvan (1998), Pérez-Leroux and Roeper (1999), Travis (2001), Heycock and Zamparelli (2003), Borthen (2003), Déprez (2005), Munn and Schmitt (2005), Matushansky and Spector (2005).

5 Chinese, Japanese and Thai make extensive use of classifiers, which are combined with cardinals and other determiners, cf. Chierchia (1998b), Krifka (1995), Cheng and Sybesma (1999). An example is given in (i) (from Chierchia, 1998b).

(i) liǎng   zhāng   zhuōz   [Mandarin Chinese]
     two   CL   table
     'two (pieces of) table'

Thus, other faithfulness constraints are ranked above *FUNCTN in this language, and a more fine-grained set of constraints than what we can establish here is required to spell out the full grammar. Let us call them FX for reference. But clearly, *ART is ranked high in Chinese, i.e., higher than the faithfulness constraint $FNOM_1$, $FNOM_2$, ...$FNOM_N$, introduced in Sections 2.3 and 2.4 below, that would trigger number morphology on the noun, or the use of definite or indefinite articles. The ranking *ART >> FX >> *FUNCTN >> {$FNOM_1$, $FNOM_2$, ... $FNOM_N$} accounts for these further complexities, but we will not illustrate the role of FX in the tableaux.

6   The notation pl(x) in the input is taken from Farkas and de Swart (2003), and means that we predicate plurality of x, so x denotes a complex (sum) individual.

7   We will not be concerned here with the full range of plural forms that Corbett (2000) discusses, and which includes the dual, trial and paucal forms, but restrict ourselves to singular/plural oppositions. We will also ignore the interaction with animacy, and the mass/count distinction.

8   Other languages in this class are Bambara (a language in the Niger-Kordofanian family, spoken in Mali, Rijkhoff, 2002) and Quechua (a language in the Amerind family, spoken in Ecuador, Argentina, Bolivia, Chile, Peru, Rijkhoff, 2002).

9   Some languages reverse markedness, and use a special form for the singular, e.g., Babungo, Bukyiyip, Kisi, Nasioi and Ngiti (Rijkhoff, 2002:150) and Endo-Marakwet (Zwarts, 2007). These languages call for a highly ranked constraint FSG, which requires the expression of singular when the plural is neutralized for a particular class of nouns. A full discussion of number is outside of the scope of this study, so we limit ourselves to the most common case. We refer the interested reader to Corbett (2000), Rijkhoff (2002) and de Swart and Zwarts (2009) for further discussion of singular number expressions.

10 Case distinctions are used by some languages to realize meaning oppositions involving specificity that are closely related to the definite/indefinite contrast (Turkish, Finnish). Cantonese uses a classifier to express definiteness (Cheng and Sybesma, 1999). In this chapter, we limit ourselves to the prototypical case of a definite article, and do not consider the contribution of case marking or classifiers.

11 Most languages that express definiteness have morphological number as well, so we frequently find grammars with the ranking {FDEF, FPL} >> {*ART, *FUNCTN}. However, Corbett (2000:278, 279) points out that some languages exemplify number distinctions for definites only, e.g., Kambera an Austronesian (Central Malayo-Polynesian languages spoken in Eastern Indonesia and Basque). This

suggests a more complex interaction of constraints, and possibly more specific constraints for marking number in definite noun phrases. We leave these issues for further research.

12 Which is particularly clear with the bare expression *home*, as Jackendoff, Maling and Zaenen (1993) have shown.

8 Paradigmatic preposition patterns

8.1 The shapes of a word

What shapes the meaning of a word? We can use a graphical metaphor to make intuitively clear that words can be shaped in three different ways. Consider the following three shapes:

Figure 8.1: Three kinds of word meanings

Some words are like the first shape in Figure 8.1, which has the very simple planar geometry of a circle:

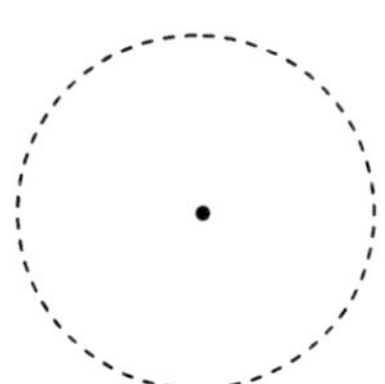

Figure 8.2: A classical word meaning

A circle can be defined by a simple equation like $x^2+y^2 = 1$. This corresponds to the kind of word meaning that is determined by one simple definition. *Bachelor*, with its definition of 'adult man who has not married yet', is the classical example of such a monosemous word (Katz and Fodor, 1963).

It is of course well-known that word meanings are rarely like this. They are often polysemous, that is, clusters of closely related, more basic meanings.[1] In this sense, they can be compared to the second shape in Figure 8.1, a complex, irregular shape built up from simple planar figures:

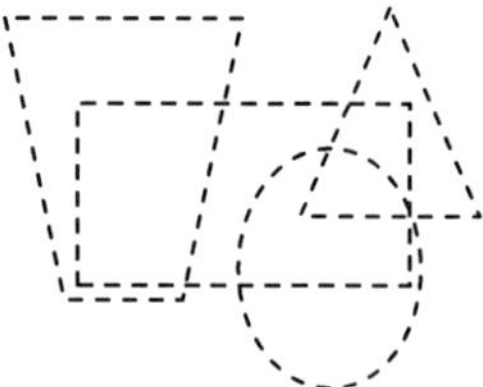

Figure 8.3: A cluster word meaning

A well-known example of such a cluster word from the literature is *over* (Brugman, 1981; Lakoff, 1987).

But there is a third way in which word meanings can be shaped, that has received much less attention in the literature and that is illustrated by the third shape in Figure 8.1. In this case the semantic outline of the word (the square) is determined by the meanings of other words that cut out parts of a regularly defined meaning and thereby create irregularity in the shape:

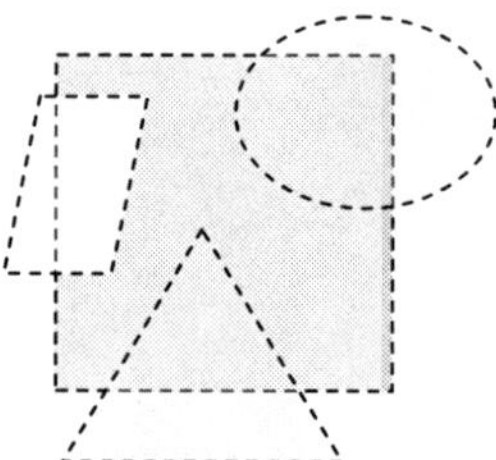

Figure 8.4: A clipped word meaning

The factor that shapes meaning in this case is not the polysemy of one single word, but interaction between different words. The idea that words and word meanings determine each other in patterns of competition and blocking is known from structuralism and Wortfeld theory (Saussure, 1974; Trier, 1972), morphology (Aronoff, 1976; Kiparsky, 1982), Gricean pragmatics (McCawley, 1978; Horn, 1984; Levinson, 2000a), acquisition (Clark, 1993; Markman, 1994) and language change (Keenan, 2003). Blutner (2000) accounted for these patterns in terms of bidirectional Optimality Theory.

The purpose of this chapter is to demonstrate that this perspective is essential for our understanding of prepositional meanings, as was also suggested in Levinson (2000b) and Solstad (2003). Levinson gives the example of *near*, that can be defined as 'location within a certain distance of the reference object', including 'zero' distance. So, strictly speaking, (1a) could be used even when the train is at the station. However, the availability of (1b), with a preposition specialized in zero distance, blocks this use, just as the square is partially occluded by the ellipse in Figure 8.4.

(1)   (a)   The train is near the station.

(b)   The train is at the station.

A similar case of blocking, but with non-spatial prepositions was brought up in Solstad (2003):

(2)   (a)   Das Fenster wurde durch einen Hammer zerstört.
'The window was broken by means of a hammer.'

(b)   Das Fenster wurde mit einem Hammer zerstört.
'The window was broken with a hammer.'

Solstad argues that *durch* 'through' has an underspecified causal meaning that he calls 'causal chain element'. Interestingly, in spite of this general meaning, *durch* cannot be used for situations where the hammer is a prototypical instrument. This is where German uses *mit*. As a result, *durch* in (2a) is used for non-prototypical (more indirect) use of instruments which is not covered by the prototype in (2b).

The purpose of this chapter is to show that these are not isolated examples, but that the meaning of many prepositions is to a large extent shaped *paradigmatically*, by its being part of a larger pattern of competing prepositions that carve up a space of meanings. This requires us to look more closely at the choice of words, i.e., the expressive perspective of optimization and the constraints that play a role there. Our focus will be on directional prepositions like *to, off, towards, through, around* and *over* in their spatial use. We will first give some background assumptions about the semantic analysis of direction in Section 8.2, before discussing four examples of the paradigmatic patterning of such prepositions. Not all competition works in the same way. There are patterns of implication, where a more specific preposition restricts the meaning of a more general preposition (developed for *through, into* and *out of* in Section 8.3), but there are also patterns where two prepositional meanings overlap (like *over* and *around*, as we will see), and spatial faithfulness conditions determine which preposition is chosen in a particular configuration (Section 8.4). With patterns of suppletion there are two forms with the same meaning, but the simple form completely blocks the complex form (like *off* and *from on*, Section 8.5). Finally, bidirectional optimization is applied to patterns of iconicity, where the division of labor between simpler and more complex forms for 'around' is determined by the underlying markedness alignment of forms and meanings (Section 8.6).

8.2   The paths of a preposition

Building on Zwarts (2004, 2005) and references cited there, we assume that directional prepositional phrases (PPs) like *to the house* and *around the park* are interpreted as sets of paths. For example (and roughly speaking), *to the house* denotes the set of paths that end at the house and *around the park* the set of paths that enclose the park. Intuitively, a path is a sequence of positions in space, but formally it can be construed as a continuous function $\mathbf{p}$ from a real interval $[0,1]$ (the indices of the path) to spatial positions. Such a function defines a directed spatial curve with a starting point $\mathbf{p}(0)$, an end point $\mathbf{p}(1)$ and intermediate points $\mathbf{p}(i)$ for every i between 0 and 1. Here are two schematic representations of paths, one that can be described as *to the house* and the other as *around the park*:

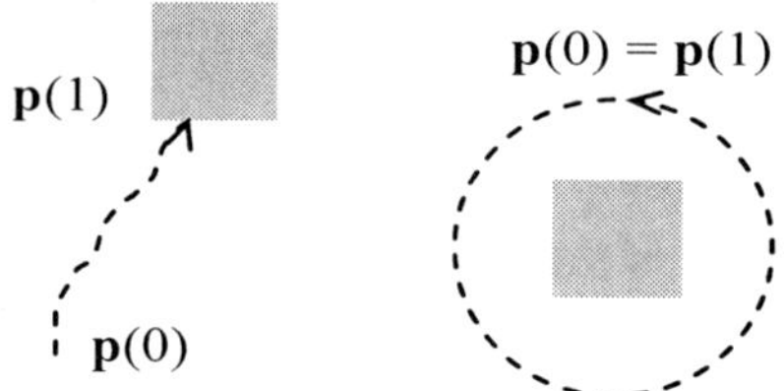

Figure 8.5: Paths of *to the house* and *around the park*

A PP defines a set of paths, by the conditions that it imposes on the shape and location of the path. Most prepositions impose conditions on either the starting point (like *from* and *out of*) or the end point (*to* and *into*), but there are also prepositions that select intermediary points (e.g., *through*) or that compare starting point and end point with respect to some property (like proximity to the reference object in the case of *towards*). *Around* is one of the prepositions that seems to make reference to the global shape of a path.

8.3   Patterns of implication: *through, into* and *out of*

Our point of departure is the assumption that lexical semantic definitions should not only be empirically adequate, but also as simple as possible, i.e., they should not contain any information that can be derived in a general way from other independent sources. We will focus here on the prepositions *through, into* and *out of*, and show that simple definitions for these items, although intuitively plausible, overgenerate.

One of the meanings of the preposition *through*, exemplified in (3a), involves paths that are entirely inside the reference object. We will write this instance of *through* as $through_\forall$, because it can be defined through universal ($\forall$) quantification over the indices of the path (3b). The double brackets [[...]] around an expression give us the set-theoretic denotation of that expression in a universe of discourse.

(3) (a) Alex walked $through_\forall$ the house.
       (i.e., back and forth, from room to room)

   (b) [[$through_\forall$ NP]] = { **p**: for every $i \in [0,1]$ **p**(i) is in [[NP]] }

In words: $through_\forall$ *NP* denotes the set of paths of which every point is in the object referred to by NP. This is an adequate definition and as simple as it can get. *Through* also has another meaning, that requires only one part of the path to be in the house and that we will therefore write as $through_\exists$:

(4) (a) Alex walked $through_\exists$ the house.
       (i.e., on his way from the gate to the barn)

   (b) [[$through_\exists$ NP]] = { **p**: there is an $i \in [0,1]$ such that **p**(i) is in [[NP]] }

It seems natural to define this version of *through* in terms of existential ($\exists$) quantification, as in (4b): some position of the path is in the house. However, despite the attractive opposition between universal and existential quantification, this existential definition of $through_\exists$ is much too liberal. In fact, the only thing it excludes are paths entirely outside the house. In the set defined in (4b) we find such paths as illustrated in the next figure:

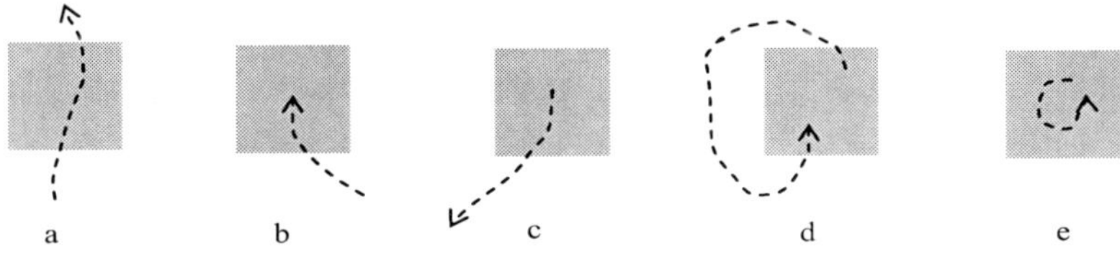

Figure 8.6: Paths in the denotation of *through*$_\exists$

All these paths have at least one point in the reference object, but we really only use $through_\exists$ for the first kind of path in Figure 8.6.

We see similar problems with simple definitions for *into* and *out of*:

(5) (a) [[into NP]] = { **p**: **p**(1) is in [[NP]] }
   (b) [[out of NP]] = { **p**: **p**(0) is in [[NP]] }

These definitions seem intuitively right. *Into* paths have their end point in the reference object and *out of* paths their starting point. But the problem is that these definitions give us also paths like the following:

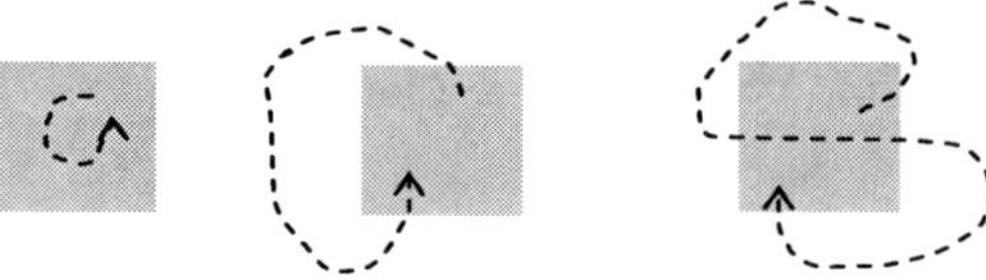

Figure 8.7: Paths in the denotation of *into* and *out of*

One conclusion could be that the definitions above (except for *through*$_\forall$) are just too simple to work and require extra restrictions. The simple definition for *through*$_\exists$ in (4b) then needs to be replaced by something like the following (Zwarts, 2005):

(6)   [[through$_\exists$ NP]] = { **p**: there is an interval $I \subset [0,1]$ that includes 0 nor 1 and that consists of all the $i \in [0,1]$ for which **p**(i) is in [[NP]] }

The definition implies that there is exactly one proper part of the path that is in the reference object. There is also the extra requirement that the starting point and the end point are not in this proper part. For *into* and *out of*, the definitions would be as follows:

(7)   (a)   [[into NP]] = { **p**: there is an interval $I \subset [0,1]$ including 1 and consisting of all the $i \in [0,1]$ for which **p**(i) is in [[NP]] }

    (b)   [[out of NP]] = { **p**: there is an interval $I \subset [0,1]$ including 0 and consisting of all the $i \in [0,1]$ for which **p**(i) is in [[NP]] }

These definitions only allow paths that consist of two 'phases' (Fong, 1997), a phase that is inside the reference object and a phase that is outside it, ordered in two different ways.

However, the problem with these more complex definitions is that they incorporate *negative* conditions to restrict the extension of the PP. The adequacy of the definition of *through*$_\exists$, for example, crucially depends on prohibiting the starting and end point of the path to be in the reference object. Such extra, negative conditions in lexical definitions are suspect, especially since there is a way to explain lexical restrictions on one item from the existence of a neighbouring item.

So let's go back again to the simple definitions of *through*$_\forall$, *through*$_\exists$, *into* and *out of*:

(8) (a) [[through$_\forall$ NP]] = { **p**: for every $i \in [0,1]$ **p**(i) is in [[NP]] }
     (b) [[through$_\exists$ NP]] = { **p**: there is an $i \in [0,1]$ such that **p**(i) is in [[NP]] }
     (c) [[into NP]] = { **p**: **p**(1) is in [[NP]] }
     (d) [[out of NP]] = { **p**: **p**(0) is in [[NP]] }

These four prepositions form a small lexical field of directionals based on the underlying locative concept 'in'. It is not an unstructured field, because the meanings are ordered. The denotation in (8a) is included in the other three denotations and (8c) and (8d) are both included in (8b), the most general meaning, but unordered with respect to each other. We can represent this in a graph, with the most specific meaning at the top and the most general meaning at the bottom.

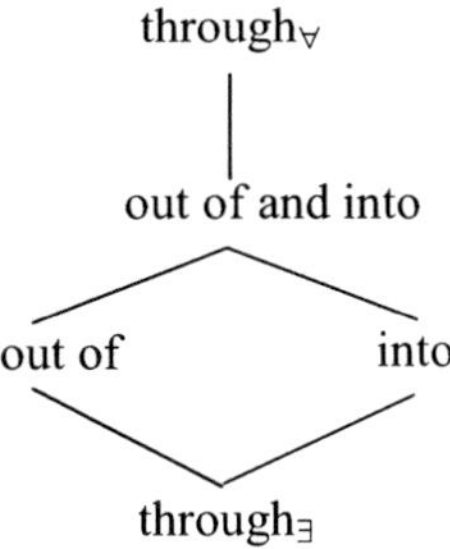

Figure 8.8: Implicational graph of directional 'in' prepositions

We have also included the intersection of the *into* and *out of* denotations, which is a subset of both *into* and *out of*, but a superset of *through*$_\forall$.

(9) [[out of and into NP]] = [[out of NP]] $\cap$ [[into NP]] = {**p**:**p**(0) and **p**(1) are in [[NP]]}

This is the set of paths that start and end in the reference object.

Notice that the graph in Figure 8.8 is a more general version of scales that we find for *all* and *some* and *and* and *or*, with the first item implicating the second (the so-called Horn scales underlying scalar implicatures, Horn, 1972). The elements of such a scale go from stronger to weaker in meaning, or, in other words, the first element implies the second element. The same is true for the prepositions in Figure 8.8 in a top to bottom fashion.

There is another way to represent these relations, using Venn diagrams, which will clarify how the meaning of one preposition can restrict the meaning of another preposition:

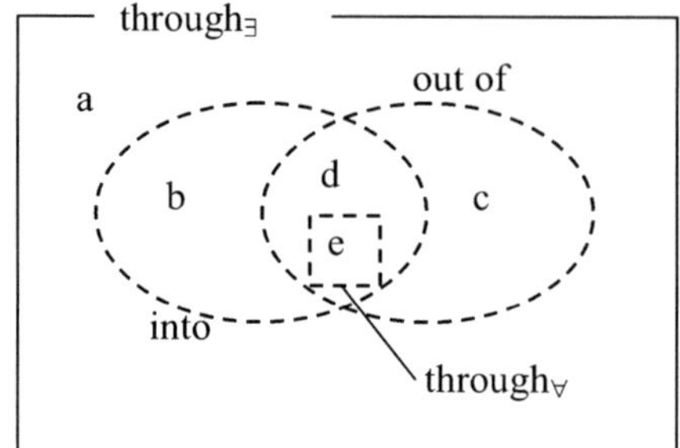

Figure 8.9: Pattern of 'in' directionals

The big rectangle represents *through*₃, the most general meaning. The two ellipses stand for *into* and *out of*. *Through*ᵥ corresponds to the small square in the middle, a proper subset of the intersection of *into* and *out of*. The letters a, b, c, d, and e refer to the paths given in Figure 8.9 and repeated here in Figure 8.10:

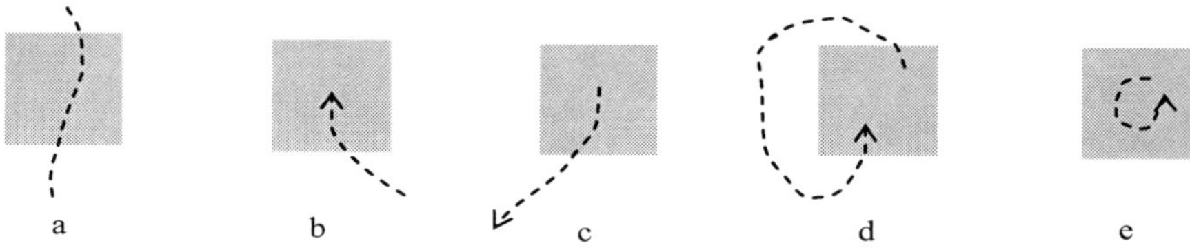

Figure 8.10: Paths in the denotation of *through*₃

We can now clearly see how the restrictions on *through*₃, *into* and *out of* can be made to result from a mechanism of partial blocking, similar to the examples that were mentioned in Section 8.1. Given the situation in Figure 8.9, *through*₃ will only apply to paths in the area, outside the *into* or *out of* area (like path **a**). *Into* is restricted to the area that does not intersect with *out of* and that includes paths like **b**, because we have the complex preposition *out of and into* for the intersection, referring to paths that are both out of and into, like path **d**. However, the expression *out of and into* does not apply to paths that are entirely in the reference object, like path **e**, because for that we have *through*ᵥ. In each case, the initial weak denotation of a preposition is strengthened by the availability of a more specific alternative that partially blocks the more general preposition in its application.

Given this, we can maintain simple and transparent definitions for prepositions. The complicating restrictions can be made to follow from the implicational pattern that these prepositions form. Prepositions compete for the space of meanings, with more specific words prevailing over more general words. We can make the competition between these two words more concrete in Optimality

Theoretic terms. The input of the optimization process is a situation in which a path **p** stands in a particular spatial relation to a reference object. The output is the prepositional sense (a set of paths **P**) that is most appropriate for that path.

Tableau 8.1: Competition between a general and specific description

	FAITH	SPECIFICITY
"through$_\forall$ the house" (8a)	*!	
"out of and into the house" (9)	*!	*
"out of the house" (8d)	*!	**
☞ "into the house" (8c)		**
"through$_\exists$ the house" (8b)		**!*

In this case, the input is a path that has its endpoint, but not its starting point, inside the reference object. The higher constraint, FAITH, is a very general constraint that is violated when the input is not included in the output. [2] The only two candidate denotations that survive this first constraint correspond to *through$_\exists$* and *into*, so the competition is between these two. The lower constraint that decides between them, SPECIFICITY, makes a translation: the position of a denotation in the partial ordering in Figure 8.8 is translated into a number of violations, making it possible to single out the more specific item *into* in this case. As a result, *into* blocks *through* for input paths like the one indicated here: a hearer will not interpret *through the house* as denoting path b in Figure 8.10, because the description *into the house* fits this path better, given the SPECIFICITY constraint.

Notice that the competition is between denotations (sets of paths) of linguistic expressions like *through the house* and *into the house*, and crucially, the outcome of the competition is not determined by the *form* of these expressions, but by their *denotation*. So, we can treat the optimization process in Tableau 8.1 as a component in the production process of OT syntax that consists of finding the descriptions that best fit a given scene. This is an instance of *categorization*, i.e., a mapping from an individual referent (path) to an extensional concept (set of paths). These concepts are then lexically linked to concrete expressions like *through* and *out of and into*, because ultimately we want to associate spatial situations to their linguistic descriptions.

The blocking pattern discussed here is quite similar to what we find in the interpretation of the existential quantifier or the disjunction in Gricean pragmatics, but there might be an important difference. It seems that the blocking effects with *through*, *into* and *out of*, described above cannot be *cancelled*. We can *never* use *through$_\exists$* for any of the paths in Figure 8.6 except for the first one. Note the following contrast:

(10) (a)   Alex ate *some* of the apples, in fact, *all* of the apples.

(b) ? Alex walked *through₃* the house, in fact, *into* the house.

Scalar implicatures of existential quantifiers can typically be cancelled, but we find no such cancellability with the 'existential' preposition *through*.[3] Obviously, the scalar implicature that arises from blocking by *into*, has somehow been 'wired' into the lexical semantics of the preposition *through*, even though it arises from pragmatic principles of use. This might be similar to the way other implicatures (like indirect speech acts) are conventionalized or 'short-circuited' into the meanings of words of expressions (Horn and Bayer, 1984). This is one of the areas where the distinction between semantics (meaning) and pragmatics (use) gets blurred.

We have seen in this section that parts of the simple denotation of a preposition can be excluded because they are 'cut out' by the denotation of a more specific preposition. We will now turn to some blocking phenomena that involve prepositions that *overlap* in meaning.

8.4   Patterns of faithfulness: around and over

Round, or its variant *around*, is one of the more polysemous items in English, having at least the same level of polysemy as *over*, the paragon example of a polysemous preposition (Brugman, 1981; Lakoff, 1987). As described in Schulze (1991, 1993), *around* does not only refer to paths that completely enclose the reference object, as in example (11a), but also to paths that go to the opposite side (11b), or to quarter paths (11c) (examples from Schulze):

(11) (a) The earth goes round the sun once in a year.

(b) We took our guests round the bay after dinner to see our house from the other side.

(c) When you get to the corner, go round carefully.

This is one dimension of the polysemy of *around*, schematically represented in Figure 8.11:

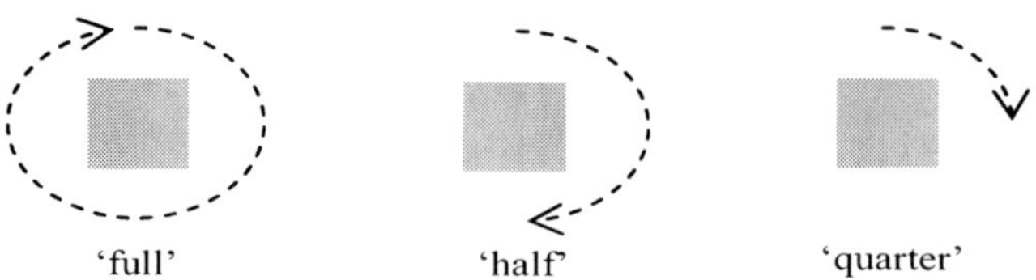

Figure 8.11: Three round paths

There are different ways to define these meanings and their relations to each other and to other meanings of *round*, not illustrated here. Zwarts (2004) analyzes the spatial meanings of *around* as sets of paths that extend the prototypical meaning of a circular path. For the purposes of this chapter we can make the rough assumption that the path shapes in Figure 8.11 differ in how much of the reference object is 'enclosed' by the path.[4]

(12) (a) [[around NP]] = { **p**: **p** encloses all of [[NP]] }
    (b) [[around NP]] = { **p**: **p** encloses half of [[NP]] }
    (c) [[around NP]] = { **p**: **p** encloses a quarter of [[NP]] }

This is intuitively clear, but two remarks are in order. One is that 'enclosure' involves some kind of convex ('outward') curvature with respect to the reference object. The other remark is that the definitions are intended to apply in a plane, i.e., they are two-dimensional, under the assumption that three-dimensional instances of *around* (like *the paper wrapped around the present*) can be reduced to two-dimensional cross-sections. See Zwarts (2004) for more discussion about these aspects.

The interesting property of *around* that we want to focus on here relates to this two-dimensional plane that we just mentioned. The observation is that some uses of *around* are restricted to a *horizontal* plane. To see this, imagine an air show near a high bridge over a river.

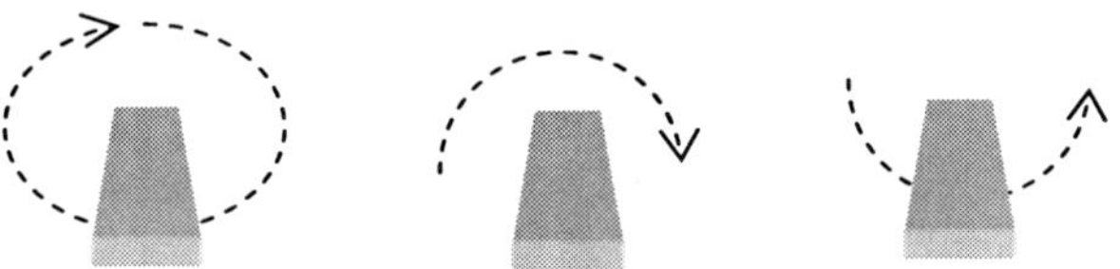

Figure 8.12: Paths with respect to a bridge

When the airplane performs a loop, as in the first situation of Figure 8.12, we have no hesitation to describe this with the following sentence:

(13) The airplane flew around the bridge.

However, even though the paths in the other two situations of Figure 8.12 'enclose' enough of the bridge to qualify as a 'round' path, we would not normally use (13) to describe them, but rather (14a) and (14b), respectively:

(14) (a) The airplane flew *over* the bridge.
    (b) The airplane flew *under* the bridge.

So, when the plane of the semicircular path is vertical, we use the vertical prepositions *over* and *under*. It is difficult to see how we could build this directional restriction into the meaning definitions of *around*. We cannot say that *around* only applies to paths in the horizontal plane, because the first situation in Figure 8.12 shows that this is not true.

We see a similar thing with paths that enclose a corner or edge of an object. When the path is in the horizontal plane, we use the preposition *around* (*around the corner*), but when that same path is in the vertical plane, *over* is used (*over the edge*).

Figure 8.13: Around the corner and over the edge

However, the division of labor between *around* and *over* depends on context. It is possible to imagine situations where *around* is also used for a path with a vertical orientation, when we want to stress the enclosure or curvature of the path:

(15) Alex climbed around the bridge (with a measuring tape).

This suggests that *around* has the definitions that we suggested earlier, without any restriction as to orientation, but that the use of *around* can be blocked by *over* or *under* when the vertical orientation of the path is salient. It is important to realize that we can't use the mechanisms of the previous section, because *over* is not a more specific (vertical) instance of *around* in the same way as *into* is a specific instance of *through*$_3$. The two prepositions only overlap in meaning. The definition of the relevant sense of *over* can be formulated as follows:[5]

(16) $[[\text{ over NP }]] = \{$ **p**: there is an interval $I \subset [0,1]$ that does neither include 0 nor 1 and that consists of all the $i \in [0,1]$ for which $\mathbf{p}(i)$ is above $[[\text{ NP}]] \}$

Every path that has one proper part above the reference object counts as an *over* path, which includes also straight paths, not in the denotation of *around*. *Around*, on the other hand, can refer to horizontal paths, which are not in the denotation of *over*. This means that the definitions of *around* and *over* are not ordered with respect to each other. We therefore need another way to make *over* the dominant preposition in vertical situations.

When the input is the *horizontally* oriented half circular path of Figure 8.11, the output should be (12b), with *around*, but for the *upwardly* curved semi-circle in Figure 8.12 it should be based on *over*, in (16). We would like to suggest that the competition between *around* and *over* is basically a competition between the properties of *shape* and *orientation* and, corresponding to this, two faithfulness conditions: one for shape and for orientation. The idea is that *around* faithfully expresses the shape of a path, while *over* faithfully expresses the upward orientation of a path with respect to the reference object. English does not have an item that satisfies both constraints, i.e., that is faithful to both orientation and shape of the input path (a gap that we come back to later). Therefore, a choice has to be made, which property to give priority to. English gives priority over the expression of orientation, by ranking 'faithfulness to orientation' (FAITHORIENT) over 'faithfulness to shape' (FAITHSHAPE). We can represent this as follows in a tableau:[6]

Tableau 8.2: Interaction of orientation and shape in the naming of paths

	FAITHORIENT	FAITHSHAPE
"around the bridge" (12b)	*!	
☞ "over the bridge" (16)		*

Neither of the two prepositions is ideal for the given input, but *over* comes out as the winner because of the way the constraints are ranked. The general picture is clear, but a number of questions require an answer.

First, what is the definition of these two faithfulness constraints that play such an important role here? We can informally state these constraints as follows, understanding them as relations between an input path **p** and an output denotation **P**:[7]

(17) FAITHORIENT: Output **P** is faithful to the orientation of input **p** iff all the paths in **P** are based on the same orientation w.r.t. the reference object as **p**.

(18) FAITHSHAPE: Output **P** is faithful to the shape of input **p** iff all the paths in **P** are based on the same shape property as **p**.

The input path in Tableau 8.2 has an upward orientation with respect to the bridge and this orientation also holds for all the paths in the output 'over the bridge', but not in the output 'around the bridge'. The input path also partially encloses the bridge, a property which is true of all the paths in 'around the bridge', but only some of the paths in 'over the bridge', because the latter set also includes straight horizontal paths. Working this out in more formal detail would require a model in which orientations and shapes can be represented, but the general rough idea should be clear.

Secondly, is there any independent evidence for these constraints? We mention here a few phenomena that illustrate that the salience of vertical orientation is not restricted to directional prepositions. As shown in Blutner and Solstad (2001), the dimensional adjective *long* is used for the major dimension of elongated objects, but only when these objects do not have a vertical orientation, because then we would use *high* or *deep*, depending on whether the orientation is upward or downward:

(19) (a) *The tower is 10m long.   (a') The tower is 10m high.
     (b) *The well is 10m long.   (b') The well is 10m deep.

High and *deep* block the use of *long* for vertically oriented objects, because of the importance to faithfully express the verticality in the output. Something similar can be seen in the use of the spatial part noun *side*. As shown already in Leech (1969), the applicability of *side* is restricted by the competing part nouns *top*, *bottom*, *front*, and *back*. We can call the six faces of a mathematical cube *sides* because there is no salient orientation. But if the cube would get a salient vertical orientation, then it has only four sides, because two of the sides are labelled *top* and *bottom*. Objects with a front-back orientation are left with only two sides. In short, if the input has a vertical orientation, then there is a strong preference to show this orientation in the output description.

The third question concerns the ordering of the two constraints. Is this ordering universal or does it vary across languages? Our hunch is that the predominance of orientation over shape is a universal phenomenon, at least in prepositional systems, but we lack enough comparative data to seriously back this up. If there is a universal ordering, then this might very well reflect a complexity hierarchy of spatial notions, grounded in perception. Even though orientation and shape are both fundamental parts of spatial perception, there is well-known evidence for the basic role of orientation in the visual neural system (Hubel and Wiesel, 1959) and its effect on spatial language (Landau and Jackendoff, 1993; Regier, 1995; O'Keefe, 1996).

In the fourth place, why would a language have to choose between *over* and *around*? Why don't we find in English a preposition *curver*, for example, that specifically means 'over something in a round curve', satisfying both FAITHSHAPE and FAITHORIENT?

(20) [[curver NP]] = { $\mathbf{p}$: there is an $i \in [0,1]$ such that $\mathbf{p}(i)$ is above [[NP]] and $\mathbf{p}$
     encloses half of [[NP]] }

We suggest that there is a high ranked semantic markedness constraint that prohibits items that combine too many (spatial) distinctions. The scope of this constraint within the lexicon needs to be determined, but it seems at least relevant for the prepositional domain. This constraint, let's call it *LEXCOMPLEX, yields a violation for every conjunction of properties in the definition of a lexical item. We then get the following tableau:

Tableau 8.3: The role of semantic markedness

	*LexComplex	FaithOrient	FaithShape
"around the bridge" (12b)		*!	
☞ "over the bridge" (16)			*
"curver the bridge" (20)	*!		

*LexComplex has the effect of restricting the lexical inventory of a language, so that a smaller number of items compete with each other on the basis of the underlying hierarchy of spatial faithfulness constraints.

Finally, what does our account say about the first situation in Figure 8.12? We have seen that a fully circular path with a vertical orientation is always called *around,* and that the use of *over* for such a path is totally inappropriate, even though the path is included in the denotation in (16) (there is one point of the path above the reference object). What this shows is that a preposition can only be faithful to the orientation of an input path if there actually is a unique direction to that orientation. The input path is in the vertical plane, but because of its shape it lacks the upward orientation with respect to the bridge to allow faithfulness to be determined. So, this is the tableau that we get:

Tableau 8.4: The inertness of faithfulness to orientation

	FaithOrient	FaithShape
☞ "around the bridge" (12a)		
"over the bridge" (16)		*!

We have seen two examples now of how the meaning of a preposition is shaped by 'neighbouring' prepositions. Although both patterns can be described as blocking, they each have their own underlying competition factor. One pattern was determined by the implicational relation between prepositions, the other pattern by their faithfulness properties. We will now look at a third situation, in which a complex prepositional item is completely suppleted by a simpler form.

8.5   Patterns of suppletion: *off* and *out of*

Suppletion or total blocking is a well-known phenomenon from morphology. It occurs when a form f with a meaning m completely disappears from the system, because there is a simpler form f' that expresses that same meaning m. In morphology regularly derived or inflected forms can be blocked by the existence of non-derived, sometimes irregular, forms (like the blocking of the form **glorious-ity* by *glory* or **good-est* by *best*).

In the prepositional system there is a regular way of deriving source expressions from locative expressions through the preposition *from* (Jackendoff, 1983):

(21)   *Location*   *Source*
         under the bed   →   from under the bed
         near the fire   →   from near the fire
         between trees   →   from between the trees

The syntax makes use of recursion of PP:

(22) $[_{PP}$ from $[_{PP}$ under the bed $]]$

The semantics involves an operation that maps a set of places to a set of paths (Jackendoff, 1983; Zwarts and Winter, 2000; Kracht, 2002):

(23)   *Location*   *Source*
         [[under the bed]]   →   { $\mathbf{p}$: $\mathbf{p}(0) \in$ [[under the bed]] }

The *from* PP denotes the set of paths that have their starting point in the set of locations denoted by the embedded locative PP.

Having said this, the interesting thing is now the absence of structures like the following:

(24) (a)   *from on the wall
     (b)   *from in the box

A blocking approach seems appropriate here. We don't find the forms *from on* and *from in*, because there are specialized forms for these cases, namely *off* and *out of*, that have the meaning of the explicit forms *from on* and *from in* cases, respectively:

(25) (a)   [[$[_{PP}$ from $[_{PP}$ on NP]]]] = [[$[_{PP}$ off NP]]] = { $\mathbf{p}$: $\mathbf{p}(0)$ is on [[NP]] }
     (b)   [[$[_{PP}$ from $[_{PP}$ in NP]]]] = [[$[_{PP}$ out of NP]]] = { $\mathbf{p}$: $\mathbf{p}(0)$ is in [[NP]] }

A simple markedness constraint on structure will derive the preference for the output without recursion:

Tableau 8.5: Total blocking of *from on*

{ **p**: **p**(0) is on the wall }	FAITHPATH	FAITHLOC	*STRCOMPLEX
from on the wall			*
from the wall		*	
on the wall	*		
☞ *off the wall*			

To make the tableau more realistic, we have also added the outputs *from the wall* and *on the wall*. We assume that faithfulness constraints for direction and location mark these outputs as sub-optimal. Notice that the optimization that we see in Tableau 8.5 is different from what we saw in the previous two sections, where a single input path was mapped to a denotation (a spatial 'concept'). Here, we are interested in mapping a set to an expression. The two mappings taken together (from input path to denotation and from denotation to linguistic expression) constitute the relation between a spatial situation and a linguistic expression that describes that situation. Notice that *STRCOMPLEX is a formal markedness constraint on syntactic or morphological *structure*, to be distinguished from the *LEXCOMPLEX constraint of the previous section that restricts the *semantic* complexity of a concept.

Of course, as always with blocking effects, many difficult but interesting questions arise, that would not have come up with an account that is less general in scope. Firstly, why do we find total blocking here, but not with the well-known partial blocking example *kill – cause to die*, also a contrast of lexical (simple) and structural (complex). What keeps *from on* from taking on a special, marked meaning? And, why would *out of* be able to block *from in*, even though the two forms seem to be equally complex? Questions like these show that our treatment of blocking effects should not too lightly pass over questions about the grammatical status of small words like *in, on* and *of*.

8.6   Patterns of iconicity: *around* in Dutch

Prepositions turn out to be an important area for studying the role of bidirectional optimization and the pragmatic principles that it incorporates (the 'division of pragmatic labor' from Horn, 1984; the M-principle in Levinson, 2000a; or Haiman's, 1980, iconicity): marked forms for marked meanings and unmarked forms for unmarked meanings. An example given by Levinson (2000b) is the contrast between *on the desk* and *on top of the desk*: *on the desk* is used for normal, canonical situations, while *on top of the desk* is used for situations that deviate from the canonical 'on' situation. There are many more cases where we find two or three near-synonymous prepositions contrasting with each other in this way, in different languages. The *on – on top of* contrast in English is paralleled by the very similar Dutch example *op – bovenop*. For internal location we can find three closely related prepositions in Dutch and English:

(26) (a) in – binnen – binnenin
     (b) in – within – inside

The short preposition *in* is used for canonical, (stereo)typical location in both languages, but as soon as the complex prepositions *binnenin* and *inside* are used, there seems to be an emphasis on the hollow, container-like capacity of the reference object (see also McIntyre, 2001, and p.c.):

(27) (a) Alex is (binnen)in het ziekenhuis.
           'Alex is in(side) the hospital.'

     (b) Alex heeft een pijp in/?binnenin zijn mond.
           'Alex has a pipe in/?inside his mouth.'

With the unmarked preposition *in*, Alex is in the hospital in the normal way, typically as a patient, but as soon as the preposition is made more complex, this reading disappears and the sentence gets a marked spatial interpretation. In Chapter 7 we already saw the importance of this semantic distinction for the omission of articles in PPs like *in hospital*. The second example in (27) shows how the smaller preposition *in* is used for the stereotypical way of holding a (specific part of a) pipe in one's mouth, smoking it, while the bigger preposition *inside/binnenin* is used for complete spatial containment.

Another, slightly different, example of this kind of iconicity involves the description of enclosure paths. As we saw in the previous section, one part of the polysemy of *around* concerns the degree of enclosure, roughly speaking: 'full' > 'half' > 'quarter'. The interesting thing is that languages tend to describe more 'complete' meanings with more complex expressions. Here are some examples of contrasting pairs from Germanic languages:

(28) (a) rondom het huis – om het huis   [Dutch]
     (b) runt umkring huset – runt huset   [Swedish]
     (c) (rings) um das Haus herum – um das Haus   [German]

The first member of these pairs refers to a path that completely encloses the house, but the second pair can also refer to a path that only encloses half of the house. In Biblical Hebrew reduplication of the word for 'around' is used to stress complete enclosure:

(29) saviv   saviv   labbayit   saviv   [Hebrew, Eze. 41:5]
     around   around   to-the-house   around
     'all around the house'

However, the form that is used for enclosure of corners is always a less marked form. None of the more complex forms for 'around' in Dutch are possible with 'corner':

(30) (a)   om   de hoek
            around   the corner

     (b) * om   de hoek   heen
            around   the corner   DIR

     (c) * rond   de hoek
            round   the corner

     (d) * rondom   de hoek
            round-round   the corner

The circumpositional *om...heen*, the preposition *rond* and the compound preposition *rondom* are all formally more complex than the unmarked form *om* and none of these can be used in this situation (see Zwarts, 2006, for a full treatment of the contrast between *om* and *rond* in Dutch).

There is no easy way to explain the differences between the simple and complex forms in a compositional semantic way based on fixed lexical meanings, given the variety of structures and lexical building blocks that are used across languages. Bidirectional optimization offers us a way to view these patterns in a different, more global, way, as resulting from the iconic alignment of expressive and interpretive complexity, as suggestively shown in the following table:

Table 8.1: Iconicity in the Dutch 'round' domain

	'quarter'	'half'	'full'
om	<-->		
om...heen		<-------------------------------------->	
rond(om)			<------------->

The generalization is that *om*, as the least marked 'round' preposition, covers all the three senses and that growing complexity on the formal side restricts the coverage of the preposition (or circumposition) to more complex meanings. This can be done in a bidirectional diagram. There are three meanings ('at least quarter', 'at least half' and 'full') and three forms (*om*, *om...heen* and *rond(om)*). Both the meanings and the forms are ordered from less marked to more marked. This leads to an ordering of the nine form-meaning pairs indicated by the small ° signs. According to the weak optimization algorithm explained in section 1.3.2, three of these pairs come out as optimal: <*om*,'at least quarter'>, <*om...heen*,'at least half'> and <*rond(om)*,'full'>. This accounts for the iconicity pattern that we see in Table 8.1.

Diagram 8.1: Bidirectional optimization in the 'round' domain

	'at least quarter'		'at least half'		'full'
om	○ ✌	←	○	←	○
	↑		↑		↑
om...heen	○	←	○ ✌	←	○
	↑		↑		↑
rond(om)	○	←	○	←	○ ✌

However, this analysis raises a number of interesting issues that require further research. First, it is not immediately clear why *rond* and *rondom* would be more marked than the circumposition *om...heen*. Clearly, words and constructions do not wear their degree of formal markedness on their sleeves. We need to carefully study the syntactic, statistical, and historical properties of these expressions to motivate their markedness in an independent way. Second, as pointed out in Blutner (2005), there is also a problem in grounding the markedness ordering on the semantic side: the ordering of 'quarter', 'half', 'full' cannot be determined by the relative *strength* or *prototypicality* of these senses, as in most other lexical examples of bidirectional optimization. It is in fact the weakest, most general meaning ('at least quarter') that is treated as the unmarked meaning, to be bidirectionally linked up with the unmarked form. The strict, prototypical meaning ('the full circle'), on the other hand, associates with the marked form. This seems to be at odds with the observation in lexical pragmatics that unmarked forms have stereotypical meanings. What is badly needed is a careful definition of the kind of markedness that is needed for bidirectional optimization. If the strongest or prototypical meaning is not necessarily the unmarked one, then there must be other factors playing a role. Blutner (2005) suggests that the decisive factor is the frequency with which a particular sense occurs, but a thorough study of relevant data is required to test whether this is actually true.

8.7 Conclusion

In this chapter we have looked at a few optimization patterns in the lexical domain, focusing on spatial prepositions. Our main purpose has been to show the *paradigmatic* nature of the lexicon, i.e., a lexicon in which lexical items compete for 'semantic space' and shape each other's meanings. We have seen four types of competition, each with their own distinct classes of constraints and constraint interaction. Patterns of implication arise when there is an inclusion relation between two prepositions (like with *on* and *near*). In this case the SPECIFICITY constraint governs the choice of the more specific preposition. Patterns of faithfulness arise when two prepositions *overlap* in meaning (as argued for *over* and *around*). In this situation, SPECIFICITY does not help, but we need to prioritize which spatial features in the semantic input are most important to express. It is more important to express the vertical orientation of a path, than its curved shape, leading to *over* taking priority over *around*. Patterns of suppletion occur when a syntactic combination of two prepositions (like *from on*) is blocked by a simpler form (*off*), in virtue of the general markedness constraint against morphosyntactic complexity that we also saw in other chapters. Patterns of iconicity, finally, can be made to result from the weak optimization process that we have seen at work in various places in this book. The division in semantic labor between *in* and *inside*, for instance, can be made to follow from their formal asymmetry. Taken all together, these patterns show how the structure of the lexicon is determined by the interaction of different types of faithfulness constraints and markedness constraints, operating at different points in the mapping between meanings and words. From this point of view, the lexicon is not just a simple listing of arbitrary form-meaning pairs, but in important ways the result of a constraint-governed optimization process.

Notes

1   Even *bachelor* has more senses besides that of 'adult man who has not married yet'.

2   Formally, for all paths **p** and sets of path **P**, FAITH(**p,P**) = * iff **p** $\notin$ **P**.

3   In fact, the opposite seems more acceptable: *Alex walked into the house, in fact, (all the way) through the house.* This is probably because a path *into* the house can always be extended to become a path *through* the house, but not the other way round, suggesting that the temporal dimension might play a role here.

4   Zwarts (2004) formalizes this notion of 'enclosure' in terms of vectors pointing outward from the reference object. The first path in Figure 8.11 has vectors pointing in every direction, the second path in at least two opposite directions and the third path in at least two orthogonal directions, each property being an implication of the preceding one.

5   In order to focus here on the interaction between *over* and *around*, we adopt the strong definition of *over* here. We assume that this strong definition can be made to result from the interaction between a basic weak definition and blocking effects, although *over* might be less straightforward than *through*.

6   For simplicity's sake, the general Faith constraint of the previous section, which only selects PP denotations that include the input path, is left out here.

7   These two semantic constraints can perhaps be understood as semantic correspondence constraints (like Max and Dep in phonology).

9 Conclusions

9.1 Conflicts in interpretation

In the previous chapters we have shown that the task of linguistic interpretation can be viewed as a process of optimization. According to this view, the optimal meaning for a given form is determined on the basis of the transparent mechanism of conflict resolution provided by Optimality Theory. Conflicts may arise at different levels of interpretation: at the level of the discourse (Chapter 2), at the interface between discourse and sentence (Chapters 3, 4 and 5), at the sentence level (Chapters 6 and 7), and at the level of word meaning (Chapter 8). These conflicts are the result of the different, and often incompatible, demands the grammar places on forms, meanings and the relation between the two. To decide among the potential meanings for a given form, these potential meanings must be evaluated on the basis of a set of ranked violable constraints. The meaning that optimally satisfies these constraints will be selected by the hearer. Such an optimization approach is the dominant approach in phonology and has been proposed for explaining phenomena in the areas of morphology and syntax. In this book we have shown that an optimization approach is able to provide a straightforward explanation for several phenomena in the area of semantics and pragmatics as well.

In addition to balancing between the demands of conflicting constraints, hearers also have to balance between their own demands and the typically conflicting demands of the speaker. Speakers tend to be 'lazy' and try to minimize their efforts, whereas hearers benefit from elaborate utterances in which all the meaning components are carefully laid out. One of the main results of this book is that speaking and understanding often require the language user to consider the opposite perspective in communication. Hearers must take into account the alternative forms the speaker could have used but did not use. This allows them to select a marked meaning for a marked form, in accordance with Horn's division of pragmatic labor. Similarly, speakers must take into account the way a hearer will interpret a potential form. Thus they will be able to avoid producing unrecoverable forms. As we have argued for, this bidirectional perspective restricts the possible forms and meanings of a language in several ways. The effects of bidirectional optimization are visible in the adult pattern of forms and meanings within a particular language, in children's pattern of acquisition of the meanings of their native language, as well as in the semantic variation among languages. In the next three sections, we will briefly summarize the results of this book with respect to these three domains.

9.2   Cross-modularity and bidirectionality in interpretation

By extending the optimization approach to grammar to the area of semantics and pragmatics, we are in the strong position of being able to contribute to, and test, a unified theory of language that aims to account for all aspects of the grammar. Such a unified theory allows for a better understanding of issues at the interface between modules of the grammar. Because constraints are assumed to apply in parallel, and all constraints (whether they are prosodic, syntactic, semantic, or pragmatic in nature) are part of the same constraint hierarchy, constraint interaction in Optimality Theory is inherently cross-modular. As a result, the interaction between clause order and rhetorical structure (Chapter 2), between word order and sentence stress (Chapter 3), and other interactions between two or more modules can be modeled straightforwardly through the interplay between constraints of various nature. Another advantage of a unified theory of grammar is that it now makes sense to look for commonalities across different modules of the grammar. Can we distinguish common stages in the acquisition of phonology, syntax and semantics on the basis of the unified optimization model of language? Can we account for cross-linguistic variation in the domains of phonology, syntax and semantics in a similar way? Do we see similarities in the notion of markedness as used in phonology, syntax and semantics, or is markedness of form different from markedness of meaning? We will return to these questions below.

If, as a result of cross-modular constraint interaction, constraints pertaining to rhetorical structure and prosody determine sentence meaning, then what exactly distinguishes semantics from pragmatics? Traditionally, semantics is seen as the study of word meaning and sentence meaning independent of context, whereas pragmatics is seen as the study of word meaning and sentence meaning in relation to context and language use. In this book we have shown that speaker influences on comprehension are not only found for phenomena that are traditionally categorized as pragmatic, such as rhetorical structure and contrastive stress. We also provided evidence for speaker influences on comprehension for phenomena that are traditionally categorized as belonging to the grammar or the lexicon, for example, the word order effects discussed in Chapters 3 and 4, the presence or absence of articles discussed in Chapter 7, and the polysemous prepositions studied in Chapter 8. These phenomena were all explained in exactly the same way, namely through bidirectional optimization. In all of these cases, the adult pattern of forms and meanings was argued to be the result of speakers taking into account the hearer's perspective and hearers taking into account the speaker's perspective. Consequently, not only the use of the grammar of a language but also important aspects of the grammar itself and of the lexicon are shaped by the essentially pragmatic principle of bidirectional optimization. This suggests that the traditional distinction between the representation of linguistic knowledge and the use of linguistic knowledge may have to be reconsidered. Certain aspects of what is commonly seen as the reflection of linguistic knowledge may be better explained as resulting from language use, in particular the interplay between the speaker's perspective and the hearer's perspective.

9.3 The acquisition of meaning

In the area of phonology, Optimality Theory makes specific claims with respect to language acquisition and language variation. An important assumption is that languages share the same set of constraints but differ in the ranking of these constraints. When acquiring their native language, children have to learn the particular ranking of the constraints in their language. To obtain the adult constraint ranking, they have to re-rank the pre-specified constraints on the basis of positive evidence provided by the language input. Several constraint re-ranking algorithms have been proposed to account for this process of language acquisition (e.g., Boersma and Hayes, 2001; Tesar and Smolensky, 1998). The constraint re-ranking model of language acquisition not only accounts for phonological acquisition, but has also been applied in OT syntax and OT semantics to account for the pattern of acquisition of young children with respect to their production of tense and agreement inflection (Legendre, Vainikka, Hagstrom, and Todorova, 2002; Legendre, 2006) and for young children's comprehension of subject-object word order (Hendriks, de Hoop, and Lamers, 2005).

This book argues that acquiring the adult constraint ranking is not sufficient for acquiring adult semantic competence. In addition to constraint re-ranking, the acquisition of the adult pattern of meanings requires a second step. In comprehension, children also have to learn to take into account the forms the speaker could have used but did not use. This allows them to discard potential meanings that are nevertheless not optimal for adults. Children initially optimize unidirectionally on the basis of the constraints of the grammar, and have to develop the ability to block these potential meanings through bidirectional optimization. Developing the ability to optimize bidirectionally occurs relatively late in child language, in general around or even after the age of 6. Differences between the child's output, which results from unidirectional optimization, and the adult's output, which results from bidirectional optimization, give rise to comprehension delays in language acquisition. These comprehension delays typically occur relatively late in language acquisition. For example, children as old as 11 sometimes fail to assign a marked meaning to a marked form when interpreting indefinite subjects or objects (Chapter 4). With respect to sentences involving contrastive stress, the majority of children until the age of 7 make errors when interpreting marked stress (Chapter 5). Because unidirectional optimization is direction-sensitive and hence different form-meaning pairings may arise in production and comprehension, the OT grammar predicts that correct production may sometimes precede correct comprehension. This was illustrated by children's acquisition of contrastive stress in Chapter 5. Although children produce marked and unmarked stress in an adult-like way from an early age on, they make errors when interpreting marked stress until the age of 7. Only when children are able to optimize bidirectionally, these production/comprehension asymmetries disappear. Whether children's initial failure to optimize bidirectionally arises as a result of their lack of a well-developed Theory of Mind, their lack of sufficient working memory capacity, or their lack of sufficient processing speed, still remains an open issue.

9.4   Cross-linguistic variation of meaning

In contrast to children, adult speakers have a full mastery of their bidirectional grammar, but grammars are not the same across languages. In all languages, speakers and hearers must balance their often conflicting needs. However, languages vary in the way they establish a balance between the needs of speakers and hearers. This was illustrated by the cross-linguistic variation in negation (Chapter 6) and the cross-linguistic variation in the use of articles with nominals (Chapter 7). For example, all languages express negation, but languages differ in the way they express negation. Semantically, languages differ with respect to whether two instances of negation are interpreted as a single negation (negative concord) or as a double negation. The attested patterns of negation in natural language were shown to arise as a result of the different possible rankings of the same set of partially conflicting constraints, in the same way as language variation is explained in OT phonology and OT syntax. Furthermore, in Chapter

6 it was shown that the attested patterns of negation could be linked to the diachronic development of negation, known as the Jespersen cycle, through gradual constraint re-ranking.

However, to explain the expression of double negation in negative concord languages the mechanism of constraint re-ranking is not sufficient. Rather, a grammar is required that employs the recursive mechanism of weak bidirectional optimization. Otherwise, double negation would never emerge as the optimal form, since double negation is a highly marked form and hence should be strongly dispreferred. In Chapter 7, a similar analysis is presented for the cross-linguistic interpretation and distribution of nominals with and without articles in Germanic and Romance languages. In languages such as Dutch and English, the absence of an article results in a shorter and hence unmarked form, which indicates a stereotypical meaning. This explains why *in jail* carries the meaning 'incarcerated'. In contrast, the presence of an article indicates an unexpected meaning, for example the meaning 'just visiting' for *in the jail*. This distribution of meanings follows if the stereotypical meaning is the unmarked meaning. Thus, markedness in the domain of meanings is governed by expectations: Highly expected meanings are unmarked. The stereotypical meaning and the general meaning can be placed on an implicational scale, with the stronger and hence unmarked meaning (i.e., the stereotypical meaning) implying the weaker general meaning. Because the unmarked form receives the unmarked stereotypical meaning, this stereotypical meaning is blocked for the marked form. As a result, the marked form is associated with the complement of the stereotypical meaning, that is, the unexpected meaning. This pattern of forms and meanings is difficult to explain through constraint re-ranking. Both Chapter 6 and Chapter 7 thus provide evidence that constraint re-ranking only explains part of the cross-linguistic data. To be able to account for Horn's division of pragmatic labor, which says that unmarked forms are associated with unmarked meanings, and marked forms are associated with marked meanings, a bidirectional optimization perspective is essential.

9.5 Future directions

Optimality Theory was conceived as a way to breach the gap between two fundamental paradigms in the study of cognition: the symbolic approach, in which cognitive computation consists of the manipulation of symbolic representations, and the connectionist approach, which replaces this with spreading activation in a neural network. The symbolic level is grounded in a subsymbolic level of neural associations, making the symbols and their manipulations meaningful and allowing for a notion of optimality that is rooted in the connectionist property of harmony. Nevertheless, within this attractive overall perspective, important questions remain about the specific grounding of linguistic distinctions, constraints and generalizations. The cognitive plausibility of a linguistic theory depends on its potential to link, where possible, the existence and nature of its theoretical entities to language-independent facts about human perception, cognition and communication. It has been argued that basic aspects of the phonological system follow from phonetic properties of articulation and perception (Boersma, 1998; Hayes, 1999). When dealing with meaning, we also need to consider what parts of the semantic system can be independently grounded. Although this book focuses on the system of linguistic distinctions and linguistic constraints, we have tried to point out links with other domains of cognition where possible. Hopefully, this book opens up new directions of thinking about the relation between language and cognition.

References

Aissen, J. (1999) Markedness and subject choice in optimality theory. *Natural Language and Linguistic Theory* 17: 673–711.

Aissen, J. (2003) Differential object marking: iconicity vs. economy. *Natural Language and Linguistic Theory* 21: 435–483.

Aloni, M., Butler, A. and Hindsill, D. (2007) Nuclear accent in bidirectional Optimality Theory. In M. Aloni, A. Butler and P. Dekker (eds) *Questions in Dynamic Semantics*, 257–273. Amsterdam: Elsevier.

Anderson, S. and Keenan, E. (1985) Deixis. In T. Shopen (ed.) *Language Typology and Syntactic Description*, 259–308. Cambridge: Cambridge University Press.

Anttila, A. and Cho, Y.-M. Y. (1998) Variation and change in Optimality Theory. *Lingua* 104: 31–56.

Aronoff, M. (1976) *Word Formation in Generative Grammar*. Cambridge, MA: MIT Press.

Ashby, W. (1981) The loss of the negative particle *ne* in French: a change in progress. *Language* 57: 674–687.

Ashby, W. (2001) Un nouveau regard sur la chute du *ne* en français parlé tourangeau: s'agit-il d'un changement en cours? *French Language Studies* 11: 1–22.

Atkinson, J., Campbell, R., Marshall, J., Thacker, A. and Woll, B. (2004) Understanding 'not': neuropsychological dissociations between hand and head markers of negation in BSL. *Neuropsychologia* 42: 214–229.

Baldwin, T., Beavers, J., van der Beek, L., Bond, F., Flickinger, D. and Sag, I. A. (2006) In search of a systematic treatment of determinerless PPs. In P. Saint-Dizier (ed.) *Computational Linguistics Dimensions of Syntax and Semantics of Prepositions*, 163–180. Dordrecht: Kluwer Academic.

van Balen, T. and de Hoop, H. (2005) Kruiperige voornaamwoorden en de kracht van klemtoon. *Tabu* 34: 145–158.

Barbosa, P., Fox, D., Hagstrom, P., McGinnis, M. and Pesetsky, D. (eds) (1998) *Is the Best Good Enough? Optimality and Competition in Syntax*. Cambridge, MA: MIT Press.

Beaver, D. (2004) The optimization of discourse anaphora. *Linguistics and Philosophy* 27: 3–56.

Beaver, D. and Lee, H. (2004) Input-output mismatches in OT. In: R. Blutner and H. Zeevat (eds) *Optimality Theory and Pragmatics*, 112–153. Houndmills, Basingstoke, Hampshire: Palgrave/ Macmillan.

Biberauer, T. (2007) A closer look at negative concord in Afrikaans. *Stellenbosch Papers in Linguistics PLUS* 35: 1–51.

Bloom, P. (2000) *How Children Learn the Meanings of Words*. Cambridge, MA: MIT Press.

Blutner, R. (1998) Lexical pragmatics. *Journal of Semantics* 15: 115–162.

Blutner, R. (2000) Some aspects of optimality in natural language interpretation. *Journal of Semantics* 17: 189–216.

Blutner, R. (2004) Pragmatics and the lexicon. In L. Horn and G. Ward (eds) *Handbook of Pragmatics*. Oxford: Blackwell.

Blutner, R. (2005) Embedded implicatures, fossilization and incremental interpretation. Paper presented at the NWO/DFG Workshop *Modeling Incremental Interpretation*, Nijmegen, November 28–29, 2005.

Blutner, R., de Hoop, H. and Hendriks, P. (2006) *Optimal Communication*. Stanford, CA: CSLI Publications.

Blutner, R. and Solstad, T. (2001) Dimensional designation: a case study in lexical pragmatics. In E. Németh (ed.) *Pragmatics in 2000: Selected papers from the 7th International Pragmatics Conference Vol. 2*, 543–554. Antwerp: International Pragmatics Association.

Blutner, R. and Zeevat, H. (eds) (2004a) *Optimality Theory and Pragmatics*. Houndmills, Basingstoke, Hampshire: Palgrave/ Macmillan.

Blutner, R. and Zeevat, H. (2004b) Editor's introduction: pragmatics in Optimality Theory. In R. Blutner and H. Zeevat (eds) *Optimality Theory and Pragmatics*, 1–24. Houndmills, Basingstoke, Hampshire: Palgrave/ Macmillan.

Blutner, R. and Zeevat, H. (to appear) Optimality-Theoretic Pragmatics. In C. Maienborn, K. von Heusinger and P. Portner (eds) *Semantics: An International Handbook of Natural Language Meaning*. Berlin: Mouton de Gruyter.

Boersma, P. (1998) *Functional Phonology*. The Hague: Holland Academic Graphics.

Boersma, P. and Hayes, B. (2001) Empirical tests of the Gradual Learning Algorithm. *Linguistic Inquiry* 32: 45–86.

Borer, H. (2004) *Structuring Sense*. Oxford: Oxford University Press.

Borer, H. and Wexler, K. (1987) The maturation of syntax. In T. Roeper and E. Williams (eds) *Parameter Setting*, 23–172. Dordrecht: D. Reidel Publishing Company.

Borsley, B. and Jones, B. M. (2005) *Welsh Negation and Grammatical Theory*. Cardiff: University of Wales Press.

Borthen, K. (2003) *Norwegian Bare Singulars*. PhD Dissertation, Norwegian University of Science and Technology, Trondheim.

Bouma, G. (2006) Production and comprehension in context: the case of word order freezing. In C. Sidner, J. Harpur, A. Benz and P. Kuehnlein (eds) *Proceedings of the Workshop on Constraints in Discourse*, 35–43. Maynooth, Ireland.

Bouma, G. (2008) *Starting a Sentence in Dutch: A Corpus Study of Subject- and Object-Fronting*. PhD Dissertation, University of Groningen.

de Boysson-Bardiès, B. and Bacri, N. (1977) The interpretation of negative sentences. *International Journal of Psycholinguistics* 4: 73–81.

Bréal, M. (1897) *Essai de Sémantique*. Paris: Hachette.

Bréal, M. (1900) *Semantics*. New York: Henry Holt. Translation of Bréal (1897).

Breitbarth, A. and Haegeman, L. (2008) *Not Continuity, but Change: Stable Stage II in Jespersen's Cycle*. Ms. University of Cambridge and Université de Lille III.

Bresnan, J. (2000) Optimal syntax. In J. Dekkers, F. van der Leeuw and J. van de Weijer (eds) *Optimality Theory: Phonology, Syntax, and Acquisition*, 334–385. Oxford: Oxford University Press.

Bresnan, J. (2001) The emergence of the unmarked pronoun. In G. Legendre, J. Grimshaw and S. Vikner (eds) *Optimality-Theoretic Syntax*, 113–142. Cambridge, MA: MIT Press.

Bresnan, J. and Aissen, J. (2002) Optimality and functionality: objections and refutations. *Natural Language and Linguistic Theory* 20: 81–95.

Brugman, C. (1981) *The Story of* over. MA Thesis, University of California, Berkeley.

Carlson, G. (1980) *Reference to Kinds in English*. New York: Garland.

Cheng, L. and Sybesma, R. (1999) Bare and not-so-bare nouns and the structure of NP. *Linguistic Inquiry* 30: 509–542.

Chien, Y.-C. and Wexler, K. (1990) Children's knowledge of locality conditions on binding as evidence for the modularity of syntax and pragmatics. *Language Acquisition* 13: 225–295.

Chierchia, G. (1998a) Reference to kinds across languages. *Natural Language Semantics* 6: 339–405.

Chierchia, G. (1998b) Plurality of mass nouns and the notion of 'semantic parameter'. In S. Rothstein (ed.) *Events and Grammar*, 53–103. Dordrecht: Kluwer.

Choi, H.-W. (1996) *Optimizing Structure in Context: Scrambling and Information Structure*. PhD Dissertation, Stanford University.

Chomsky, N. (1957) *Syntactic Structures*. The Hague/Paris: Mouton.

Chomsky, N. (1959) A review of B. F. Skinner's Verbal Behavior. *Language* 35: 26–58.

Chomsky, N. and Halle, M. (1968) *The Sound Pattern of English*. New York: Harper and Row.

Cinque, G. (1993) A null theory of phrase and compound stress. *Linguistic Inquiry* 24: 239–298.

Clark, E. V. (1993) *The Lexicon in Acquisition*. Cambridge: Cambridge University Press.

Cohen, A. (2006) Bare nominals and optimal inference. In C. Ebert and C. Endriss (eds) *Proceedings of Sinn und Bedeutung* 10: 71–84.

Comrie, B. (1989) *Language Universals and Linguistic Typology: Syntax and Morphology*. Oxford: Basil Blackwell.

Corbett, G. (2000) *Number*. Cambridge: Cambridge University Press.

Corblin, F. and Tovena, L. (2003) L'expression de la négation dans les languages romanes. In D. Godard (ed.) *Les Langues Romanes: Problème de la Phrase Simple*, 279–342. Paris: CNRS Editions.

Crain, S., Philip, W., Drozd, K.F., Roeper, T. and Matsuoka, K. (1992) *Only* in child language. Paper presented at the 17th Boston University Conference on Language Development, Boston, MA.

Cutler, A. and Swinney, D. (1987) Prosody and the development of comprehension. *Journal of Child Language* 14: 145–167.

Dahl, Ö. (1979) Typology of sentence negation. *Linguistics* 17: 79–106.

Dalrymple, M. and Nikolaeva, I. (2006) Syntax of natural and accidental coordination: evidence from agreement. *Language* 82: 824–849.

Dayal, V. (1999) Bare NPs, reference to kinds and incorporation. In *Proceedings of SALT IX*. Ithaca: Cornell University Press.

Dayal, V. (2003) *A Semantics for Pseudo-Incorporation*. Ms. Rutgers University.

Dayal, V. (2004) Number marking and indefinites in kind terms. *Linguistics and Philosophy* 27: 393–450.

Dekker, P. and van Rooy, R. (2000) Bi-directional Optimality Theory: an application of Game Theory. *Journal of Semantics* 17: 217–242.

Delfitto, D. and Schroten, J. (1991) Bare plurals and the number affix in DP. *Probus* 3: 155–185.

Déprez, V. (2005) Morphological number, semantic number and bare nouns. *Lingua* 115: 857–883.

van der Does, J. and de Hoop, H. (1998) Type-shifting and scrambled definites. *Journal of Semantics* 15: 393–416.

Doron, E. (2004) Bare singular reference to kinds. In R. B. Young and Y. Zhou (eds) *Proceedings of Semantics and Linguistic Theory* 13: 73–90.

Drozd, K. and van Loosbroek, E. (1998) Dutch children's interpretations of focus particle constructions. Poster presented at the 23rd Annual Boston University Conference on Language Development, Boston, MA.

Dryer, M. (1988) Universal of negative position. In M. Hammond, E. Moravcsik and J. Wirth (eds) *Studies in Syntactic Typology*, 93–124. Amsterdam: John Benjamins.

Dryer, M. (2008) Verb-object-negative order in central Africa. In N. Cyffer, E. Ebermann and G. Ziegelmeyer (eds) *Negation Patterns in West African Languages*. Amsterdam/New York: Benjamins (in press).

Eisenbeiss, S. (1994) Kasus und Wortstellungsvariation im Deutschen Mittelfeld: Theoretische Überlegungen und Untersuchungen zum Erstspracherwerb. In B. Haftka (ed.) *Was Determiniert Wortstellungsvariation?* 277–298. Opladen: Westdeutscher Verlag.

Elenbaas, N. and Kager, R. (1999) Ternary rhythm and the lapse constraint. *Phonology* 16: 273–329.

Farkas, D. (2002) Specificity distinctions. *Journal of Semantics* 19: 1–31.

Farkas, D. (2006) The unmarked determiner. In S. Vogeleer and L. Tasmowski (eds) *Non-Definiteness and Plurality*, 81–105. Amsterdam: Benjamins.

Farkas, D. and de Swart, H. (2003) *The Semantics of Incorporation*. Stanford, CA: CSLI Publications.

Farkas, D. and de Swart, H. (2007) Article choice in plural generics. *Lingua* 117: 1657–1676.

Feeney, A., Scrafton, S., Duckworth, A. and Handley, S. J. (2004), The story of *some*: Everyday pragmatic inference by children and adults. *Canadian Journal of Experimental Psychology* 58, 121–132.

Féry, C. (2005) *The Prosody of Topicalization*. Ms. University of Potsdam.

Flobbe, L. (2006) *Children's Development of Reasoning about other People's Minds*. MSc., University of Groningen.

Flobbe, L., Verbrugge, R., Hendriks, P. and Krämer, I. (2008) Children's application of Theory of Mind in reasoning and language. *Journal of Logic, Language and Information* 17, 417–442.

Foley, C., Lust, B., Battin, D., Koehne, A. and White, K. (2000) On the acquisition of an indefinite determiner: evidence for unselective binding. In S. C. Howell, S. A. Fish and T. Keith-Lucas (eds) *Proceedings of the 24th Annual Boston University Conference on Language Development*, 286–298. Somerville, MA: Cascadilla Press.

Fong, V. (1997) *The Order of Things: What Directional Locatives Denote*. PhD Dissertation, Stanford University.

Gennari, S., Gualmini, A., Crain, S., Meroni, L. and Maciukaite, S. (2001) How adults and children manage stress in ambiguous contexts. *Proceedings of 1st Workshop on Cognitive Models of Semantic Processing*. University of Edinburgh, Edinburgh.

Gennari, S., Meroni, L. and Crain, S. (2005) Rapid relief of stress in dealing with ambiguity. In J. Trueswell and M. Tanenhaus (eds) *Processing World Situated Language: Bridging the Language-as-product and Language-as-action Traditions*. Cambridge: MIT Press.

German, J., Pierrehumbert, J. and Kaufmann, S. (2006) Evidence for phonological constraints on nuclear accent placement. *Language* 82: 151–168.

Giannakidou, A. (2006) N-words and negative concord. In M. Everaert and H. van Riemsdijk (eds) *The Syntax Companion*, 327–391. Oxford: Blackwell.

Givón, T. (1983) Introduction. In T. Givón (ed.) *Topic Continuity in Discourse: A Quantitative Cross-Language Study*, 5–41. Amsterdam: John Benjamins.

Godard, D. (2004) French negative dependency. In F. Corblin and H. de Swart (eds) *Handbook of French Semantics*, 351–390. Stanford, CA: CSLI Publications.

Greenberg, J. (1963) Some universals of grammar with particular reference to the order of meaningful elements. In J. Greenberg (ed.) *Universals of Language*, 73–113. Cambridge, MA: MIT Press.

Greenberg, J., Ferguson, C. and Moravcsik, E. (1978) *Universals of Human Language*. Stanford, CA: Stanford University Press.

Grimshaw, J. (1997) Projections, heads and optimality. *Linguistic Inquiry* 28: 373–422.

Grimshaw, J. and Rosen, S. T. (1990) Knowledge and obedience: the developmental status of the binding theory. *Linguistic Inquiry* 21: 187–222.

Grimshaw, J. and Samek-Lodovici, V. (1998) Optimal subjects and subject universals. In P. Barbosa, D. Fox, P. Hagstrom, M. McGinnis and D. Pestsky (eds) *Is the Best Good Enough? Optimality and Competition in Syntax*, 193–219. Cambridge, MA: MIT Press.

de Groot, C. (1993) Hungarian. In P. Kahrel and R. van den Berg (eds) *Typological Studies in Negation*, 143–262. Amsterdam: Benjamins.

Gualmini, A. (2002) Children do not lack some knowledge. *Working Papers in Linguistics 12*, 49–74. University of Maryland.

Gualmini, A., Maciukaite, S. and Crain, S. (2003) Children's insensitivity to contrastive stress in sentences with *only*. *University of Pennsylvania Working Papers in Linguistics* 8. University of Pennsylvania, Philadelphia, PA: Penn Linguistics Club.

Haegeman, L. and Zanuttini, R. (1996) Negative concord in West Flemish. In A. Belletti and L. Rizzi (eds) *Parameters and Functional Heads*, 117–180. Oxford: Oxford University Press.

Haiman, J. (1980) The iconicity of grammar: isomorphism and motivation. *Language 56*: 515–540.

Halbert, A., Crain, S., Shankweiler, D. and Woodams, E. (1995) Children's interpretive use of emphatic stress. *Paper presented on the 8th Annual CUNY Conference on Human Sentence Processing*. Tucson, AZ.

Harris, A. (1981) *Georgian Syntax: A Study in Relational Grammar*. Cambridge: Cambridge University Press.

Haspelmath, M. (1997) *Indefinite Pronouns*. Oxford: Clarendon Press.

Haspelmath, M. (2006) Against markedness (and what to replace it with). *Journal of Linguistics 42*: 25–70.

Haspelmath, M. (2007) Coordination. In T. Shopen (ed.), *Language Typology and Linguistic Description*, 2nd edition, 1–51. Cambridge: Cambridge University Press.

Hayes, B. (1995) *Metrical Stress Theory: Principles and Case Studies*. Chicago: University of Chicago Press.

Hayes, B. (1999). Phonetically-driven phonology: the role of Optimality Theory and inductive grounding. In M. Darnell, E. Moravscik, M. Noonan, F. Newmeyer and K. Wheatly (eds) *Functionalism and Formalism in Linguistics, Volume 1: General Papers*, 243–285. Amsterdam: John Benjamins.

Hedden, T. and Zhang, J. (2002) What do you think I think you think? Strategic reasoning in matrix games. *Cognition* 85: 1–36.

Heim, I. (1982) *The Semantics of Definite and Indefinite Noun Phrases in English,* PhD Dissertation, University of Massachusetts, Amherst.

Heine, B. and Kuteva, T. (2002) *World Lexicon of Grammaticalization.* Cambridge: Cambridge University Press.

Hendriks, P., Hendrickx, S., Looije, R. and Pals, C. (2005) Hoe perfect is ons taalsysteem? Een bidirectionele OT-analyse van de verwerving van klemtoonverschuiving. *Tabu* 34: 71–97.

Hendriks, P. and de Hoop, H. (1997) On the interpretation of semantic relations in the absence of syntactic structure. In P. Dekker, M. Stokhof and Y. Venema (eds) *Proceedings of the 11th Amsterdam Colloquium,* 157–162. Amsterdam: ILLC, University of Amsterdam.

Hendriks, P. and de Hoop, H. (2001) Optimality Theoretic Semantics. *Linguistics and Philosophy* 24: 1–32.

Hendriks, P., de Hoop, H. and Lamers, M. (2005) Asymmetries in language use reveal asymmetries in the grammar. In P. Dekker and M. Franke (eds) *Proceedings of the 15th Amsterdam Colloquium,* 113–118. Amsterdam: ILLC, University of Amsterdam.

Hendriks, P. and Spenader, J. (2004) A bidirectional explanation of the Pronoun Interpretation Problem. In P. Schlenker and E. Keenan (eds) *Proceedings of the ESSLLI '04 Workshop on Semantic Approaches to Binding Theory.* Nancy, France.

Hendriks, P. and Spenader, J. (2006) When production precedes comprehension: an optimization approach to the acquisition of pronouns. *Language Acquisition* 13, 319–348.

Hendriks, P., van Rijn, H. and Valkenier, B. (2007) Learning to reason about speakers' alternatives in sentence comprehension: a computational account. *Lingua* 117, 1879–1896.

Heycock, C. and Zamparelli, R. (2003) Coordinated bare definites. *Linguistic Inquiry* 34: 443–469.

Higginbotham, J. (1985) On semantics. *Linguistic Inquiry* 16: 547–593.

Hinrichs, E. (1981) *Temporale Anaphora im Englischen.* MA Thesis, University of Tübingen.

Hoeksema, J. (1997) Negation and negative concord in Middle Dutch. In D. Forget, P. Hirschbühler, F. Martineau and M. Rivero (eds) *Negation and Polarity: Syntax and Semantics,* 139–158. Amsterdam: John Benjamins.

de Hoop, H. (2000) Optimal scrambling and interpretation. In H. Bennis, M. Everaert and E. Reuland (eds) *Interface Strategies,* 153–168. Amsterdam: KNAW.

de Hoop, H. (2003) Scrambling in Dutch: optionality and optimality. In S. Karimi (ed.) *Word Order and Scrambling,* 201–216. Oxford: Blackwell.

de Hoop, H. (2004) On the interpretation of stressed pronouns. In R. Blutner and H. Zeevat (eds) *Optimality Theory and Pragmatics,* 25–41. Houndmills, Basingstoke, Hampshire: Palgrave/MacMillan.

de Hoop, H. and Krämer, I. (2006) Children's optimal interpretations of indefinite subjects and objects. *Language Acquisition* 13: 103–123.

de Hoop, H. and Lamers, M. (2006) Incremental distinguishability of subject and object. In L. Kulikov, A. Malchukov and P. de Swart (eds) *Case, Valency and Transitivity*. Amsterdam/ Philadelphia: John Benjamins.

de Hoop, H. and de Swart, H. (2000) Temporal adjunct clauses in Optimality Theory. *Revista di Linguistica/Italian Journal of Linguistics* 12: 107–127.

Horn, L. R. (1972) *On the Semantic Properties of Logical Operators in English*. PhD Dissertation, University of California, Los Angeles.

Horn, L. R. (1984) Towards a new taxonomy of pragmatic inference: Q-based and R-based implicature. In D. Schiffrin (ed.) *Meaning, Form, and Use in Context: Linguistic Applications*, GURT84, 11–42. Washington: Georgetown University Press.

Horn, L.R. (1989) *A Natural History of Negation*. Chicago: University of Chicago Press.

Horn, L. R. and Bayer, S. (1984) Short-circuited implicature: a negative contribution. *Linguistics and Philosophy* 7: 397–414.

Hornby, P. A. and Hass, W. A. (1970) Use of contrastive stress by preschool children. *Journal of Speech and Hearing Research* 13: 395–399.

van der Horst, J. and van der Wal, M. (1979) Negatieverschijnselen en woordvolgorde in de geschiedenis van het Nederlands. *Tijdschrift voor Nederlande Taal en Letterkunde* 95: 6–37.

Hubel, D. H. and Wiesel, T. (1959) Receptive fields of single neurones in the cat's visual cortex. *Journal of Physiology* 148: 574–591.

Jackendoff, R. (1983) *Semantics and Cognition*. Cambridge, MA: MIT Press.

Jackendoff, R. (2008) Construction after construction and its theoretical consequences. *Language* 84: 8–28.

Jackendoff, R., Maling, J. and Zaenen, A. (1993) *Home* is subject to Principle A. *Linguistic Inquiry* 24: 173–177.

Jäger, A. (2008) *History of German Negation*. Amsterdam: John Benjamins.

Jäger, G. (2004) Learning constraint sub-hierarchies. In R. Blutner and H. Zeevat (eds) *Optimality Theory and Pragmatics*, 251–287. Houndmills, Basingstoke, Hampshire: Palgrave/MacMillan.

Jäger, G. and Rosenbach, A. (2006) The winner takes it all – almost: cumulativity in grammatical variation. *Linguistics* 44: 937–971.

Jespersen, O. (1917) *Negation in English and Other Languages*. Copenhagen: A.F. Høst. Reprinted in: *Selected Writings of Otto Jespersen* (1962), 3–151. London: George Allen and Unwin.

Jespersen, O. (1924) *The Philosophy of Grammar*. London: George Allen and Urwin.

Jespersen, O. (1933) *Essentials of English Grammar*. Reprinted 1964, University of Alabama Press.

Kamp, H. and van Eijck, J. (1997) Representing discourse in context. In J. van Benthem and A. ter Meulen (eds) *Handbook of Logic and Linguistics*, 179–237. Amsterdam: Elsevier.

Kamp, H. and Reyle, U. (1993) *From Discourse to Logic.* Dordrecht: Kluwer Academic Press.

Karmiloff-Smith, A. (1979) *A Functional Approach to Child Language: A Study of Determiners and Reference.* Cambridge: Cambridge University Press.

Katz, J. J. and Fodor, J. A. (1963) The structure of a semantic theory. *Language* 39: 170–210.

Keenan, E. (2003) A historical explanation of some binding theoretical facts in English. In J. Moore and M. Polinsky (eds) *The Nature of Explanation in Linguistic Theory*, 152–189. Stanford, CA: CSLI Publications.

Kennedy, G.A. (1991) *Aristotle, On Rhetoric: A Theory of Civic Discourse.* New York/Oxford: Oxford University Press.

Kiparsky, P. (1982) Lexical morphology and phonology. In I.-S. Yang (ed.) *Linguistics in the Morning Calm*, 3–91. Seoul: Hanshin.

Kiparsky, P. (1983) Word-formation and the lexicon. In F. Ingemann (ed.) *Proceedings of the 1982 Mid-America Linguistic Conference.* Kansas: Lawrence.

Klein, W. (1996) *Specificity in Child Dutch: An Experimental Study.* MA Thesis, Utrecht University.

Kracht, M. (2002) On the semantics of locatives. *Linguistics and Philosophy* 25, 157–232.

Krämer, I. M. (2000) *Interpreting Indefinites. An Experimental Study of Children's Language Comprehension.* PhD Dissertation, Utrecht University, MPI Series in Psycholinguistics 15.

Krifka, M. (1995) Common nouns: a contrastive analysis of Chinese and English. In G. Carlson and J. Pelletier (eds) *The GenericBook*, 398–411. Chicago: University of Chicago Press.

Kuhn, J. (2003) *Optimality-Theoretic Syntax – A Declarative Approach.* Stanford, CA: CSLI Publications.

Lakoff, G. (1987) *Women, Fire, and Dangerous Things: What Categories Reveal about the Mind.* Chicago: University of Chicago Press.

Lambrecht, K. (1984) Formulaicity, Frame Semantics and pragmatics in German binomial expressions. *Language* 60: 753–796.

Lamers, M. and de Hoop, H. (2005) Animacy information in human sentence processing: an incremental optimization of interpretation approach. In H. Christiansen, P.R. Skadhauge and J. Villadsen (eds) *Constraint Solving and Language Processing* (Lecture Notes in Artificial Intelligence 3438), 158–171. Berlin/Heidelberg: Springer- Verlag.

Landau, B. and Jackendoff, R. (1993) 'What' and 'where' in spatial language and spatial cognition. *Behavioral and Brain Sciences* 16: 217–265.

Lascarides, A. and Asher, N. (1993) Temporal interpretation, discourse relations and commonsense entailment. *Linguistics and Philosophy* 16: 437–493.

Le Bruyn, B. (2005) Looking for the bare necessities. MA thesis, Utrecht University.

Lee, H. (2001) Markedness and word order freezing. In P. Sells (ed.) *Formal and Empirical Issues in Optimality Theoretic Syntax*, 63–128. Stanford CA: CSLI Publications.

Lee, H. (2003) Parallel optimization in case systems. In M. Butt and T. King (eds) *Nominals: Inside and Out*. Stanford, CA: CSLI.

Leech, G. N. (1969) *Towards a Semantic Description of English*. London: Longman.

Legendre, G. (2006), Early child grammars: qualitative and quantitative analysis of morphosyntactic production. *Cognitive Science* 30: 803–835.

Legendre, G., Grimshaw, J. and Vikner, S. (eds) (2001) *Optimality-Theoretic Syntax*. Cambridge, MA: MIT Press.

Legendre, G., Miyata, Y. and Smolensky, P. (1990a) Harmonic Grammar – a formal multi-level connectionist theory of linguistic well-formedness: theoretical foundations. In *Proceedings of the Twelfth Annual Conference of the Cognitive Science Society*, 388–395. Hilldale, NJ: Lawrence Erlbaum.

Legendre, G., Miyata, Y. and Smolensky, P. (1990b) Harmonic Grammar: a formal multi-level connectionist theory of linguistic well-formedness: an application. In *Proceedings of the Twelfth Annual Conference of the Cognitive Science Society*, 884–891. Hilldale, NJ: Lawrence Erlbaum.

Legendre, G., Vainikka, A., Hagstrom, P. and Todorova, M. (2002) Partial constraint ordering in child French syntax. *Language Acquisition* 10: 189–227.

Levinson, S. C. (2000a) *Presumptive Meanings: The Theory of Generalized Conversational Implicature*. Cambridge, MA: MIT Press.

Levinson, S. C. (2000b) H.P. Grice on location on Rossel Island. In S.S. Chang, L. Liaw and J. Ruppenhofer (eds) *Berkeley Linguistics Society* 25: 210–224.

Lidz, J. and Musolino, J. (2002) Children's command of quantification. *Cognition* 84: 113–154.

Lidz, J. and Musolino, J. (2006) On the quantificational status of indefinites: the view from child language. *Language Acquisition* 13: 73–102.

Link, G. (1983) The logical analysis of plurals and mass terms: lattice-theoretical approach. In R. Bäuerle, C. Schwarze and A. von Stechow (eds) *Meaning, Use, and Interpretations of Language*, 302–323. Berlin: de Gruyter.

Lyons, C. (1999) *Definiteness*. Cambridge: Cambridge University Press.

Maratsos, M. (1974) Preschool children's use of definite and indefinite articles. *Child Development* 45: 446–455.

Markman, E. M. (1994) Constraints on word meaning in early language acquisition. In L. Gleitman and B. Landau (eds) *The Acquisition of the Lexicon*, 199–227. Cambridge, MA: MIT Press.

Mattausch, J. (2004) *On the optimization and grammaticalization of anaphora*. PhD Dissertation, Humboldt University Berlin. Published as *ZAS Papers in Linguistics 38*, 2005.

Mattausch, J. (2007) Optimality, bidirectionality & the evolution of binding phenomena. *Research on Language & Computation* 5: 103–131.

Matthewson, L. (1998) *Determiner Systems and Quantificational Strategies: Evidence from Salish*. The Hague: Holland Academic Graphics.

Matthewson, L. (2005) Some Other St'átimcets Quantifiers. Talk at the workshop on QP structure, nominalizations, and the role of DP, Saarbruecken, December 15–17.

Matushansky, O. and Spector, B. (2005) Tinker, tailor, soldier, spy. In E. Maier, C. Bary, and J. Huitink (eds) *Proceedings of SuB9*, 241–255. Nijmegen: NCS.

Mazzon, G. (2004) *A History of English Negation*. Harlow: Pearson Longman.

McCarthy, J. and Prince, A. (1993a) *Prosodic Morphology I: Constraint Interaction and Satisfaction*. Ms. University of Massachusetts, Amherst, and Rutgers University, New Brunswick, NJ.

McCarthy, J. and Prince, A. (1993b) Generalized alignment. In G.E. Booij and J. van Marle (eds) *Yearbook of Morphology 1993*, 79–153. Dordrecht: Kluwer.

McCawley, J. D. (1978) Conversational implicature and the lexicon. In P. Cole (ed.) *Syntax and Semantics 9: Pragmatics*, 245–259. New York: Academic Press.

McDaniel, D. and Maxfield, T. (1992) Principle B and contrastive stress. *Language Acquisition* 2: 337–358.

McIntyre, A. (2001) *Functional Interpretations: Borderline Idiomaticity in Prepositional Phrases, Complex Verbs and other Expressions*. Ms. Leipzig University.

Meisel, J.M. (ed.) (1992) *The Acquisition of Verb Placement: Functional Categories and V2 Phenomena in Language Acquisition*. Dordrecht: Kluwer.

Miller, K. and Schmitt, C. (2004) Wide-scope indefinites in English child language. In J. van Kampen and S. Baauw (eds) *Proceedings of GALA [Generative Approaches to Language Acquisition] 2003*, 317–328. Utrecht: LOT.

Miller, K. and Schmitt, C. (2005) The interpretation of indefinites and bare singulars in Spanish child language. In D. Eddington (ed.) *Proceedings of the 6th Conference on the Acquisition of Spanish and Portuguese as First and Second Languages*, 92–101. Somerville, MA: Cascadilla Press.

Milsark, G. (1977) Toward an explanation of certain peculiarities of the existential construction in English. *Linguistic Analysis* 3: 1–29.

Mitchell, E. (2006) The morpho-syntax of negation and the positions of NegP in the Finno-Ugric languages. *Lingua* 116: 228–244.

Moens, M. and Steedman, M. (1988) Temporal ontology and temporal reference. *Computational Linguistics* 14: 15–28.

Morimoto, Y. (2001) Deriving the directionality parameter in OT-LFG. In M. Butt and T. King (eds) *Proceedings of the LFG01 Conference*. Stanford, CA: CSLI Publications.

Munn, A. and Schmitt, C. (2005) Number and indefinites. *Lingua* 115: 821–855.

Murray, A.F. (1995) *Applications of Neural Networks*. Dordrecht: Springer.

Musolino, J. (1998) *Universal Grammar and the Acquistion of Semantic Knowledge: An Experimental Investigation into the Acquisition of Quantifier Negation Interaction in English*. PhD Dissertation, University of Maryland.

Nederstigt, U. (2001) The acquisition of additive 'focus particles' in German. In A. H.-J. Do, L. Dominguez and A. Johansen (eds) *BUCLD 25 Proceedings*, 554–565. Sommerville, MA: Cascadilla Press.

Neeleman, A. and Reinhart, T. (1998) Scrambling and the PF interface. In W. Geuder and M. Butt (eds) *The Projection of Arguments: Lexical and Compositional Factors*, 309–353. Stanford, CA: CSLI.

Newmeyer, F. (2002) Optimality and functionality: a critique of functionally-based Optimality-Theoretic Syntax. *Natural Language and Linguistic Theory* 20: 43–80.

Noveck, I. (2001) When children are more logical than adults. *Cognition* 78: 165–188.

O'Keefe, J. (1996) The spatial prepositions in English, Vector Grammar and the Cognitive Map Theory. In P. Bloom, M. A. Peterson, L. Nadel and M. F. Garrett (eds) *Language and Space*, 277–316. Cambridge, MA: MIT Press.

Onishi, K. H. and Baillargeon, R. (2005) Do 15-month-old infants understand false beliefs? *Science* 308: 255–258.

Ouali, H. (2003) Sentential negation in Berber: a comparative study. In J. Mugany (ed.) *Linguistic Description. Typology and Representation of African Languages*, 243–256. Trenton: Africa World Press.

Ouali, H. (2005) Negation and negative polarity items in Berber. In M. Ettlinger, N. Fleisher and M. Park-Doob (eds) *Proceedings of the Thirtieth Annual Meeting of the Berkeley Linguistics Society*, 330–340. Berkeley: Berkeley Linguistics Society.

Papafragou, A. and Musolino, J. (2003) Scalar implicatures: experiments at the semantics-pragmatics interface. *Cognition* 86: 253–282.

Partee, B. (1984) Nominal and temporal anaphora. *Linguistics and Philosophy* 7: 243–286.

Payne, J. (1985) Negation. In T. Shopen (ed.) *Language Typology and Syntactic Description I: Clause Structure*. Cambridge: Cambridge University Press.

Pérez-Leroux, A. and Roeper, T. (1999) Scope and the structure of bare nominals: evidence from child language. *Linguistics* 37: 927–960.

Philip, W. and Termeer, M. (2002) *Specific Indefinite Subjects and Quantifier Scope Ambiguity in Child Dutch*. Ms. University of Utrecht.

Posner, R. (1985) Post-verbal negation in non-standard French: a historical and comparative view. *Romance Philology* 39: 170–197.

Postal, P. (2004) A remark on English double negatives. In Eric Laporte et al. (eds) *Syntaxe, Lexique, et Lexique-Grammaire*, 497–508. Amsterdam: Benjamins.

Prince, A. and Smolensky, P. (1993) *Optimality Theory: Constraint Interaction in Generative Grammar*. Technical Report CU-CS-696–93, Department of

Computer Science, University of Colorado at Boulder, and Technical Report TR-2, Rutgers Center for Cognitive Science, Rutgers University, New Brunswick, NJ. Published by Blackwell in 2004.

Prince, A. and Smolensky, P. (1997) Optimality: From neural networks to universal grammar. *Science* 275: 1604–1610.

Regier, T. (1995) A model of the human capacity for categorizing spatial relations. *Cognitive Linguistics* 6: 63–88.

Reinhart, T. (2004) The processing cost of reference set computation: acquisition of stress shift and focus. *Language Acquisition* 12: 109–155.

Reinhart, T. (2006) *Interface strategies*. Cambridge, MA: MIT Press

Rijkhoff, J. (2002) *The noun phrase*. Oxford: Oxford University Press.

Roodenburg, J. (2004) French bare arguments are not extinct: the case of coordinated bare nouns. *Linguistic Inquiry* 35: 301–313.

Rooth, M.E. (1985) *Association with Focus*. PhD Dissertation, University of Massachusetts, Amherst.

Rooy, R. van (2004) Signalling games select Horn strategies. *Linguistics and Philosophy* 27: 493–527.

Samek-Lodovici, V. (1996) *Constraints on Subjects: An Optimality Theoretic Analysis*. PhD Dissertation, Rutgers University, New Brunswick, NJ.

de Saussure, F. (1974) *Course in General Linguistics*. London: Fontana. [Translated by W. Baskin]

Schaeffer, J. (1997) *Direct Object Scrambling in Dutch and Italian Child Language*. PhD Dissertation, University of California, Los Angeles.

Schaeffer, J. and Matthewson, L. (2005) Grammar and pragmatics in the acquisition of article systems. *Natural Language and Linguistic Theory* 23: 53–101.

Schafer J. and de Villiers, J. (2000) Imagining articles: what *a* and *the* can tell us about the emergence of DP. *Proceedings of BUCLD 24*, 609–620. Somerville, MA: Cascadilla Press.

Schulze, R. (1991) Getting round to *(a)round*: towards a description and analysis of a spatial predicate. In G. Rauh (ed.) *Approaches to Prepositions*, 251–274. Tübingen: Gunter Narr Verlag.

Schulze, R. (1993) The meaning of *(a)round*: a study of an English preposition. In R. A. Geiger and B. Rudzka-Ostyn (eds) *Conceptualizations and Mental Processing in Language*, 399–431. Berlin/New York: Mouton de Gruyter.

Selkirk, E. (1984) *Phonology and Syntax: The Relation Between Sound and Structure*. Cambridge, MA: MIT Press.

Sells, P. (ed.) (2001) *Formal and Empirical Issues in Optimality Theoretic Syntax*. Stanford, CA: CSLI Publications.

Smolensky, P. (1986) Information processing in dynamical systems: foundations of Harmony Theory. In D. E. Rumelhart, J. L. McClelland and the PDP Research Group (eds) *Parallel Distributed Processing: Explorations in the Microstructure of Cognition*. Vol.1: Foundations, 194–281. Cambridge, MA: MIT Press.

Smolensky, P. and Legendre, G. (2006) *The Harmonic Mind: From Neural Computation to Optimality-Theoretic Grammar*. Cambridge, MA: MIT Press.

Solstad, T. (2003) Towards the optimal lexicon. In M. Weisgerber (ed.) *Proceedings of the Conference SuB7 – Sinn und Bedeutung*, 282–294. Konstanz: Universität Konstanz.

Stvan, L. S. (1998) *The Semantics and Pragmatics of Bare Singular Noun Phrases*. PhD Dissertation, Northwestern University.

Su, Y.-C. (2001) Scope and specificity in child language. *Proceedings of BUCLD 25*, 744–755. Somerville, MA: Cascadilla Press.

de Swart, H. (1999) Position and meaning: time adverbials in context. In P. Bosch and R. van der Sandt (eds) *Focus: Linguistic, Cognitive and Computational Perspectives*, 336–361. Cambridge: Cambridge University Press.

de Swart, H. (2006) Marking and interpretation of negation: a bi-directional OT approach. In R. Zanuttini, H. Campos, E. Herburger and P. Portner (eds) *Negation, Tense and Clausal Architecture: Cross-Linguistic Investigations*, 199–218. Georgetown: Georgetown University Press.

de Swart, H. (2009) *Expression and Interpretation of Negation. An OT Typology*. Springer.

de Swart, H. and Sag, I. (2002) Negation and negative concord in Romance. *Linguistics and Philosophy* 25: 373–417.

de Swart, H., Winter, Y. and Zwarts, J. (2005) Bare predicate nominals in Dutch. In E. Maier, C. Bary and J. Huitink (eds) *Proceedings of SuB9*, 446–460.

de Swart, H., Winter, Y. and Zwarts, J. (2007) Bare nominals and reference to capacities. *Natural Language and Linguistic Theory* 25: 195–222.

de Swart, H. and Zwarts, J. (2009) Optimization principles in the typology of number and articles. In B. Heine and H. Narrog (eds) *Handbook of Linguistic Analysis*. Oxford: Oxford University Press.

Szendröi, K. (2004) Acquisition evidence for an interface theory of focus. In J. van Kampen and S. Baauw (eds) *Proceedings of Generative Approaches to Language Acquisition 2003 Volume 2*, 457–468.

Termeer, M. (2002) *'Een meisje ging twee keer van de glijbaan': A Study of Indefinite Subject NPs in Child Language*. MA Thesis, Utrecht University.

Tesar, B. and Smolensky, P. (1998) Learnability in Optimality Theory. *Linguistic Inquiry* 29: 229–268.

Thornton, R. (1995) Referentiality and wh-movement in child English. Juvenile D-linkuency. *Language Acquisition* 4: 139–175.

Tomasello, M. (2003) *Constructing a Language: A Usage-Based Theory of Language Acquisition*. Cambridge, MA: Harvard University Press.

Travis, L. (2001) The syntax of reduplication. In M. Kim and U. Strauss (eds) *Proceedings of the Northeast Linguistics Society (NELS)* 31, 455–469. Amherst, MA: GSLA Publications.

Trier, J. (1972) *Aufsätze und Vorträge zur Wortfeldtheorie*. In A. van der Lee and O. Reichmann (eds). The Hague: Mouton.

Unsworth, S. (2005) *Child L2, Adult L2, Child L1: Differences and Similarities. A Study on the Acquisition of Direct Object Scrambling in Dutch*. PhD Dissertation, Utrecht University.

Valkenier, B. (2006) *Bidirectionality in Language Acquisition*. MSc Thesis, University of Groningen.

Vogel, R. (2004) Remarks on the architecture of optimality theoretic syntax grammars. In R. Blutner and H. Zeevat (eds) *Optimality Theory and Pragmatics*, 211–228. Houndmills, Basingstoke, Hampshire: Palgrave/Macmillan.

Widrow, B., Rumelhart, D.E. and Lehr, M.A. (1994) Neural networks: Applications in industry, business and science. *Communications of the ACM* 37: 93–105. New York, NY: Association for Computing Machinery.

Williams, E. (1997) Blocking and anaphora. *Linguistic Inquiry* 28: 577–628.

Wilson, C. (2001) Bidirectional optimization and the theory of anaphora. In G. Legendre, J. Grimshaw and S. Vikner (eds) *Optimality-Theoretic Syntax*, 465–507. Cambridge, MA: MIT Press.

Wimmer, H. and Perner, J. (1983) Beliefs about beliefs: representation and constraining function of wrong beliefs in young children's understanding of deception. *Cognition* 13: 103–128.

Yang, N. (2008) *The Indefinite Object in Mandarin Chinese: Its Marking, Interpretation and Acquisition*. PhD Dissertation, Radboud University Nijmegen.

Zamparelli, R. (2005) Introduction: some questions about (in)definiteness. *Lingua* 115: 759–766.

Zanuttini, R. (1991) *Syntactic Properties of Sentential Negation: A Comparative Study of Romance Languages*. PhD Dissertation, University of Pennsylvania.

Zanuttini, R. (1994) Reexamining negative clauses. In G. Cinque, J. Koster, J.-Y. Pollock, L. Rizzi and R. Zanuttini (eds) *Paths Towards Universal Grammar. Studies in Honor of Richard S. Kayne*, 427–451. Georgetown: Georgetown University Press.

Zanuttini, R. (1996) *Negation and Clausal Structure: A Comparative Study of Romance Languages*. Oxford: Oxford University Press.

Zeevat, H. (2000) The asymmetry of Optimality Theoretic syntax and semantics. *Journal of Semantics* 17: 243–262.

Zeevat, H. and Jäger, G. (2002) A reinterpretation of syntactic alignment. In D. de Jongh, H. Zeevat and M. Nilsenova (eds) *Proceedings of the 3rd and 4th International Symposium on Language, Logic and Computation*. Amsterdam: ILLC.

Zehler, A. M. and Brewer, W. F. (1982) Sequence and principles in article system use: an examination of a, the and null acquisition. *Child Development* 53: 1268–1274.

Zeijlstra, H. (2004) *Sentential Negation and Negative Concord*. PhD Dissertation, Utrecht: LOT Dissertation Series.

Zeijlstra, H. (2007) Emphatic multiple negative expressions in Dutch. Amsterdam: *ACLC working papers* and lingBuzz/000344.

Zwarts, J. (2004) Competition between word meanings: the polysemy of (a) round. In C. Meier and M. Weisgerber (eds) *Proceedings of SuB8*, 349–360. Konstanz: University of Konstanz Linguistics Working Papers.

Zwarts, J. (2005) Prepositional aspect and the algebra of paths. *Linguistics and Philosophy* 28: 739–779.

Zwarts, J. (2006) *Om* en *rond*: een semantische vergelijking. *Nederlandse Taalkunde* 11: 101–123.

Zwarts, J. (2007) Number in Endo-Marakwet. In M. Reh and D. Payne (eds) *Advances in Nilo-Saharan Linguistics: Proceedings of the 8th Nilo-Saharan Linguistics Colloquium* 281–294. Cologne: Rüdiger Köppe Publishers.

Zwarts, J. and Winter, Y. (2000) Vector Space Semantics: a model-theoretic analysis of locative prepositions. *Journal of Logic, Language and Information* 9: 169–211.

Author Index

Subject index